THE EXISTENTIAL CORE
OF PSYCHOANALYSIS

Reality Sense and Responsibility

The Existential Core

REALITY SENSE AND RESPONSIBILITY

LITTLE, BROWN AND COMPANY

of Psychoanalysis

Avery D. Weisman, M.D

ASSISTANT CLINICAL PROFESSOR OF PSYCHIATRY, HARVARD MEDICAL
SCHOOL; PSYCHIATRIST AND DIRECTOR OF THE PSYCHIATRIC CONSULTATION
UNIT, DEPARTMENT OF PSYCHIATRY, MASSACHUSETTS GENERAL HOSPITAL;
TRAINING ANALYST, BOSTON PSYCHOANALYTIC INSTITUTE

BOSTON

Published in Great Britain by J. & A. Churchill Ltd., London

PRINTED IN THE UNITED STATES OF AMERICA

To Erma

Preface

THIS BOOK is about neither existentialism nor psychoanalysis but about both. It deals with the existential in man and the existential in psychoanalysis. Few publications about existentialism fail to discuss some aspects of psychoanalysis, but only occasionally do articles about psychoanalysis refer to work done beyond its own province, especially when that work has been done by existentialists.

By inclination and training I am an analyst. Along with many others who have given thought to the matter, however, I have discovered that we have been unofficial "existentialists" all along. In his daily work the psychoanalyst contends with many so-called existential issues. He is concerned not with existentialism as an explicit philosophy but with an *existential attitude* toward man, including himself.

If existential writers depend upon case reports and readings in psychoanalytic theory for their understanding of psychoanalysis, they are almost sure to misinterpret the entire analytic process.

Preface

The immediate sense of reality for the substance of psycho-analysis, as it is confronted each day, grows both in time and in depth. The nature and ramifications of the analytic encounter have been described at length and from different viewpoints by many authors; yet the encounter has not been fully appreciated as a significant source of psychoanalytic theory. The wide gulf between psychoanalytic theory and psychoanalytic practice is the result of ignoring realities inherent in actual, daily encounters between patient and analyst. It is a thesis of this book that the ideas and practices of psychoanalysis emerge from an existential attitude within the psychoanalyst and that this attitude influences his perceptions and permeates his generalizations.

Psychoanalysis is a merger of the aesthetic with the scientific, but, first and last, it is a venture in communication. The existential attitude is not just a subjective distortion of objective reality, nor is it a viewpoint that advocates a special interpretation of reality. The existential attitude, so crucial for psychoanalysis, recognizes that each person's version of reality is determined by his unique way of polarizing existence. Ordinary communication assumes that between one man and another there is only one world. Psychoanalytic communication accepts the relativity of reality and the ultimate correspondence between man's sense of reality for the world and his image of responsibility for himself.

I do not intend to document any particular controversy between psychoanalysis and existentialism in this work. However, without primarily presenting a concordance or a critique, the text will illustrate how many psychoanalytic and existential concepts, problems, and inquiries intersect and fuse at the existential core of psychoanalysis. Because I go beyond the limited version of psychoanalysis which is concerned only with diagnosis and treatment of patients and do not restrict the discussion of existentialism to the aspect which appeals only to philosophers, I hope that the relevance of this book may extend beyond the fields of psychiatry and medicine to other intellectual and aesthetic disciplines.

A. D. W.

Boston

Acknowledgments

IT IS PATENTLY IMPOSSIBLE for an author to cite the various people who have presumably influenced his viewpoint and to list the different places where they have done so. Such citation would be, in any case, profoundly uninteresting to a reader. Acknowledgments of this kind are in most instances a cross between a bibliography and a passport. There are, however, some people whose influence and assistance, direct and indirect, I would like to recognize and a few to whom I am genuinely indebted. Among these are Raymond Adams, John Dorsey, Donald Ramsdell, Beata Rank, and Paul Yakovlev. I have been influenced particularly by Erich Lindemann, whose work in the field of crisis theory and psychosomatic disorders has been so germinal. I also consider my earlier association with Edward Bibring and Hanss Sachs to be decisive. For over twenty years I have had an opportunity at the Massachusetts General Hospital to engage in both congenial discussion and clinical investigation with many stimulating colleagues, both older and younger. I hope they will understand that

Acknowledgments

the omission of their names does not detract from my appreciation. Finally, like many of my associates at the Boston Psychoanalytic Society and Institute, I have been proud to train and to teach at this center of psychoanalytic education.

Since 1956 Dr. Thomas P. Hackett and I have collaborated on a number of clinical studies, some of which are cited in the bibliography. At the present time we are investigating "Death and the Denial of Death," a project (No. 62-247) sponsored by the Foundations Fund for Research in Psychiatry. In fact, Chapter 8 is a résumé of the theoretical principles that have guided this research and so may be considered an introduction to what will be reported separately in another book.

Contents

Contents

THE EXISTENTIAL CORE OF PSYCHOANALYSIS

Reality Sense and Responsibility

1. Existentialism and Psychoanalysis

THAT COPERNICUS, DARWIN, AND FREUD sired three great revolutions in man's attitude toward himself is a familiar truism. Man was first displaced from his central position in the zodiac; then he was no longer a unique biological entity; finally he was deprived even of the distinction of directing his own thoughts or controlling his own actions. These collective claims allege that, with each advance of science — the discovery of his planet's insignificance, the long phylogeny of his species, and the meager scope of his consciousness — man has been progressively humbled, disillusioned, and minimized.

Acceptance of man's minor position in the universe, or among other animals, or even within the full scope of his inner processes, is not necessarily a demeaning experience. That he could pass beyond his nakedness and ignorance to create instruments that out-see his eyes, out-hear his ears, and out-think his brain is sufficient to set man apart, so that he may be viewed from a unique perspective. Among other great men with no less significant innovations, Copernicus, Darwin, and Freud did not discover new facts. They discovered new perspectives for familiar facts, through which they can be said to have liberated other facts for future generations to discover. In a similar sense, the attitudes and perspectives of all men provide precious continuity from one generation to the next, so that discovery is always fresh.

While the consequences of these discoveries have unquestionably changed man's way of life, it is doubtful that the inner attitudes of the average man today differ very much from his ancient Athenian counterpart. Stripped of the external trappings of time, place, and custom, man is probably no more disillusioned or uncertain about his personal significance today than he was before Copernicus, Darwin, or Freud — or any other decisive genius. The tangible gods, who controlled his destiny by divine mandate, did not allow ancient man more autonomy than his contemporary descendant has, as he teeters on the edge of imminent incineration.

Man has no reason to be either proud or humble. Central heating and air conditioning protect him against the extremes of daily weather but not against the heat of distant novae or the rigors of another ice age. Whether or not he is central in our galaxy, the zenith of organic life, or the quintessence of consciousness, his first concern is with his own survival, plus a degree of harmonious fulfillment of appetites and a reconciliation of the conflicts and contradictions that the manifold of circumstance puts before him. The most abiding realities are his sense of life and the existential event of being alive. Every other reality he produces by probing the enigmas of existence. Caught between what is real and what he can understand, man is obliged to acknowledge that reality without rules is an amorphous mystery and that rules without reality are empty myths.

It is the sense of reality for his own existence that makes even the most miserable wretch cling to his fragment of life. His self-perpetuating belief in his unique reality is both a premise for understanding purposeful conduct and a problem to be understood. Investigation of man and nature requires a judicious mingling of the empirical and the empyrean merely to give experience a tangible form. Physiological processes, biochemical reactions, psychological analyses, and theological conjectures delineate certain kinds of meaning that can be attributed to man, but it is his sense of reality for the world and his sense of responsibility for himself which endow his conduct with both value and validity.

Reality is to the world what responsibility is to the self. Neither can be sought, or recognized, without a strong sense of the other. Responsibility — the capacity to respond selectively, and to bring about similar responses in the world — is limited by the structure of reality. Since reality, in turn, consists of every proposition which is believed, and every belief which is acted upon, responsible acts can alter the shape of reality.

Not too long ago psychology, philosophy, and theology were natural companions. They were usually taught by a professor who combined a divinity degree with philosophical scholarship and drew his knowledge of psychology from speculations advanced by other philosophers. Laboratories and clinical facilities for psychology were primitive, at best. For the most part, psychology consisted of deductions based upon traditional metaphysics and epistemology.

Whenever a philosophical problem becomes sufficiently investigated, it tends to split off from the parent discipline, by a kind of parthenogenesis, and achieves an autonomy of its own. Consequently, there is no philosophical "knowledge" which can be discovered and applied to other fields. Physical and natural scientists have long looked upon traditional metaphysics as a somewhat lugubrious study of semantic ambiguities. Social scientists too suspect that philosophical studies of ethics and values are veiled theological premises in search of logical justification.

In spite of these complaints, every discipline that purports to examine the world, and to reflect upon its problems, owes a debt to philosophy which cannot be settled. The scientist who is not content to be a mere technician recognizes that no science is self-sufficient, that his observations must always be related to other ideas transcending the arbitrary limits of his own field.

Some highly developed disciplines, like physics and mathematics, in the days of their maturity return to their original sources to take up the philosophical issues they had put aside. Others, like psychology, not yet wholly independent, are too close to parental antecedents in philosophy to acknowledge their indebtedness.

Psychoanalysis is a somewhat scientific pursuit, but it is scarcely a science [60b, 111a]. Unless the analyst is willing to accept the firm standards imposed by other sciences, and to draw upon their experience, he exiles himself to dwell in some sacred grove, exempt from outside influence. Part of his task is to recognize contributions from workers in related fields, but he must also clarify his own implicit philosophical principles. In his daily practice the analyst is confronted with philosophical issues which could well occupy him for the remainder of his life, were not even more problems presented on the following day. It is often forgotten that Freud described himself as a "conquistador." Among other things, he used his neurological knowledge and his interest in art and archeology to penetrate further into psychology, beyond mere syndrome description and beyond academic restrictions [4]. Despite his misgivings about philosophers [7], he repeatedly raised philosophical issues in the course of his work [46n, o].

Today's intellectual climate does not encourage unmitigated orthodoxy or reliance upon revealed truths. Philosophical principles directly participate in the psychoanalyst's working attitudes, as well as in his attitudes toward work, by inconspicuously defining his standards of health and disease, normality and psychopathology.

In a field where there is no standard technology, the analyst cannot be merely an artisan whose workshop is the couch and chair. The competent clinician derives his competence from *not* being a pure technician who is detached from the processes he sets in motion. His total participation [96] in the analytic process is not covered by the concepts of transference and countertrans-

6

ference. Books on psychoanalytic technique fall short in so far as they dogmatically assume what any analyst needs to prove for himself. No manual can account for the personal contribution — philosophical as well as emotional — which an analyst brings to his work. It is, therefore, somewhat irrelevant to ask how "couch data" can contribute to an understanding of pressing human problems. The significance of what the patient says is not determined by his verbal reports alone; nor does the analyst restrict himself to the positivism he often espouses. He operates on several levels of knowledge at once [137c], whether or not he acknowledges some levels and ignores others.

It is possible to investigate experience on at least four levels: scientific, categorical, phenomenal, and existential. From the psychological standpoint, these levels may be called *psychophysical, psychodynamic, descriptive, and existential.*

The image of "levels" always suggests that one level is higher or lower than another, and even that one is better or worse. However, the purpose of levels is to detach events from the relative chaos of ordinary experience, and from the relative crudity of everyday language, inasmuch as scientific appraisal requires both generality and clarity of concepts.

Theoretically, each level of investigation and experience is a refinement of the level just beneath it. It is wholly possible, however, that the order of levels can be completely reversed for certain purposes, and that experience can be understood best by regarding it as an hourglass whose contents run in either direction, from the concrete to the abstract, and from pure reason back to bare existence.

Although the content of each level is sustained by the methods and materials of the underlying levels, it does not replace these levels, nor does it make study on less refined levels superfluous. Nevertheless, like snobs, students on one level tend to look down upon the crudities of their forebears, who subsisted on the rugged fare of less highly developed investigations. Obviously, the fine quantification of the psychophysical laboratory cannot be applied to psychodynamics, and psychoanalytic research is inclined to bypass even the most exquisite descriptions of clinical phenomena in order to extract and examine metapsychological theories. Similarly, clinical psychiatry, concerned as it is with taxonomy and treatment of large numbers of cases, finds even the language purporting to describe existential issues curious, baffling, and, for the most part, useless.

The polemics between students on each level suggests a warfare between states instead of a federation of related disciplines. Science on any level is an nth-degree abstraction, arising from concrete sources in existence. Only outsiders, unfamiliar with research, venerate the vast impersonality and objectivity of science. Those who know what it means to comb data for strands of truth realize that pertinent facts are not easily discovered amid extraneous observations and that formulas are the end products of arduous adventures. Subjective experience and objective facts are polarities, not opposites. In any field there is a critical difference between discovering what is true and simply being told what is true.

There have always been people who understood that the immediate content of living experience is the final source of judgment for itself. They know that what is real is only what is real for some living person, that whatever evokes a consistent response gradually acquires the status of an independent entity, and that generalizations are useful only in so far as experience is interpreted for the sake of existence. Everyone is an existentialist of sorts, depending upon how he comes to terms with existence and what he expects from the fact of being alive. According to Heinemann [58], who distinguishes between dead philosophies of existence and living philosophers of existence, there is no school of thought called "existentialism." Those who call themselves "existentialists," including those who merely don the terminological robes of existentialism, *speak for themselves and no one else.* Existentialists seem to share a common attitude toward man, rather than an explicit philosophy. Among ancient philosophers, Plotinus [108] was concerned with "existential" issues and used language that, with only slight modification, could be used readily in existential circles today. In certain passages St. Thomas Aquinas [90b] sounds like a modern existentialist. Kaufman [69, 70] has traced many existential themes in the great literary works of our Western tradition, and Watts [139] has under-

8

scored the points of similarity between Oriental religion and the Western world. In our own times, it would be supererogation to document the existential attitudes of Bergson, James, Whitehead, Dewey, and other great contemporary thinkers not usually classified as existentialists. Similar documentation could be extracted from the body of Freudian writings, were it not already acknowledged that Freud was wholly aware of the variety of experience that we call "existential" [123].

The ascendance of existentialism in Europe since World War II can be attributed to an effort to resolve the perpetual dilemma of man [8]. He has lived through the fall of old institutions and transmogrification of traditional values and now yearns for abiding harmony and truth in a world that has both defeated and deserted him. The grand philosophies of faith have failed; rationalism and scholarship have been ironically inadequate shelters against the shattering events of his time. Left to find his solitary way through moral and metaphysical shambles, he feels that the future will be no less bleak than what is already past. Indeed, it is this recent past that still seems to be gathering momentum for some ultimate catastrophe.

In addition to the use of such well-known, but ambiguous, terms as *being, existence, anguish, becoming, dread,* and so forth, the personality of the existentialist philosopher seems to shine through his writings more clearly than it does in the works of more traditional and systematic philosophers. While their common theme is the fate of man, existentialists have, naturally, different interpretations of man [87]. Some eulogize man as a species and glorify his name by capitalizing it as Man — a distinction usually reserved for the deity and the first person singular. Others have found despair, estrangement, and nonbeing among the ashes of tradition and have offered them as new guiding principles. In the act of combating rationalism, certain existentialists have converted the existential viewpoint into a new rationalism, replete with categories as murky as any found in Kant or Hegel. Existence itself becomes a new version of old-fashioned "essence."

Religion is rarely an explicit issue among existentialists — with exceptions, to be sure [59, 90, 135]. However, when held up to the light, even their most secular writings seem to be oddly inverted sermons which praise man's choice, will, consciousness, intelligence, and responsibility in superlatives once applied only to God. The existentialist may profess that what he is, or believes, is entirely a matter of indifference to the universe, but he is also a devout skeptic who regrets that the universe cares so little. Existential pronouncements often carry the imperative ring of moral injunctions [89]. Making a few terminological adjustments, such as substituting "Divine Being" for being, "Nature" for existence, "love" for care, and "sin" for nonbeing, would cause the latent religious orientation to be even more apparent. It is not unfair, and by no means pejorative, to say that existentialists advocate a *theology of man.*

For reasons already cited, scientists seek the more abstract and precise, rather than the crude and concrete. Consequently, evaluation of subjective events has largely been relegated to the implausibilities and imprecisions of theologians, literary men, and essayists, who have neither clinical nor scientific training. This has meant that predominantly existential problems have not been of significant scientific concern. In psychiatry, where these problems are most relevant, existential formulations have not lent themselves to operational analysis.

Psychoanalysis has been reproached both for not being more "scientific" and, at the same time, for not giving more attention to "human values" [94]. Double criticism like this is more or less inevitable, because psychoanalysis stands midway between objective science and subjective experience. Emphasis on one implies that the other is ignored. Psychoanalysis studies psychodynamic processes as well as human problems, but they are by no means synonymous. Human problems are the substance *of* man while psychoanalytic theory is *about* man. The so-called mental apparatus in psychoanalysis is a scientific model, at best, and does not refer to the "mind" or problems of anyone in particular [46m]. Existentialists seem to devote themselves to the hiatus between the *formulations* of psychoanalytic theory and the *problems* with which individual men are involved.

The most significant contribution that existentialists can

make to psychoanalysis is to underscore those subjective, intrapersonal factors which apply directly to a unique, responsible
person from the *inside* of his experience, and which defy conventional categories and descriptions [61, 121b]. It is the *existential attitude*, therefore, that psychoanalysts will find most congenial, since it stresses man's unique responsibility in relation to
reality. Far more than most men, and certainly more than even
the theologian, philosopher, or literary essayist, the psychoanalyst
is immersed in the reality of human suffering. Moreover, he realizes that categories, rating scales, rational standards, and impersonal explanations fail to capture the living, stinging moment
of reality when people are caught in a tangle of stoloniferous
conflict. He does not need to be told that the here-and-now of
existence is far richer than the attenuated generalizations by
which he seeks to order it. Through the existential attitude, implicit in his practice as well as in his own personality, he recognizes that the spread of space and surge of time are irrelevant
phantoms unless they contain the fresh reality sense of an individual human being enmeshed in existence.

Although it is not true of everyone practicing in the field, psychoanalysis itself is permeated with profound regard for human
values because it respects the irrational motives of man and the
highly specialized structure of his conflicts [44]. The existential
attitude toward the utterly subjective in man has sharpened the
contrast between psychoanalysis as an intellectual discipline and
psychoanalysis as a human encounter. However, unless existential
principles can be brought out of the sphere of elusive pronouncements into that of clear scientific investigation of psychoanalytic
problems, the existential attitude will merely rouse us from ra-
tionalistic slumbers in order to give us a sleeping pill.

To think is to challenge categories, just as existence itself
challenges the categorical. Deep within himself the psychoanalyst
knows that insight emerges from the shadows of intuition rather
than from the bright illuminations of reason. He is aware that
his thoughts and theories are vagrant beams which first must pass
through the lens of his own personality before becoming the
light of understanding [47]. Although he seeks relevant facts to

11

incorporate into reliable principles, he cannot overlook the existential core of his discipline which escapes the written, and even the spoken, word.

There is a paradox, then, between analytic practice and analytic literature. Somewhere between the patient and the analyst, and between the author and the reader, the sense of reality, which brings both coherence and conviction to clinical events, evaporates. What remains is a dry, expository skeleton. When the inner spontaneity of discovery vanishes, the living reality of a psychoanalytic encounter no longer can be recognized in the residue.

Even the most convincing private events are rarely communicable when put into print. Psychoanalytic formulations condense so many clinical observations that the symbol replaces the reality; the very means of rational containment becomes a means of forsaking thought. The psychodynamic formulation is like a bucket without a bottom: the more that is poured into it, the less it holds [140b]. Furthermore, in some circumstances the quest for clarity itself may be self-defeating. The public word necessarily points up the similarities between people, either in their symptoms or in their principles. But this fact alone may undermine the unique appeal which first attracted the investigator.

The rubric and the reality are readily confused, but disciplines do not decide their own subject matter. Existential events are not the special province, or discipline, of existentialists; nor, for that matter, are dreams and childhood events the fief of psychoanalysis alone. Unfortunately, however, habits of thought that insist upon pigeonholing ideas also insist upon fomenting friction instead of upon clarifying the genuine issues between one ism and another. Accordingly, the relevance of the *existential attitude* must be examined apart from any controversial and confusing *existential theories* that pertain to it.

Parochial animus is appropriate only for devotees of a sect, not for reflective human beings, and surely not for serious investigators. Egregious distortions of psychoanalytic perspectives and existential conceptions are probably unavoidable. Some existentialists, such as Frankl [45], further their own philosophies by making straw men out of analysts. Because psychoanalysis has many theoretical and practical limitations, these authors conclude that any other viewpoint is an improvement — particularly their own, which they call "existential psychotherapy." Some analysts, too, look upon classical psychoanalytic writings as a kind of sacred text that must never be modified. That Freud may have erred is seldom mentioned and rarely documented [68]. In their misguided devotion, proponents of one viewpoint or another often resort to the familiar device of coupling their controversial notions with some undisputed principle. As a result, it becomes difficult to examine one without seeming to repudiate the other, as, for example, when it is claimed that only psychoanalysis is truly "scientific," or that existentialism alone is concerned with "human values." Those who support the first notion are afraid that the use of information from other fields will somehow befoul analytic aims, while those who espouse the second idea suppose that, without the unique contributions of existentialism, psychoanalysis is blind pedantry.

To argue the uniqueness or originality of any viewpoint is of doubtful value. Although enthusiasts proclaim that some idea or other is a new window of truth or a panacea for every malady, its uniqueness does not assure its validity. Unless its value can be demonstrated by painstaking study, no hypothesis gains authenticity by authoritarian proclamation. Thinkers have long been aware of the synthetic priority of experience over conceptual systems and are prepared to acknowledge that most philosophical positions are strategies whereby innate convictions and private temperaments are reconciled with explicit propositions and world views. A thinker's ideas surely cannot be reduced to his autobiography, but his basic acceptances do belong to his style of life and to his orientation toward existence. This viewpoint is an axiom of psychoanalysis, not a special discovery of existentialists. Moreover, if this is true, then it is also true for analysts themselves, as well as for every other person. Hence, the existential core of psychoanalysis proposes that the living reality of analytic experience itself pervades the *theory of analysis*, the *act of analyzing*, the *profession of psychoanalysis*, and the *personal dimensions of the analyst*.

Out of the personal reality of being an analyst, then, the psychoanalyst must account for his own participation in what is real. Self-scrutiny enables him to clarify the kind of reality he brings to the analytic encounter. More than this, he must recognize that he too is caught within an unending oscillation between meaning and being. Thus he typifies the problems of finding significance amid the disappointments, errors, pains, and false faiths that undermine existence.

Why has it fallen to the psychoanalyst — that curious and arcane physician who deals in both personal maladies and protoscientific theories — to represent the existential dilemma of mankind? In his person, profession, practice, and theories he exemplifies a fusion of inner organic experience with abstract philosophical principles. When he affirms that some things are more real and responsive than others, he makes use of reality sense. At the same time, his sense of responsibility insists that he also make sense out of his own reality before he can even conjecture about anyone else's reality and responsibility. His existential core is shared with no one else, yet this is typical of everyone. He is concerned about human problems yet is detached from the swirl of everyday events. He is isolated yet is perpetually immersed in whatever happens during human suffering. In a word, the psychoanalyst must face in two directions at once: toward the utterly subjective, irrational elements in men who differ from each other according to intangible qualities, and toward the completely objective, scientific principles by which man reckons what he means and what he means to do.

On what level of existence does psychoanalysis operate? How far can the existential attitude reach? Even though the writings of existentialists call attention to domains of experience that more systematic philosophers have conveniently overlooked, the existential attitude is too pervasive to be chronicled and contained by books and articles. The philosophical problems that tumble out of each day's analytic hours are often overlooked by analysts, so that philosophers have very little opportunity to acquaint themselves with these problems. Because they must rely upon second- or third-hand sources, most critical appraisals of psychoanalysis by philosophers are limited to its most peripheral manifestations. Nevertheless, just as the ancients conceived of minor gods to preside over property and households and of major gods to inspire universal theologies and different kinds of worship, there are philosophical principles which seem to govern every phase of an analyst's life, professional and personal, and influence his style of examining reality.

The existential attitude reminds man that whether he seeks scientific truth, aesthetic illumination, or practical performance he cannot move beyond the boundaries of his own diversified reality. The chapters that follow will trace the existential core of psychoanalysis from its root reality in organic events to its emergence in emotion and in the development of meaning, motivation, and conduct. It can be traced by following the parallel threads of reality sense and responsibility through the transformations that each undergoes. The existential core of psychoanalysis is not confined to the consultation room. It is found in any version of reality and on any level of experience; it is dispersed by conflict but brought together again in concordant conduct; it is discovered in the vicissitudes of emotional crises and in the quavering uncertainty of hope and despair. The abiding principle is that reality is primarily a human experience and that man creates his own conditions for what is true, what is effective, and, finally, what is responsible.

The ensuing sequence of chapters forms neither a closed circle of argumentation nor a symmetrical pyramid of self-contained theory. It is intended to be like the audacious and open-ended act of thinking itself — a catenary holding within itself the shape of existence, the substance of reality, the ways in which we intuitively reach out for truth, and the circumstances under which time snatches it away.

2. The Categorical and the Existential

The Human Conditional

That each person regards himself as a unique and significant entity is an unquestioned fact of existence. He may resemble his fellow humans more than he differs from them, but, deep within, he is convinced that whatever he thinks or feels has a claim to general validity and cannot be dismissed simply as his own prejudice or preference. Whether or not he is prepared to acknowledge his beliefs openly, or even to formulate them clearly, he cherishes them and feels, therefore, that his thoughts unquestionably correspond to reality.

The Categorical and the Existential

Many people declare themselves ready to accept criticism and even profess to welcome it, but secretly they prefer praise. This is natural, because to damage the beliefs with which a man confronts the world is to damage the man himself. A personal aura of reality and truth brackets whatever is seen, felt, and thought, so that anyone else's beliefs are accepted or rejected according to their compatibility with pre-existing convictions [27]. The certainty clinging to personal experience fosters another belief: that the ultimate source of truth and reality is to be found among the data of self-observation. Psychoanalysts call this tendency toward augmented self-esteem "narcissism" [46g], and it is clear that narcissistic aims are served when man identifies his objectives with those of the universe. The concept of nature herself is, like Eve, a specific creation cast in man's own image. When man declares that self-preservation is the first law of nature, he means that nature's first concern is with his own survival.

Positivism is a kind of philosophical narcissism. It is bred by coupling complete confidence in the reliability of thinking with certainty about the data of consciousness. According to that branch of positivism called phenomenology, experience seems so unambiguously real that what is thought about it seems unequivocally true. Belief in our thinking processes and in the facts of observation has an elementary appeal as a theory, but it is notoriously unreliable as a base for a method of investigation. Positivism cannot claim to be valid merely because its principles are supposedly determined by the phenomena of experience. These phenomena require interpretation, which, in turn, is derived from previous ideas, concepts, and attitudes. A strict positivism may limit the scope of meaning to what is already believed. There are many mentally ill patients whose skewed convictions and distorted reality sense firmly restrict their interpretations of experience and therefore make "positivists" of them. It is an illusion to believe that principles of thought can be derived solely from the data of experience and self-observation. The growth of ideas depends upon stretching the boundaries of circumscribed convictions by believing just as firmly in our capacity to doubt and to tolerate uncertainty [154].

The Existential Core of Psychoanalysis

Self-recognition and judgment of others depend upon root convictions and axioms of certainty called acceptances [151]. These are primitive ideas and inclinations whose reality sense is so strong that, even if their possessor were wholly aware of explicit acceptances, no alternative would be conceivable. Acceptances are the implicit grounds on which other ideas are judged true or false. For this reason, acceptances themselves are neither true nor false. In fact, as we define them, acceptances are rarely distinct ideas; more often they are special *attitudes* toward experience and *inclinations* toward different kinds of acts. Were there a personal creed to reflect collective acceptances, it, too, would be only a derivative of the actual sources of belief. Our established "principles" are not the reasons we believe as we do; they are the result of believing a great many other things. What any man professes in his philosophy is more often a distilled, bowdlerized version of what he would like to believe than what he does believe or what he really acts upon.

These axioms of certainty are at the core of both meaning and motivation and give rise to the collective acts and activities known as *mind*. Acceptances shape the questions asked of nature, instead of supplying the answers. Their unspoken certitude allows no compromise or qualification until other acceptances, bearing an equal sense of reality, moderate the force of the original ideas. Man first emerged from the darkness of foreordained fact into the dawn of the thinking process when his derived attitudes offered a *choice* between alternative possibilities. Although, by definition, acceptances are unquestioned attitudes, derived attitudes can lose a portion of their original sense of reality. As a result, ideas become less certain, attitudes less entrenched. It is this unsettled aspect of existence that precedes both thinking and truth. To subject a cherished belief to open examination is to change its sense of reality from certainty to doubt. When this noble event happens — an act celebrated by genuine skeptics — then acceptances become *conditionals* and are no longer *certainties*. Among unconscious attitudes there is no logical alternative to "*Since . . . then. . . .*" But when conditionals replace absolutes, reality testing is able to choose between alternatives and to select a premise: "*If . . . then. . . .*" At this point the processes of trial-and-error thinking and provisional generalization have begun.

The enigmatic process by which objects, images, acts, ideas, attitudes, and facts are brought together into a cohesive sense of reality transcends our knowledge of reality itself. However, to accumulate information about existence without understanding why *this* experience is convincing, or *that* object is real, and why other objects or experiences are neutral or indifferent, distorts the purpose of inquiry and even defeats it. Prejudices are often preferred to truth, and modest conditionals have less appeal than do comprehensive absolutes, but we cannot capitulate to ignorance and elevate it to the level of knowledge simply because it has a strong sense of reality. Certainty about our own existence is a primitive acceptance. However, in the midst of the errors and terrors of life, the animal validity of personal experience is an unsatisfactory explanation. Although reason, logic, and proof do not decide which ideas are important enough to be acted upon, it is our *belief* in the processes of reasoning, logic, and proof that makes them relevant to our inquiries.

"WE" AS A CONDITIONAL

For the most part, the ideas motivating man are seldom conscious, rarely explicit, and never well defined. His attitudes and inclinations are predicates of the times in which he lives, the product of his own history. One of his favorite acceptances is that, *since* thought and reality are so much alike, his perception of another person is *then* equivalent to full knowledge about that person. For example, when a writer or speaker refers to "we," he is not always being modest or generous. More often he is testifying that "what is true for me is true for thee." He believes not only that it is possible to communicate with other people but that because they share mutual acceptances their decisive realities must be identical. However, this claim of "we" is a conditional. Compared with the vast information gathered from lifelong self-examination and from observation of the surrounding world, our knowledge of what another person is like on the inside is paradoxically limited to a few scattered impressions encircled by a host of inferences. I am obliged to look at people from the viewpoint of my own preconceptions, to assume that my inevitable distortions and special interests will reveal the truth about another person in my impressions of him. I must mitigate this bitter truth by assuming that you, too, share this isolation. Therefore, I justify my use of "we" when I think that your beliefs, habits, attitudes, or ideas, on the basis of our common experience, correspond to some extent with mine. Nevertheless, in casual, everyday encounters, we do not always specify the difference between what a person does and what he intended to do, or between what he seems to be and what he is. Instead, we automatically accept that the other person is just what we judge him to be.

Psychoanalysis is challenged by this issue. Who is the other one, and what do we make out of him? A "patient," for example, is a tender abdomen to a surgeon's hand, a cry of pain to a nurse, an open mouth to the diet kitchen, and a financial risk to the front office. To his bank he is a series of numbers and to his employer he is a body who performs more or less predictably. Psychoanalysis could not proceed without heeding the disparity between a man's image of himself and another person's ideas about him. It must ask how people are able to use the same words and yet mean different things, or to talk about issues without really conveying their full sentiments. Judgment of another person may indeed be fragmentary, but self-perception, too, is often self-deception. Thus, it is crucial that psychoanalysis mistrust the motives which are so easily assigned to outward acts and inquire into how people develop their unique stamp of reality.

PARADOXICAL JUDGMENTS

What if it were possible to perceive the whole existence of another person, instead of just the masks he wears or the noises he makes? If a domineering, arrogant businessman were simultaneously judged to feel diffident and impoverished because he lacked education, he would no longer be labeled "boorish" or "ruthless," because his entire effect upon us would be different. In turn, if he did not look upon us as educated detractors, his veneer of arrogance and bullying might well dissolve. What if the posture of a vain, self-centered woman were understood as a plea for reassurance that she is worthy of love? Suppose we could fully appreciate that an indolent, frivolous playboy wastes his life for no other reason than that he is ashamed of his own merit; or that a noble, self-sacrificing missionary is partially spurred by some nameless remorse; or that a devoted mother dedicates her life to her children in order to atrophy their independence and keep them forever helpless. In a strange balance of nature it is often found that tyrants create martyrs, martyrs call forth tyrants, and both may have similar motives.

These paradoxical judgments are at once the pride and despair of psychodynamic psychiatry. If the private convictions and acceptances that motivate people could be appreciated with the same sense of reality with which we affirm ourselves, then we would truly pass from categorical group thinking and pigeonhole classification of man into full comprehension of what it means to be a human being. By shedding some of the values that register unqualified admiration or contempt, we could gently discover how people come to terms with themselves. Recognition of the devious paths that primitive acceptances follow to fulfillment and federation is not a vision of a psychodynamic utopia. If there is pride in being able to recognize what people are like from the inside — as opposed to their public definitions — there is also despair at the persistent categorical judgments which these same people form about others.

THE HUMAN CONDITION

The phrase *human condition* has a curious and contrite banality. It is often uttered as an unfathomable answer to some unformulated question about human destiny and suffering. Whether this vapid term encourages an optimistic or a pessimistic attitude, we can be sure that neither is justified. Affirmations about man's melancholy fate are often everted ecstasies, just as a depressed patient will blame himself, or his stars, in order to affirm his discovery of the ultimate standard of judgment. Truth does not necessarily hurt, nor is bitterness the test of a medicine. Reality is not determined wholly by what is harsh or hopeless, and wisdom is not always an ineffective by-product of experience, withheld until we are too old to care. Coming to terms with existence, like "adjustment to reality," is something more than a bad bargain that costs too much. To be responsible, finally, does not mean being blamed for what we did not cause in the first place. In short, the "human condition" is not "humanity in a critical condition." According to Sherrington [128], "We have an inalienable prerogative of responsibility which we cannot devolve, no, not as once was thought, even upon the stars. We can share it only with each other."

What any man believes is determined by his sense of reality. His acceptances — premises of both motivation and meaning — are the unspectacular conditionals which guide his search for reality. Thus, the *human conditional* is the productive and affirmative side of man's efforts to resolve the paradoxes of existence. Its shadowy undersurface is the *human condition.*

Dimensions of the Personal

Human conditionals depend upon the root reality of the *I* — the first person singular of both grammar and existence — who acts and, by acting, repudiates the fact of being acted upon. The *I* is able to explore the full range of its dimensions because of the *ontological acceptance*, which combines three axioms: existence is prior to knowledge; the sense of reality corresponds to what is real; there are other entities with an autonomous existence of their own. Thus, while it is an exaggeration to claim that no man is an island, neither is he immersed in an ocean, with receding horizons as his only limits. The concept of a shared, public reality depends upon ontological assumptions that the sense of reality is not confined to our own *I*, that the world is populated by many independent beings who act, and that there are objects which allow themselves to be acted upon. The private cloister of personal encounter with the world is not, therefore, a prison in which we are doomed to serve a life sentence of solitary confinement.

Although it is wholly possible for me to accept the autonomous existence of another person, and even to understand a few shared properties of his existence, his independent experience is as elusive to me as my inner experience is to him. There is a paradoxical union between *ontological acceptance* and *existential solitude*. The paradox occurs because each of us is sealed in a transparent cocoon of reality. We gesticulate and shout, and, hearing our own sounds and seeing the nodding and grimaces of others, we conclude that they have heard and, therefore, understand a message. The cocoon stretches but never yields. The fact of solitude means that in each man's eyes we catch glimpses only of ourselves, and when we shield our eyes it is to reduce the glare of self-discovery. The logical conditions which impel us to our own general view of reality arise from existential absolutes. Styles of life and ways of thinking become types of reality [73]. The ubiquitous conditionals guiding our conclusions are also the specific conditions on which the autonomous existence of other people is accepted. Whoever proclaims that he is, in fact, "involved in all mankind" is involved with no one in particular. Since reality sense is rooted in private being, not in public contexts, reality is as much created as it is encountered, and merely being able to acknowledge the independent existence of others becomes almost a miracle of reality sense. The cacophony set off by teeming hordes of humanity is not to be confused with the tolling of a bell calling us to mutual meditation. Instead of the Cartesian "I think, therefore I am," or the existentialist "I exist, therefore I think," ontological acceptance holds that the *I* is the first reality — "I am real, therefore the world is real." Existential solitude is both a conviction and a condition for the human act of living in and through experience, and for acting upon people and things, without always being aware of doing so. The absolute relevance of this "metaphysical" solitude is often overlooked unless it emerges in such pathological shapes as loneliness, despair, desolation, or abandonment.

ACTIVITIES AND THINGS

Perhaps the most primitive distinction between mind and matter is that between *activity* and *thing*. Activity is a property of organisms [35c], whereas things are characteristically inanimate. The term *object*, which is usually opposed to *subject*, refers both to things of the world and so-called objects of thought. The difference between them is determined by their participation in some organic activity: a *thing* is unchanged, while an *object of thought* is altered by its participation. For example, the chemical structure of water is unchanged throughout the activities of preparing ice, liquid, or steam. Water is, therefore, a thing — an entity recognized by the formula H_2O. In some respects a thing is a *postulated* entity, with constant, durable components that allow it to be more or less independent of the human acts in which it participates. As we think about water, however, it is an object of thought, whose regular changes are conveniently called its *properties*. The idea of a thing is a wholly *impersonal* reality — an obdurate fiction that belongs to the domain of objective science and to knowledge *about* the world.

According to the existential attitude, explanations and scientific accounts of objects are the products of categorizing the world; they are not literal expressions *of* the world. Because the fact of existence is prior to knowledge, science, as a human, organic activity, becomes a systematic way to regulate existential facts of experience.

So-called objective reality is conventionally represented only by things, but without a sense of reality *for* things, objective reality would contain neither objects nor reality. Although our abiding sense of personal identity — the *I* — is usually accepted as the prototype of the wholly mental, in some respects it is as constant, obdurate, and impenetrable as are things.

The *I* is a dynamic participant in organic events, while the idea of *self*, with which it is often confused, is only a static sample of what exists in its full significance as *I* [3, 64a]. The *I* is an existential phenomenon, but the *ego*, with which it is also confused, is a categorical concept designating an integrated hierarchy of functions that evolve through time [40a, b]. The difference between *I* and *ego* may be described as the difference between the sensation of warmth and light from the sun, as a purely personal, unshared experience, and an analysis of the event according to the perception of regulated body temperature and intensity of illumination.

The Categorical and the Existential

THE THREE WORLDS OF PERCEPTION

The existential attitude puts the *I* at the center of existence as the ultimate referent. Admittedly, this viewpoint is proto-scientific and preanalytic, and perhaps even precognitive. In any case, it generates a personalized reality. Existentialists have emphasized three ways of perceiving the world [94]. The *Eigenwelt* is our own inner world and is the means by which we reach out to whatever else exists. The *Mitwelt* is the world of human beings in relation to each other. It is not a world of static relations but a sphere of mutual responsibility and responsiveness. Finally, the *Umwelt* is that aspect of the world which exists apart from our immediate awareness. It includes such issues as instincts, natural laws, drives, forces, and things.

These three worlds may be roughly translated as *dimensions of the personal* [53]. They define the order and direction of different types of reality with respect to the nodal *I*. Thus, the *intrapersonal dimension* consists of purely private events, wherein the vividness and conviction of acceptances, meanings, and motivations arise. The *interpersonal dimension* relates the *I* to other human beings, whose existence substantially modifies the naked reality of personal experience. Finally, the *impersonal dimension* is that in which the *I* is just one object, or set of forces, among other objects, or forces, that influence each other simply because they are subject to laws or principles.

The reality of being a person among other persons is not conveyed by the bleak term *object relations* [117]. The difference between a static object relation and the dynamic interpersonal dimension of reality is like the difference between the logical relation *next to*, in "A is next to B" and the human relation implied by, for example, a husband lying next to his wife. An inert object can be identified, but only a living subject has its own identity [83]. The interpersonal dimension makes of man neither an impersonal thing nor an intrapersonal phantom. When Caudill [25, 26] compares the interpersonal dimensions of our contemporary mother-child relationships with those of the Japanese, he does not merely define their differences in terms of "society" or "culture" but includes the subjective attitudes and acceptances of people as they influence each other.

The impersonal dimension is made up of alien forces that indifferently impinge upon us. In its impersonalized form, the unique character of the *I* is lost. Instead of being able to initiate a response in another person, man becomes a thing which responds only to some outside influence. When a man is struck by a falling stone, the event is an impersonal one in the impersonal dimension. If the stone is thrown by another man, with a specific intent to hurt, the event also becomes relevant in the interpersonal dimension. When the victim is subsequently treated for his injury, both the trauma and the method of treatment are further impersonalizing forces, because they could happen to anyone. The pain and humiliation resulting from an unprovoked attack, however, are uniquely intrapersonal.

There are also impersonal biological forces that operate within the organism. Unlearned and relatively stereotyped instinctual patterns characteristically erupt and impose themselves upon a person, depriving him of all but the most primitive means to fulfill or to avoid their intents. The psychoanalytic *id* of unconscious images, ideas, and impulses is, indeed, an impersonal *it* which periodically overpowers more highly evolved, less stereotyped mechanisms.

Existential solitude and ontological acceptance confine man to a sphere from which he cannot be extruded. Dimensions of the personal define his latitude within this sphere. It is wholly consistent with the existential attitude to emphasize one dimension and negate the others [cf. p. 220]. This selectivity certainly occurs in scientific investigation, where the intrapersonal and interpersonal dimensions are ignored in favor of the world of forces and things. Being a thing is still a feature of being a person, just as being an organism is a property of being a person. *Feeling like* a thing is an intrapersonal experience, not an impersonal event. However, different views of reality [106*a*], whether found in theories of society, religion, art, or psychology, may be the unconscious outcome of using data from one dimension to draw conclusions about other dimensions. The notion of *fate*, for example, is the result of assigning interpersonal significance to the impersonal operation of forces and things [36]. In contrast, the doctrine of *determinism* asserts that it is impossible to be anything other than an impersonal object that responds to inflexible or intractable forces. Reality sense is distributed throughout all three dimensions, but the capacity to impersonalize, interpersonalize, and intrapersonalize experience is a function of reality testing.

Categorical and Existential Views of Man

In what dimension shall man himself be viewed? A psychiatric consultant is often asked to evaluate patients whose complaints cannot be explained by the nature of their medical disease or surgical lesion. He is almost never asked to appraise patients who have fewer complaints and problems than other patients with similar ailments. The physician who seeks the consultation is disturbed only because he is unable to contain the excessive and unexpected complaints within the conventional limits of impersonal and categorical knowledge [140c].

Why do excessive and unexpected complaints and problems challenge the physician himself? He is likely to ask the psychiatrist a pseudo-quantitative question: "How much is organic, and how much is functional?" This is, of course, a meaningless question. It shows that the physician is trying to maintain a false distinction between the *patient*, as an impersonal, categorical system of biological processes, and the *person*, who seemingly defies the determination of forces and things by insisting, through his complaints, that he is not like the other people with whom he shares the same kind of organs, symptoms, or illnesses. Physician and patient may be equally perplexed, because their harmonious interpersonal relationship, which is based upon the conformity of each to the categorical image of the other, is now disrupted.

If the underlying acceptance of the physician is that man, the patient, is wholly subject to categorical predication and clinical prediction, he is then obliged to believe that further appraisal will disclose still other categorical issues within the impersonal dimension, and that these will account for unexplained complaints by adding up to exactly 100 percent, with no interpersonal or intrapersonal remainders. However, neither physician nor patient can ignore these two dimensions. It is no more possible to dismiss a patient by making a diagnosis of "atypical" than it is to appraise a physician by his bedside manner alone.

It is uniquely distressing to the physician to discover that his medical knowledge has abruptly become inadequate. He is confronted no longer with a categorical patient but with a person whose complaints and problems are often responses to the physician as a person. The physician is forced to adopt an existential viewpoint, along with his familiar categorical viewpoint. Baffled, he tries to overcome the diplopia of a dual viewpoint by closing his eyes to one aspect or the other. When he finally calls upon the psychiatrist, the fact of mutual alienation or despair has often already happened, and he has subsequently become angry with the patient, who seemingly has violated his clinical, impersonal assignment by "choosing" to be recalcitrant. At other times the physician may feel ashamed of his own inadequate knowledge, or of his inability to forgive either the patient or himself for being a person. At this enduring moment the physician and the patient are each split off from their categorical properties, from their knowledge, their previous relationship, and even their sense of time.

An occasional physician is able to contend with the split between a person who is sick and a patient with a disease without repudiating the patient or reproaching himself. He is prepared to commit himself to caring, even in the presence of incurable disease. He accepts the challenge by learning to live with despair and makes a scapegoat of neither the patient nor himself.

The psychiatrist is not exempt from the diplopia of two views of man. By the nature of his work, he may experience even more frequent moments of despair, but perhaps only because he concerns himself with situations in which definitions fail, and with areas where a patient's unique existence transgresses categories. Like his medical colleagues, however, he rarely complains about "too little" resistance or "too flexible" defenses. When he says his patients are "doing well," he means that there have been no particular challenges recently. Nevertheless, he may be as baffled by the patient who does well and recovers, without leaving a hint of the reason why, as he is by the patient who stubbornly clings to his illness. He may attribute unexplained success to his "relationship" with the patient; yet, when faced with failure, he will ignore relationship and tacitly accuse the patient of being "too narcissistic," or "unwilling to give up secondary gain." These pejorative explanations clearly reveal that the psychiatrist has imputed a hidden voluntarism to the patient and that the patient's existential attitude is the latent cause of his intractable symptoms. In a sense, it is the patient's "intention" to remain in despair.

Constant oscillation between the existential and categorical viewpoints during psychoanalysis suggests that many problems of transference and countertransference result from skewed attitudes of both the analyst and the patient [18]. Problems of this kind are almost invariably due to a confusion between categorical necessity and existential choice. Transference diplopia is readily recognized in the patient whenever his sense of reality for the analyst is distorted by special images inherited from the past and transposed into the present. Countertransference problems arise in the analyst whenever he relinquishes categorical observations of process and content — the psychoanalytic equivalent of forces and things — and responds as though he believes the patient is voluntarily defying both unconscious determinants and the institution of psychoanalysis. The ensuing struggle is precipitated by viewing the patient simultaneously as an example of inexorable, categorical processes and as a self-determined, responsible individual [137a].

DISTINCTIONS BETWEEN THE TWO VIEWS

There is inherent contradiction between the existential and categorical viewpoints only when will and determinism are assigned to the same dimension [85]. Cause and choice, indeed, presuppose each other. Despite our pretense of a belief in immutable laws of nature, the existential view is implicit in everyday life. Even hard-shelled determinists assume that everyone has some degree of latitude, conscious choice, and responsibility for what he does. Most actions, Sherrington says, have "an unquestioned tinge of freedom" [128]. The prototype of both causal determinism and existential freedom, not surprisingly, is found in the relation of *wish* to *deed*. Whenever a deed follows a wish for it to be so, the swift certainty is no less a model of freedom than it is a paradigm of determinism. The intimate relation of wish to deed illustrates that the existential and categorical cannot be reduced to one or the other but that, like reality sense and reality testing, they appeal to each other for confirmation.

The distinction between categorical man and existential man is not simply another great dichotomy, such as that of reason and emotion, intellect and passion, the rational and the empirical; nor is it another antithetical tradition, such as classic or romantic, priestly or prophetic, Apollonian or Dionysian; nor yet is it another perplexing antinomy, such as permanence and change, being and becoming, one and many. These are all examples of problems and paradoxes that have meandered down through the ages, clothed in the intellectual raiment fashionable in their times. The recurrent civil war of these alternative viewpoints has long since degenerated into a ritual combat which settles nothing because the issues are no longer living. Each antithetical position is a value judgment, not a method of inquiry. There is no such need to "choose" between existential man and categorical man. Each is *there*, within his own proper coordinates. When we inquire about reality we do not choose between height and weight, rest and movement, time and space, or even spirit and matter. As with reality sense and reality testing, each makes a case for the other. The genuine question is, "Which is the most reliable way to discover what is real and what is illusory, the method of the fixed criterion or of the transient event?"

Categorical man is cross-sectional man. As an object that shares characteristics with others, he is known by his anatomy and politics, chemistry and occupation, credit card and color, social standing and religion. Depending upon the category in which he is catalogued, he is citizen, taxpayer, animal organism, face in the crowd, thing to be feared, or, among other things, patient with disease. In his extreme form, categorical man is a statistical fiction, regardless of how skillfully the statistics are put together.

The Categorical and the Existential

Existential man is seen from inside his own world instead of as a distant object in an orderly universe. Because he believes in his own unique existence, the circumstances in which he acts are perceived as inseparable from the acts. In his extreme form, existential man believes that his own choice and control alone create the reality of the world.

Since the distinction between existential man and categorical man is largely determined by perspective, it is not surprising to find that each perspective tends to have a vocabulary of its own. At any moment, we simultaneously match our thoughts *about* an event with our intrapersonal perception *of* that event. Consequently, we often ambiguously use words that sound alike but have different meanings in each perspective.

CATEGORICAL AND EXISTENTIAL LANGUAGE

Because thinking itself is inherently dichotomous — we must negate as well as generalize — and reality is relative — whatever is real is real only from a particular viewpoint — categorical and existential language are both in use at any one time. Reality is compounded of an *activating subject*, from the viewpoint of reality sense, and of *activated objects*, from the viewpoint of reality testing. Reality sense spreads out centrifugally to the world, and the language of existence conveys the special intrapersonal flavor of direct experience. Reality testing captures objects and events and pulls them inward for categorical inspection. Categorical language is precise, as only an object-language can be. Existential language, as it strives for total comprehension, is imprecise, reflecting the ambiguity of its subject matter. *Existential language is not to be confused with the language, or terminology, used by existentialists.* The issue here is to distinguish between two general *aims* of language, not to devise new terminology. The categorical aim is that of dualistic thought and the relation of substantives to predicates. The existential aim is that of direct affirmation of reality in all of its relative impermanence. A list of typical expressions illustrates how contrasting terms are related, without being contradictory. Both can occur in the same context and supplement each other's meaning without incompatibility.

31

Existential	Categorical
Reality sense	Reality testing
Affirmation	Negation
Intuition	Logic; reason
Absolutes	Conditionals
Being	Categories; properties
Organic meaning	Objective meaning
Immediacy	Contingency
"It is"	"It might"
"and"	"or not"
"Since . . . then . . ."	"If . . . then . . ."
I	Self; ego
Conviction; belief	Corroboration; information
Organic activity	Objective ordering
Equivalents	Sequences
Metaphors	Symbols

Reality Sense and Reality Testing

Characteristics of reality sense may be briefly compared with those of reality testing. Their more detailed analysis has been published elsewhere [140a].

1. Reality sense is concerned with *what* is real. Reality testing discovers *how* it is real.
2. Reality sense refers to an *entire event*, not to any one part, unless that part has established an independent existence of its own. Reality testing separates the content of events into *component parts*.
3. For reality sense, events are unequivocal, complete objects that can be *comprehended as a whole*. For reality testing, objects are events that belong to many contexts and hence can be only *approximately understood*.
4. Reality sense may be shared by different events, which thereby become *affective equivalents*. Reality testing may arrange events in sequences according to a common meaning or according to different meanings of a common event.
5. Reality sense is *synthetic*. Reality testing is *analytic*.
6. Reality sense is largely *emotional, intuitive, and percep-*

tual. Reality testing tends to be *rational, intellectual, and conceptual.*

7. Reality sense experiences an event from the *inside.* Reality testing appraises an event from the *outside.*
8. Reality sense deals with *convictions.* Reality testing operates with *conditionals.*
9. Reality sense uses *certainty as a measure of value and validation.* Reality testing begins with *contingency,* ends with *proof,* and, with the exception of truth, is more or less *free of value judgments.*
10. Reality sense is the *discovery* of experience as it happens. Reality testing is the *consequence* of experience and of the rules governing it.
11. Reality sense depends upon the *intensity* of experience. Reality testing depends upon the *invariance* of experience.
12. Reality sense consists of self-sufficient, *private acts.* Reality testing shares *public events* that have a common meaning.
13. Reality sense is expressed as *evocative affirmations,* often couched in metaphor, paradox, or adumbrative language. Reality testing may be expressed as *informative propositions.*
14. Reality sense *requires no justification,* since proof, rationality, logical demonstration, and reasonable argument use reality sense for their own justification. Reality testing *achieves plausibility* through a kind of calculus of observation and meaning.
15. Reality sense is based upon the priority of the *knower.* Reality testing depends upon variations in objects *known.*

This list is neither exhaustive nor exclusive. It is inserted here in an attempt to clarify the role of reality sense as the creative, self-enriching *I,* which cuts across categories and transmits conviction about reality, apart from full knowledge of its inner structure or operations. Reality testing, which shall only secondarily concern us, assiduously assigns meanings to events and gradually builds a scaffolding of premises and inferences. Reality sense appeals to nothing other than its own luminous validity.

Reality sense and reality testing are only the coordinates of experience, not its content. They cannot fill the vessel of existence and thought, nor do they exhaust the potential of motivated acts. Yet reality sense and reality testing generate whatever human reality there is. The animal validity of reality sense pounces upon the facts it encounters and swallows them whole. Then it either discards these facts as unreal and worthless or makes them its own. The comparatively civilized, more or less reasonable method of reality testing judiciously intervenes in the public realities of time, place, and action by taking events apart, piecemeal. Then, by means of compromise, qualification, and reconciliation, it fosters individual autonomy. Thus, reality is not merely an unyielding horde of brute facts which we face with obsolete equipment and according to rules we do not or cannot comprehend. It is created, as well as confronted. The dictum "I am real, therefore the world is real" implies that, through unspoken beliefs, passions, principles, perceptions, and dispositions, we have the means of recognizing and accounting for a public reality.

If we were to declare that the difference between reality sense and reality testing is merely the difference between emotion and reason, or between affective inclination and rational thought, the problem of understanding how organic meaning arises would be greatly oversimplified. Our task is to find out how private meanings, arising from inner experience and personalized reality, become translated into common language and objective events. The distinction between emotion and reason, for example, deals with the categorical view of man because it imposes an extrinsic form which the facts themselves do not justify. Man is neither an existential phantom nor a categorical fiction. The categorical and existential perspectives are not synonymous with statistical problems of classification, on the one hand, and existential problems of intuition, on the other. The creative conspiracy of reality sense and reality testing produces more than a world of objects and things; it produces a world of mutual meaning to be shared with others. The mediating influence between isolated, separate cubicles that each human being inhabits depends upon organic acts, not objective facts. After all, nature is a dynamic assembly of beings who know, perceive, and activate objects, and things which are known, perceived, and acted upon.

The penalty of oversimplification is the penalty of intellectual ambition; it destroys the substance of what first evokes the wish to understand. What prompts man to assume that he is adequate to the impossible task of contending with the surprises, disappointments, and suffering of living itself? We are not concerned with demonstrating again what needs no proof — that infinite combinations of circumstances and facts baffle understanding. To discover how man articulates his motives, prejudices, and inclinations with the manifold meanings of the world, we must first clarify the way in which organic meaning arises. Compared with this problem, the distinctions between subject and object, act and fact, instinct and intelligence, object and thing, synthesis and sequence, and, finally, mind and matter are wholly secondary consequences.

3. Organic Meaning

Organic and Objective Meaning

Neither man, as the knowing subject, nor the world, as objects known, affords a completely appropriate perspective for the interpretation of nature. Any viewpoint from which, in extreme form, the world is seen as an extension of consciousness, or the self as merely a diaphanous replica of the world of hard objects, is too restricted to do more than prejudice perception and distort understanding. The categorical and existential views of man do not together account for his vicissitudes in the world, nor do reality sense and reality testing explain the inner intricacies of psychological processes. At best, these are only gross approximations of different ways in which we may understand our actual attitudes.

Ordinary people prefer certainty to proof. Their obdurate dogmatism and blind prejudice are derived from an animal conviction that their own reality has a share in the structure of the world and that whatever seems real can be accepted on its own terms as a tangible extension of themselves. The ultimate equivalence between being real and being alive depends upon a wholly private belief that whatever has any meaning derives its meaning from human responses to the world. The meaning of meaning is more than an arid academic field tilled with semantic harrows. Because it is the meaning of reality *for* us which prompts our subsequent thought *about* both reality and meaning, the proper study of man begins with how his meanings are created [24b].

Nothing has meaning apart from its reference to something else. The concept of meaning itself usually refers to a link between a more or less abstract idea and a concrete experience [35b]. A novel or isolated event can be recognized only when it already has some meaning. Hence, it is neither absolutely novel nor totally isolated. A child seeing a chess knight for the first time recognizes only an unusual toy which looks like a horse; he does not see it as a chess piece. Rattles are manufactured in the shape of animals to impress parents, not infants. One reason why so-called intellectual insight is ineffective in psychoanalysis is that the patient is unprepared to relate the meaning of what the analyst says to his own body of personal meanings. Figure 1, adapted from Ogden and Richards [103], diagrams the relation between *symbol, thought,* and *thing.* Each of these terms refers primarily to events in the interpersonal, intrapersonal, and impersonal dimensions. A symbol is not made up just of those items of dream life and waking experience which are conventionally called symbols. It may be defined as *anything* that acquires meaning by standing for something else.

It is possible to maintain a militant monism toward reality only by acknowledging that we are committed to a dogmatic dualism in the act of knowing reality. The distinction between the knower and the known is basically a distinction between two

37

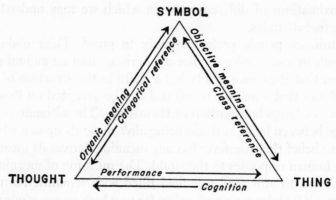

FIG. 1.

The meaning of meaning. (Adapted from C. Ogden and I. Richards, *The Meaning of Meaning*, Harcourt, Brace and Co., New York, 1946.)

kinds of meaning — *organic meaning* and *objective meaning*.

Objects have meaning, plus an accepted existence. Subjects — *subject* is a drab word for the *I* who knows and creates — have existence, plus an accepted meaning. How can this *I* understand its own organic meaning? There is seemingly no end to the introspective data that knowing subjects provide. However, sooner or later an investigator discovers the *looking-glass phenomenon*: the more closely he studies the intrapersonal dimensions, the more readily the subject who knows turns into a familiar, yet detached, object of knowledge.

Objective meaning depends upon the relation between symbols and things. The result is community meaning, or that meaning which is shared by everyone for whom the symbol designates similar objects. Organic meaning is determined by the relation between thoughts and symbols. It is generated by sources within the knowing subject, rather than in objects thought of. When a psychoanalyst speaks about the particular meaning of an episode, an object, or an act, he refers to its organic meaning — the meaning which is unique to his patient's personal experience. In short, organic meaning is the significance of different purposeful acts and attitudes with respect to some object or set of objects.

Organic Meaning

The meaning of anything, therefore, may be both public and private, narrow and broad, or organic and objective, depending upon the perspective from which it is viewed [80]. The organic meaning of "watch," for example, is the personal significance *this* watch has for me, and for any purposeful act that I undertake with respect to it. Its objective meaning is the community meaning of the entire class of watches, not merely this one.

The concept of organic meaning is based upon acceptance of the prior existence of a reality which can be sought, discovered, and understood, without merely postulating its existence or violating its unique character. Although outward signs may be bizarre or baffling, inner experience always has some kind of order or style. Events which are chaotic in some respects may be precisely patterned in others. Regressed schizophrenic patients, for example, always retain some link with objects and objective meaning, even if it is only with their own excrement. The kind of link is determined by the organic meaning of those objects and by the patient's orderly perspectives about experience.

ORGANIC MEANING AND ORDERLY PERSPECTIVES

Man must think according to one or another perspective, but he does not always think according to the perspective he prefers, or believes that he follows. Organic meaning is produced by collections of orderly perspectives [35b], which can be roughly described as somewhat more explicit versions of acceptances. However, it is equally proper to regard orderly perspectives as the ways in which acceptances interpret symbols, or, indeed, create symbols. Truth and error are instances of orderly perspectives, as are more tentative types of meaning, such as interpretations of dreams, or regressive behavior.

Orderly perspectives exert their influence on anyone who ponders his own responses and his place in the world, whether he is a patient, physician, or scientific investigator. When a patient is depressed, every event forebodes an imminent calamity. To a paranoid man, every man is a potential enemy. On whatever level, there is always the danger of insisting upon one viewpoint over another, with only slight reason for doing so.

The Existential Core of Psychoanalysis

Less conspicuous, but more insidious, are the one-sided perspectives indigenous to investigation of "mental" events. These may be called the *psychologist's fallacy*, the *philosopher's fallacy*, the *physiologist's fallacy*, and the *psychoanalyst's fallacy*.

The *psychologist's fallacy* confuses the products of thinking with the process of thinking. Because perception, for example, may be analyzed into components such as sensation, concepts, configurations, and so forth, the psychologist concludes that these are factors which nature has put together for the purpose of perceiving. The fallacy results from his failure to distinguish between organic meaning and objective meaning. Logic is concerned with the formal relation of thoughts, but thinking itself need not follow rules of logic.

The *philosopher's fallacy* confuses the common meaning of different events with a causative principle. Rules which govern events do not necessarily control them. Objects do not obey the law of gravity, nor do people adapt because of the reality principle. Our own anthropocentric concepts, names, and perspectives are often used not only to understand events but as a magical means to control them.

The *physiologist's fallacy* confuses a recognized, but impersonal, process with the total event, of which the isolated process is a part. The total event of sleep and sleeping, for example, may be studied in part by electroencephalography. But these records are not equivalent to the sleep process, even though they closely parallel increased and decreased alertness. This kind of fallacy is like confusing a deer with the tracks it leaves in the snow.

The *psychoanalyst's fallacy* confuses a viewpoint with an explanation. Part of the analytic task is to separate events from the meanings patients have given them, and then to understand both the concrete experience and the abstract idea. The analyst, too, may follow one perspective so closely that any alternative viewpoint is excluded. If, for example, an analyst is "instinct-minded," every symptom will be the result of aggression or sexual conflict. If, on the other hand, he follows a "psychosocial" line, then his patients will tend to suffer from disruptions of interpersonal relationships. When the full scope of organic meaning is confused with a more specialized or parochial perspective, any phase of meaning which is clearly defined soon acquires the status of a principle.

SKEPTICISM

Perspectives too long fixed, like authority too long held, lose the invigorating influence of uncertainty. Genuine skepticism is a restorative tonic for established attitudes, but pseudoskepticism is a destructive virus. Pseudoskeptics are disguised doctrinaires who believe that perspectives are like independent theories which can be challenged, and hence proved or disproved. No matter how congenial some perspectives feel, they are only contexts in the making, to be disciplined, perhaps, but not to be dismissed simply because other perspectives seem equally reasonable. Since acceptances in themselves are neither true nor false, the negation of an acceptance is itself an acceptance and is no more trustworthy, in some respects, than the one displaced. The tenacity with which acceptances and perspectives are held is a product of the believing process, not a measure of their validity. Genuine skeptics recognize that perspectives are only the fulcrum which organic meaning uses to extract objective meaning out of the homogeneity of reality sense and belief. They know that facts are deceptive and that impartiality may be the most deceptive fact of all.

Intrinsic and Extrinsic Meaning

Organic meaning is by far the most common way to establish a link between the objects, events, people, and things which surround us all. As a rule, thinking passes directly to the external thing, with only slight awareness of the symbolic forms whose transparency has made its passage easy [80]. Only when this direct comprehension is interrupted by baffling events, meaningless objects, or, as frequently happens, opaque prose do we appreciate how spontaneously we usually discover meaning. Like reality, meaning varies both in scope and in intensity — even for the same person — at different times and in different ways. At one moment an object may be rich with meaning; its hues and nuances may capture an ocean in a drop of water. At other moments, perhaps because of no more than fatigue or distraction, meaning may diminish into monochromatic poverty. Since objective meaning tends to be more or less constant, these fluctuations of meaning may be attributed to organic meaning, which, in turn, is determined by the condition of the organism and the distribution of reality sense itself. At the other extreme, the transparency of natural symbols is sometimes deliberately removed by the introduction of technical symbols [29]. This is done in order to exclude organic factors and to insure both precision and universal objective meaning. For example, the formula used in the conversion of Fahrenheit to Centigrade, C. $= 5/9$ (F. $- 32$), allows for the objective meaning of temperature measurement, uncontaminated by any feeling of heat or cold.

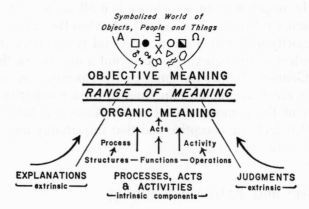

FIG. 2.
Organic and objective meaning.

The significance of organic meaning can best be understood by referring to Figure 2. It is inaccurate to speak of *the* meaning of any act or object; rather, there is a *range of meaning* which transects the fields of both organic and objective meaning. A dictionary definition is a typical example of a fairly restricted range of meaning. However, since meaning is compounded of both acts and objects, the dictionary definition of, for instance, *door* will express the broadest possible range for *objective meaning* and the narrowest possible range for *organic*

Organic Meaning

meaning. According to Webster, a door is "the movable frame or barrier of boards, or other material, usually turning on hinges or pivots, or sliding, by which an entrance-way into a house or apartment is closed or opened. . . ." Obviously, a clear and comprehensive definition of a mundane object, such as a door, is difficult to achieve, perhaps because an objective meaning for door is so seldom needed, and the organic meaning of this or that door is more relevant for our purposes. In other words, people seem to "understand" the general meaning of door and to concern themselves only with special features of individual doors. Through their actual participation in acts of passage, or opening up or closing off access, doors acquire further organic meaning. Consequently, the dictionary definition of door is decidedly narrow for organic meaning, since, in the interest of objective generality, interpersonal and intrapersonal components have been sacrificed.

Within the scope of organic meaning there are two components, which may be termed *intrinsic* and *extrinsic meaning.* Although each component can contribute independently to organic meaning, one is often confused with the other, particularly when psychological issues are being considered. Intrinsic components are those which are characteristic of the active organism — *structures, functions,* and *operations.* Extrinsic components are those which register the effect of an organic act as a whole — *explanations* and *judgments.*

EXPLANATIONS AND JUDGMENTS

Explanations and judgments are often mistaken for each other. Most discussions that go on between people every day — religious, literary, political — depend upon extrinsic judgments *about* events, and not upon events themselves. The facts that are summoned to support these judgments are, as a rule, selected afterthoughts instead of unmistakable data which demand explanation. Consequently, arguments are usually futile simply because value judgments, such as right/wrong and good/bad, are confused with explanations even if, indeed, the central meaning of the issue under discussion is clear. Unlike explanations, value judgments appeal to the highly personal perspectives of

43

reality sense rather than to reality testing. Value judgments are labor-saving devices; they allow people who know nothing about a complex subject to pass judgment and to put it in its place simply because of the total effect it has upon them. It is easy to approve or disapprove on the basis of some standard and difficult to show that the standard itself may be irrelevant or peripheral to the central issue. Truth is only one of many possible judgments, although these many other possible judgments may often be accepted as truth. For example, music may be judged as diverting, deplorable, profitable, or boring, just as people may be judged as cordial, vain, humdrum, learned, or ethical. These are all value judgments that express shades of approval or disapproval within the spectrum of organic meaning, yet none refers to the intrinsic significance of the object of judgment. In everyday life organic meaning is influenced far more by value judgments than by cautious understanding. This is the case not only with ordinary communications; the principal purpose of political addresses, sermons, and literary essays is to evoke a positive value judgment simply on the basis of emotion and pre-existing prejudice, not by the truth of their utterances.

The tendency to substitute value judgments for explanations has many examples in psychiatry. Patients who want to know whether they are "normal" are more often concerned about the effect of their acts and attitudes upon outside observers than about their own discomfort or conflict. Once advised that their conduct and feelings are "normal," they ask no further questions about their intrinsic meaning; they seek no explanation. Psychiatrists, too, have tacit standards that lead them to pseudo-quantitative, pseudo-scientific judgments which actually convey no more than their disapproval of patients.

The meaning of an event is not the same as its explanation, although an explanation is part of its meaning [131]. Like the value judgment, an explanation is *about* organic acts as whole events, but there is an important difference. Explanations do not simply register the approval or disapproval of an outside witness; they relate different sets of acts to each other through a common meaning and in this way expand the range of organic meaning. When a patient has a dream, for example, only he can experience the intrinsic component of its organic meaning. His analyst can *explain* the dream, or *interpret* it, but only from the outside. Although, by relating it to other acts and facts about the patient, the analyst may expand the meaning of the dream as an act, the organic meaning of the dream to the patient will not be expanded unless the interpretation or explanation becomes part of an intrapersonal event.

STRUCTURE, FUNCTION, AND OPERATION

Unlike extrinsic meanings, which are *about* organic acts, intrinsic meanings consist of the acts themselves. Custom has determined that organic acts have three more or less independent phases, called *structure, function,* and *operation.* As with so many similar distinctions, their differences are largely those of polarity and viewpoint, rather than of absolute qualities. Structures, as a rule, refer to relatively fixed organs, or substantives. Functions are systematic variations within different parts of the organs. Operations are the final, common acts of combined processes that exercise practical influence upon the world.

Structures differ from functions only because they tend to change more slowly, and with less systematic variation. Both are but polarized versions of *process* [143]. Similarly, the term *activity,* which is extensively used throughout this discussion, combines functions and operations. Let it be understood that an operation refers to the instrumental, or pragmatic, aspect of whatever the organism finally accomplishes [35c]. That is, operations make use of objects in order to clarify organic meaning. Without a final set of operations and objects, which themselves combine many subsidiary acts and processes, a violin would be merely an oddly shaped wooden box with longitudinal strings that vibrate whenever other strings are drawn across them. However, the decisive component of organic meaning is not restricted to its final pragmatic operation. Because they are objects which are put to use in many purposeful human acts, both doors and violins acquire organic meaning without being organisms themselves. Their full organic meaning is supplemented by the successive addition of value judgments and explanatory references.

45

The Existential Core of Psychoanalysis

It is usually easier to explain an entire context of meaning than to explain some structure or function within it. The ambiguous meaning of psychic events is due partly to our ignorance of how the mind itself works, and of the principles that govern mental data. Psychology consists largely of ways in which to interpret events, even though it is not always clear what is being interpreted. Explanation is the vehicle of science, but meaning is the substance of human activity.

If an Englishman were to ask an American friend to explain football, his comparatively simple request could be satisfied in two ways. His friend could first set down the rules of football and then point out which events on the playing field were relevant to the rules. Or he might assume that the Englishman was already familiar with games like Rugby and, as they watched a football game, he could call attention to their similarities and differences. After this demonstration the rules would then be taught. The first method is explanation by deductive principles; the second method explains by generalizing from examples. In either case, the Englishman would learn to follow a football game as a more or less knowledgeable spectator.

If the Englishman begins by asking his friend to explain what "quarterback" means, the problem becomes unreasonably complex. How can his friend clarify the meaning of quarterback without first explaining the entire context — or football as a whole? Nevertheless, let us suppose that, in the absence of a nearby game or rule book, he chooses to explain football by first clarifying the meaning of quarterback. He decides to begin with a *structural viewpoint* by describing the *organization* of a team, the number of players, and the names of the positions they play. However, since football is not a static organization of structures, he must then turn from the structural to a *dynamic viewpoint*. He will outline the various *functions* of a quarterback and show how these functions articulate with those of other players. His observant pupil may notice that the functions of a quarterback are not wholly unique — sometimes they are interchangeable

46

with the functions of other players. He may well ask whether these players are also quarterbacks. Before long his teacher will begin to hedge and will speak about the "process of quarterbacking." In this way he can account for a constant position, as well as for the variable functions, of a quarterback. But since it thus becomes apparent that one set of processes elicits other processes, the teacher now must adopt an *operational viewpoint* in order to explain how the different activities of all the players are integrated to fulfill a common practical purpose: to advance the ball. He points out that, from an *economic viewpoint*, the ball is advanced by strategic deployment of energy and skill.

At this juncture the Englishman may properly ask, "If the purpose of the game is to advance the ball, why are so many different formations required?" His teacher now proceeds to an *adaptive viewpoint* and explains how each team act contends with the organized, antagonistic acts of the opposing team.

Let us assume that the pupil is now quite satisfied but that the teacher, understandably enough, still wonders whether he has completely explored the meaning of quarterback. In fact, he may question his own understanding of football because, even with extensive knowledge of the game gathered from these many viewpoints, he cannot account for every act on the field, nor can he understand why some acts are permitted by the rules, others are prohibited, and still others are either accidental or irrelevant. Recognizing that any game is played according to prevailing rules, he may turn to a *genetic viewpoint* to find the determining factors that made the rules as they are, and also to find, perhaps, even higher abstractions.

In the course of investigation, he will undoubtedly discover, some experts maintain that *extrinsic rules* are more important than the game itself, which naturally must comply with each modification of rules. Other experts insist that, since there would be no game without players, rules are simply man-made conventions that organize the details of what began as an answer to the natural, *intrinsic needs* of students for recreation but now, after years of development, serves the needs of only particularly rugged students. If the teacher persists and interviews many players and spectators, he will also find that, while there is a consensus about the objective game called football, it means different things to different people. Some people tend to confuse the values they derive from the game with the reasons why the game is played. Furthermore, special groups emphasize their special preoccupations. Marxists, for example, note the huge income which some universities derive from the sale of tickets, and point to unscrupulous recruitment of players as indications of economic motivations. Moralists may acknowledge these facts but insist that the central issues are the beneficial effects of football upon physique, character, employment, and so forth. Still probing, the investigator may find psychiatrists who will report that some patients attend games on Saturday afternoons in order to enjoy vicarious discharge of aggressive drives and that other patients deliberately avoid games lest they become anxious at the sight of healthy young men lying on top of each other. He may also encounter existentialists who decide that the crucial issue is the individual significance of the quarterback, who, out of a series of irrevocable choices, must face, in utter solitude, the eternal either/or of calling one play or another.

What has the teacher learned? He has discovered that many events on the field are actually irrelevant to an understanding of football, even though he is unable to explain why. He can distinguish between the primary purpose of the game and secondary value judgments about it. He realizes that it is up to him to understand football as it is played, and not according to some idealized Game. Most of all, he recognizes that there is a difference between the extrinsic explanation of "quarterback" and the intrinsic meaning of "quarterbacking" — a series of purposeful acts by a player.

Although this extended illustration refers to events on a football field, instead of to psychic events and psychological theory, it could be called the *metapsychology* of football, since metapsychology may be defined as a set of viewpoints that pertain to the organic meaning of events. There is, however, no absolute metapsychology, with a set of fixed rules and theories. Ultimately, it is the way we interpret events that matters. In the psychic domain, *meaning modifies material.*

Organic Meaning

Metapsychology and Organic Meaning

When psychiatry ceased to be purely descriptive and taxonomic, it began to interpret, if not to explain, symptoms, signs, traits, and syndromes. A patient's acts and attitudes were no longer regarded as static facts but as products of mental activity. Although psychodynamic psychiatry made use of earlier philosophical concepts and psychological formulations [145], the main impetus for psychoanalysis arose from clinical experience. Freud [46] attempted to draw parallels between dreams and neurosis, conversion symptoms and hypnotic suggestion, character development and psychosexual disturbances. Psychoanalytic theory was then, as it is now, an effort to systematize clinical observations and to determine the meaning of mental activity.

Early formulations of clinical entities (as succeeding years have demonstrated) were oversimplified, just as early psychoanalytic theories tended to be merely diagrammatic metaphors. Psychoanalysis continues to have a dual purpose: to find theories which adequately cover clinical facts and to keep theories and facts separate. The outside observer who occasionally ventures into psychoanalytic literature is likely to conclude that clinical facts have long since become overgrown by a jungle of speculation and unverifiable theory. Because it is quite true that in the psychic domain meaning modifies material, he may notice how frequently theory is confused with clinical conjecture and how difficult it is to recognize facts amid the plausible inferences.

Psychoanalysis, however, consists of more than a simple division between theory and clinical facts. Psychoanalytic meaning, as well as material, is expressed in a variety of ways. Rapaport and Gill [114], for example, recognized four major types of psychoanalytic generalization: (1) empirical propositions about clinical events, (2) propositions about specific analytic issues, (3) propositions of wide analytic generality, and (4) irreducible assumptions which any theory makes.

Metapsychology as a whole consists of different versions of mental events and includes different types of generalizations. Each version is determined by two factors: a special component of organic meaning, whether intrinsic or extrinsic; and a set of acceptances, or irreducible assumptions, appropriate to a particular dimension. There is nothing esoteric about metapsychological viewpoints. Whatever has an organic meaning, whether it be football or psychology, has a "metapsychology" to contain its acceptances and activities.

Naturally Freud dealt with metapsychological issues from the beginning. In 1915 he published five basic metapsychological essays [46g]: "Instincts and their Vicissitudes," "Repression," "The Unconscious," "Metapsychological Supplement to the Theory of Dreams," and "Mourning and Melancholia." Freud did not complete his more comprehensive study of metapsychology, but, however detailed, metapsychological viewpoints only provide concepts for understanding the organic meaning of clinical events. They cannot exhaust the potential meaning of those events. Freud's original metapsychological viewpoints, or, more properly, his three versions of organic meaning, were called the *topographic*, the *dynamic*, and the *economic*. More recently, Rapaport added the *genetic* and the *adaptive* and substituted the *structural* for the topographic [113c].

VERSIONS OF ORGANIC MEANING

The topographic viewpoint had limited value until Gill's recent reformulation [48]. It was originally based upon the distinction between psychic events according to their conscious availability and quality of being conscious, preconscious, or unconscious. The structural viewpoint assumes that there are organized units, collectively termed the *psychic apparatus*, which comprise the familiar trichotomy of *id*, *ego*, and *superego*. Most psychoanalytic hypotheses, however, depend upon the dynamic viewpoint. Together with the structural version, the dynamic viewpoint contributes to the phase of organic meaning which is called *process*. Its basic metaphor is that of systems and forces, which act either together or in selective opposition. The concepts of the dynamic unconscious and of repression are central to this version of mental events.

The economic viewpoint, through its controversial assumption of *psychic energy* [9, 30, 68], nevertheless provides an explanation for the whole range of psychic activity. Oversimplified or not, the most appealing analytic hypothesis in earlier years was that of instinct theory. It asserted that instincts could be "represented" in different acts, organs, or objects and that psychic energy could be distributed through those representatives [14a, b].

The genetic and adaptive viewpoints are combinations of the structural, dynamic, and economic viewpoints set into the dimension of *time*. The genetic version is to the past what the adaptive viewpoint is to the future. Both assume that orderly sequences and homogeneous themes coexist among diversified events. Although the genetic viewpoint is often mistaken for an etiological hypothesis, it is, actually, only a way to recognize and to compare recurrent themes throughout emotional development. In so far as events may be understood according to their capacity to derive direction from the past and to influence future events, the genetic and adaptive versions combine both functions and operations. In turn, functions and operations combine to form a phase of intrinsic organic meaning that is called *activity*.

The adaptive version has both extrinsic and intrinsic significance. Sometimes "adaptive" is an extrinsic value judgment about a series of acts, quite apart from their intrinsic operations. The intrinsic act of living itself is an arabesque of adjustments, precipitated by external events, regulated by internal systems, signaled by pain, and released by performance. The whole complex is often called *adaptation*, but since not all adjustment is effective, or even appropriate, its adaptive quality is questionable. Adaptation, then, is less a quality or an aim than it is a *post hoc*, nonempirical generalization about the effectiveness of purposeful acts.

SCOPE OF ORGANIC MEANING

Because the concept of organic meaning provides for value judgments of different kinds, its scope is broader than that of traditional metapsychology. One function of superego is to make judgments according to the ruling standards of the ego ideal. However, in most accounts these seem to be largely confined to ethical and moral judgments [46i], ignoring the vast panoply of potential judgments within ordinary experience. After all, every adjective is a value judgment, and every adverb multiplies the number of judgments still further. Although science recognizes only the values of truth, every investigator imperceptibly makes additional value judgments of his own. This is why, for example, an otherwise objective investigator so frequently tends to confuse a meaning with an explanation and, in so doing, creates the fallacies typical of his discipline.

In "Negation" [46j] Freud was as concerned with values and the underlying uniformity of what is bad, false, and ugly as were Greek philosophers in their discourses about the good, the true, and the beautiful. Nevertheless, in the interest of impartial investigation he had to limit his judgments to true and false. The concept of narcissism, for example, is only a scientific concept, and not synonymous with vanity or pride, although it is often used this way pejoratively by laymen, or by professionals who try to conceal their disapproval within a technical term. The risk in legitimizing value judgments is that they can be so freely applied that they all too readily become the private prerogative of arbitrary authority. When values are repeatedly confused with explanations, value judgments tend to stifle inquiry. As a result, the scientific meaning of true and false is gradually taken over by the social values of acceptability. Value judgments are necessary and indispensable elements of existence nonetheless, apart from the specialized circumstances of science [3]. Furthermore, how values arise is itself a significant problem. For example, it is difficult to understand how neurophysiological mechanisms can distinguish between a value judgment and an explanation, or how computing machines can decide which particular value judgment is relevant. Autonomous neuronal assemblies may conceivably represent value systems that are activated by other assemblies, but at this time such constructs are personifications, not mechanisms. Current theories of psychology, and of social systems, are engaged in tracing the origins and sources of value [84, 105]. However, preference for one theory instead of another is itself often decided by another value judgment and, in most instances, probably not by the same value. The secret hope that physiological explanations may someday obviate psychological meanings seems to be an inversion of the ontological acceptance. Even though it is assumed that whatever is thought corresponds to reality according to existential premises, what is real according to brain physiology does not precisely correspond to whatever is thought. For example, the terse assertion "Sex is chemistry" contains a qualified hormonal truth, but only on a single level of investigation. The methods and materials of one discipline can redefine the crude content and problems of another, but the redefinition does not eliminate other levels of experience and other kinds of meaning. Psychoanalysis can be augmented by assimilation of relevant knowledge from other disciplines without danger of being obliterated.

Tests of Meaning

Man is not a rational animal. He is a reasoning beast who rarely gives accurate reasons for what he does. Judgment of his reasons depends upon knowing what he means and what various things mean to him. The familiar psychiatric division of mental activity into thought, emotion, and behavior is convenient but arbitrary. These words designate three phases of diversified organic processes. Although they contribute to ordinary meaning, the extremes of thought, emotion, and behavior disappear beyond the limited horizon of everyday meaning.

Except in fairly rigorous scientific investigation, precise definitions and exclusive reliance upon true and false judgments are rare. Nevertheless, in discourse between people the inexhaustible potential of organic meaning sooner or later produces a relevant range of meaning that can be shared with the world. This common range of meaning is a prerequisite for understanding what another person means and what he assumes that we mean. Political addresses, sermons, lectures, poetry, and clichés of ordinary speech intend that we believe the words but not that we judge their meanings as though they were unambiguous truths. For instance, a political speech may reek with altruism, sagacity, and wit. However, its organic meaning would be misconstrued if it were understood to be anything other than a rhetorical device for getting out the vote.

Value judgments provide an extrinsic check on what a man is expected to believe. His own organic meaning decides what

53

kind of total effect any object or act has upon him. Thus, his enemy may seem "arrogant," but his friend appears "confident." With such widely divergent, seemingly arbitrary possibilities, how can we begin to establish even a minimal range of meaning for the mutual corroboration of reality sense and reality testing?

At the most elementary level, every test of meaning depends upon dichotomizing events according to one value or another. Whatever means anything can at least be partially defined and, in order to define it, what it does *not* mean must also be clear. In logic, negation is both a fine art and a technical device [150]. But the act of negating is an integral part of meaning in general and certainly is the basic requirement for every test of meaning [115a], since in ordinary communication we tend automatically to agree or disagree without being quite sure what we are or are not agreeing to.

SYSTEMATIC NEGATION

The statements set forth in books and essays are often as meaningless and trivial as the most casual, informal conversations. However, the important issue is not to count how many meaningless statements there are but to decide whether these meaningless statements are the key propositions which enunciate the author's beliefs. The simplest way to test meaning is to negate any proposition we are asked to believe. If the negative does not seem to change its meaning, or to make any difference in how we use the idea, it is fair to conclude that the proposition is meaningless — a *vacuous verbalization*.

A negation of some pretentious propositions results in a *triviality* instead of a vacuous verbalization. If a speaker were to declare, for example, that "self-preservation is the first law of nature," its negation would be "self-preservation is *not* the first law of nature." This is not meaningless. Indeed, it expresses the speaker's meaning more clearly: he is not concerned with priority among natural laws but is merely trying to say that "survival is an important consideration in life," a proposition which few people dispute. Its negation, "survival is *not* an important consideration in life," is either absurd or self-contradictory. In actual practice, the hidden triviality is more common than the vacuous verbalization.

Rule 1. When negation does not change the meaning of a statement, the statement is meaningless.

Rule 2. When negation results in a self-contradictory or absurd statement, the original statement is self-evident or trivial.

STIPULATED CONTEXT

In contrast with many ponderous propositions that contain trivial meanings, or none at all, there are other statements that contain several different kinds of meaning. Their ambiguity leads to endless controversy because the antagonists are talking about different things. This is frequently the case when the statement happens to be couched in metaphorical terms, or in terms which condense various ideas in elliptical form. For example, it is claimed that "the hand that rocks the cradle rules the world." If this means merely that mothers influence infants, it is so banal an observation that one may wonder why it requires an epigram. Presumably, however, the declaration is intended to sum up all maternal influence in a single sentence, or at least to declare that early influence is the most decisive. There are still other interpretations of this proposition, some of them true, others false, and still others neither true nor false. Its meaning can be determined only by stipulating each context in which the proposition has significance and then deciding which is most relevant for the purpose at hand. Freud's famous remark that neurosis is the "negative" of perversion has a variety of potential meanings, none of which can be discussed until the appropriate contexts are stipulated. Most indecisive discussions contain several instances of unstipulated contexts. This is a particularly significant test of meaning in psychiatry because many statements by patients seem outwardly to be absurd, or trivial, or meaningless, or "crazy." Upon analysis, they often reveal highly relevant capsular meaning.

Each of two young men said to their psychiatrist, "Before I'd get married, I'd rather be a bachelor!" Since a bachelor is an unmarried man, this statement, at best, seems to be an obvious truth. However, to one man marriage meant the inferno in which he had been raised, with both parents in constant turmoil, sabotaging each other's existence. His statement, although apparently a logical tautology, was, in fact, a passionate declaration that he would rather be a *lonely* bachelor than a *tormented* husband. The stipulated context that clarified his meaning was not the legal institution of marriage but any intimate male-female relationship.

To the other man being a bachelor meant associating with girls from a higher level of society than his own. Although welcome as an extra man at society events, he realized that these girls would find him unacceptable as a husband, and to marry within his own class would be a painful defeat of his social ambitions. In this instance the stipulated context was *social climbing*, and neither marriage nor intimate male-female relations conveyed the central meaning behind his original statement.

Rule 3. Statements have meaning only in so far as their relevant contexts can be stipulated.

Rule 4. Statements are ambiguous when their relevant contexts cannot be stipulated.

Rule 5. Changing a stipulated context changes the meaning of statements.

PARAPHRASING

The meaning behind certain orotund utterances may often be discovered simply by rephrasing them in unambiguous terms. This test requires the use of the previous tests. For example, it is wholly possible that an orator could proclaim from a public platform, "What is, is; what is not, is not; what has been, has been; and what will be, will be!" and it would be accepted as an apocalyptic revelation. The first test — systematic negation — produces a more mystical but no more informative proposition. Furthermore, since the meaning of this statement hangs upon the meaning of *what*, or *whatever*, to stipulate a relevant context would result in a remark hardly worth uttering. However, if we try to paraphrase the original statement, it becomes clear that its only significance is in the ear of the listener, who seals it off in values of his own and presumes, without further question, that it has an objective meaning which other members of the audience will also appreciate. A statement without meaning can be expressed in only one way, since there is no meaning to carry over from one verbal form to another.

The paraphrase is used to advantage by nondirective counselors, who understand that a range of meaning is both public and private and that people can be helped to recognize their private meanings by listening to paraphrases of what they say [116a, b].

Rule 6. Whatever can be expressed in only one way belongs to the verbal form, not to the meaning of a statement.

Rule 7. Statements which have genuine meaning can be expressed in several ways.

Strong beliefs imply strong values, but the strength of a belief does not assure its validity. The sense of reality requires the modulating influence of reality testing. To cross a busy street simply because we have confidence in the meaning of green traffic lights can be a disastrous act, based on an invalid belief. Reality testing introduces other ways to cross streets safely.

The sense of reality is the most primitive way to bring different kinds of experience together into an uninterrupted whole and to discover a single direction for purposeful activity. Reality is existence plus meaning. Existential meaninglessness is different from semantic meaninglessness, ambiguity, and banality. The existential "yes" or "no" about statements is a necessary condition for any valid judgment because when nothing can be affirmed, nothing can be negated, and when nothing can be negated, nothing has meaning. Existential meaninglessness is to organic meaning what ignorance, as a mental state, is to knowledge. A man who has unwittingly detached himself from recognition of his own contributions to reality is likely to live according to semantic ambiguities and absurdities. Most people do live amidst semantic confusion [98], but this fact alone does not imply that they are also meaningless from the existential viewpoint.

The semantic relation between symbols and objects depends

upon objective meaning. In a sense, it is a function of reality testing. But in psychoanalysis semantics is secondary to the existential significance of the person who uses words and endows them with private meanings of his own. It is comparatively easy to decide what words do and do not mean, once the problem of ambiguity is recognized. The concept of existential meaning, in contrast, is nebulous. It does not fit the tests of meaning, nor is it subject to the rules of negation. Like descriptions of emotional, aesthetic, and religious experience, expressions of existential meaning seem to elude ordinary language — except, it will be shown, through metaphor, paradox, and iconic symbols.

The inherent difficulty in defining existential terms does not deter some writers, who insist that people ought to find "meaning" in their lives. Unfortunately, they do not also show people how to recognize this meaning when it is found. Moreover, the idea of existential meaninglessness seems thunderously empty to anyone who is not already acquainted with the phenomena on which it is based.

In contrast to the awkward imprecision of the term *existential meaning*, which may even be self-contradictory, the concept of organic meaning opens up a way to define ideas that ordinarily baffle people seeking to understand them. It is customary to deny that a fact has meaning unless its components can be expressed in suitably objective form, ready for inclusion in a dictionary. The scope of organic meaning is far more evanescent. Because it is conveyed in every act and motion of the human organism, organic meaning is both fixed and fluid, and scarcely the same from moment to moment. Nevertheless, organic meaning underlies every other kind of meaning, including that of reality sense and of the language of the existential viewpoint.

This somewhat lengthy excursion into the nature of organic and objective meaning has been necessary to demonstrate that psychoanalysis is an exercise which helps to distinguish between them. Furthermore, because reality sense is transmitted in every component of organic meaning and links the diversified facts of experience with acts that express them, it is the prototype of organic meaning itself.

4. The Meaning of Reality Sense

THE TRULY PERVASIVE IDEAS OF MANKIND elude efforts to contain them in definitions. Because definitions necessarily restrict the range of meaning, it is clear that the organic meaning of reality sense — the source of what we believe and the source of how we come to believe — originates beyond whatever boundaries can be put around it. Reality sense cannot be defined the way objects are defined, or even the way activities that depend upon reality sense are defined. Nevertheless, the organic meaning of reality sense can be clarified, just as any other organic process can be described. This method allows for separate discussion of four particular phases of reality sense: (1) reality sense as content, (2) reality sense as activity, (3) reality sense as judgment, and (4) reality sense as explanation.

The Existential Core of Psychoanalysis

The sense of reality arises from the centrifugal reality of the *I* who cannot escape his subjective orientation, even though he is moved and modified by the centripetal realities of objects, people, and things in the world. Because reality sense permeates existence, creates meaning, and yet conforms to the world, it is both immanent and emergent.

The *intrinsic meaning* of reality sense is made up of content and activity — the *what* and *how* of reality — as reality is lived in the immediacy of the *now*. As it is lived, reality sense is unfractionated experience of whatever commands the conviction "This is real!" Reality sense as content includes the concepts of both *structure* and *substance*. Reality sense as activity is the process of *sensing* what is real — *intuition*.

The *extrinsic meaning* of reality sense depends upon the value judgment, real or unreal, and whatever explanations are brought forward to account for cohesive, comprehensive conviction as a whole. From the existential standpoint, the value judgment — real — is identical with the validation judgment — true — because whatever is judged true or false is secondary to an initial judgment that our affirmations are real and pertain to real events.

Reality sense as explanation includes both the reality sense of explanation and the explanation of reality sense. In either case, any explanation of reality sense is obliged to transmit the same sense of conviction that it strives to account for. Such explanation, therefore, ascribes causal and motivational properties to the organic processes which give rise to reality sense, and to the secondary acts that express organic meaning.

Reality Sense as Content

The terms *being, becoming,* and *nonbeing* are the common shibboleths of existentialist writings [70, 146]. Capitalized or not, their meaning is obscure, and it is probably useless to document the subtle variations of meanings with which these simple words have been endowed. Nevertheless, it is possible to recognize a thread of reality in the tangle of rhetoric surrounding them. If we leave aside dubious works that simply glorify being, becoming, and nonbeing into metaphysical mysteries, and semi-inspirational essays that exhort the reader to pay more attention to his existence, it becomes apparent that what these concepts denote is the *content* of reality as it is encountered, and not as it is distorted by special viewpoints. This is the reality sense of both enduring and transient events. It may, in other words, be described as a *state* of being, or becoming, something that has structure *and* substance.

We must, however, immediately beware of vacuous verbalizations and concepts without content, because terminology can readily turn into demonology. The *concepts* of being and becoming do not give us any more information about what is real than the isolated concept of nonbeing tells us what is unreal.

Despite their arcane, even supermundane, usage the concepts of being, becoming, and nonbeing are intended to simplify the meaning of experience. They represent faith in the direct accessibility of ultimate referents and in the basic identity of experience with the person who experiences. In this sense, because they seek the starkest possible affirmation about what is real and the ways in which it becomes real, Dewey [35a] and Whitehead [66b] are more profoundly existential than Sartre [121c] and Heidegger [57].

The immediate, irreducible event called real is both the fact of being and the sensitivity to that fact. *Reality sense as content refers to the reality of an experience as an experience of reality.* The existential issue is always contained within the here-and-now of this event, since this real event is an image of reality. More sophisticated ways to understand the existential issue are simply ways to certify what we are already sure of.

The concept of reality sense as content is totally antagonistic to such obsolete, worn-out issues as materialism vs. idealism. Whether or not the traditional "chair is in the next room" is a pseudoquestion, whose putative answer will depend upon whether we choose to emphasize the priority of the subject who experiences or the object experienced. A chair is a configuration of electrons, a piece of furniture, or a place to sit down. Regardless of the categorical view I adopt toward myself or the chair, its being is its sense of reality in the content of my experience. Just as I have a constancy aside from my viewpoints, a chair has a constancy apart from its possible perspectives. This kind of being does not require capitalization, reification, or hypostasis in order to be experienced as real.

Unless we are to tumble into a pit of dogmatism or fly away on wings of terminology, our efforts to delineate the meaning of being, becoming, and nonbeing must be tempered by reminders that none of us can enter directly the sanctum of another person's subjective experience and, literally, see his world through his eyes. When events persist, or regularly recur, or do not yield to our efforts to embrace them with our understanding, they acquire an existence of their own. Some inner events abide, but others vaporize almost at the very moment of awareness. External events can be recognized by their invariant properties; internal events are understood according to components which are both credible and constant. The constant and credible content of personal experience gathers meaning to the degree in which it shares a context of thought either with someone else or with some other, already familiar event. A bird can be identified by its song, but only after the sounds have been recognized as a song. The absolutely unique cannot be recognized, just as the absolutely unrelated has no meaning. Facts are facts, but only within a context of meaning which can be shared without burdensome readjustments to another's idiosyncrasies. Being and becoming are dynamic concepts that allow for constancy, ordered change, and inclusiveness without imposing a "monism," or false homogeneity, upon the infinite varieties of experience. They allow for recognition of the content of reality through images which, at any instant, are accepted as real.

PSYCHOANALYSIS AND REALITY OF CONTENT

Psychoanalysis is a procedural prototype of this concept of reality. The reality sponsored by psychoanalysis, knowingly or not, is a reality of content [55]. It will gather its meaning by accepting some aspects of experience as constant and credible and ignoring other aspects as irrelevant. Whether constancy and credibility are determined by the special context of understanding that arises between the analyst and the patient or are the inevitable result of a fixed method of formulation is an issue to be decided by the reality sense of both participants.

There is considerable ado in some psychiatric circles about the "therapeutic contract" — an unwritten document which insists that the patient ought to conform to his doctor's version of how patients should act. A more fundamental pact, however, appeals to the mutual existential definition of both analyst and patient. This comprehensive pact depends upon the kind of reality generated by the psychoanalytic process itself. It commits the analyst to an acceptance of the reality of certain constant features of the analytic experience in order to challenge others [77]. Thus, he can accept a delusion as a part of the analytic content, and as an image of the patient's reality, without being deluded himself [86]. The patient may accept the reality of what he believes; the analyst may accept only the reality of the believing process. But by sharing a common reality with his patient, the analyst strives to recognize judgments that are correct in some instances and incorrect in others. In short, just as a teacher may understand incorrect answers without losing confidence in the constancy and credibility of performance itself, the analyst's sense of reality for both being and becoming will permit him to understand wrong ideas and right ideas. The immediate content of an event necessarily includes all facts about it.

BEING AND BECOMING — STRUCTURE AND PROCESS

Reality is largely a matter of perspective, and the only change that abides is a functional relationship between constants and variables [24a]. Becoming is no less real than being because both are phases of a common process. *Being is to becoming as structure is to process.* Being purports to denote a structure that has substance, with articulated parts that *endure* throughout chronological time. It is, in effect, a spatial metaphor. Becoming is the way in which *orderly change* in structure occurs within a context of chronological time. It is a temporal metaphor. Process combines both within a single organic meaning. In the context of existential time — to be discussed later — being and becoming are abstractions.

As a rule, most discussions of structure tacitly ignore the temporal factor and thereby acquire spurious constancy for structural concepts. For example, anatomy books describe the heart as if it were a constant structure, remaining unchanged throughout time. This actually confuses no one who has felt a pulse or listened to heart sounds. But its psychological analogue, the structural viewpoint, is frequently misunderstood as a literal description of the "mental apparatus." Except in its developmental hypotheses psychoanalysis, too, tends to ignore the factor of time, change, and becoming in day-by-day clinical interpretations and in moment-to-moment psychological processes. As a result, id, superego, and ego are usually thought of not as ways to cope with the flux of immediate, living issues but as somewhat intangible geographical domains, ruled by three monarchs who divide a mental continent between them. Terrestrial travelers are not surprised to learn that dots and stipplings are convenient notations made by mapmakers and that maps do not depict the actual terrain or the people who live there. But travelers in the psychic domain seem to expect that, like Gaul, all mental content may be divided, in structure and substance, according to the three offices of id, superego, and ego.

The concept of a fixed psychic structure is like that of a child practicing his piano lesson. He learns by being told that this finger goes here and that finger goes there; this is for the right hand and that is for the left hand. However, for learning to be more than this kind of rote, orderly changes in the image of reality must conform to the different perspectives of the person himself [64a]. The principle of multiple function [137b] recognizes that a fixed distinction between ego, superego, and id is an illusion. Viewpoint alone determines which aspect of an event is to be regarded as a timeless, constant, credible entity of enduring significance.

Being and becoming are defined within a process in which there is no absolute distinction between an activating subject and an object acted upon. Just as, in the content of experience, organic meaning is discovered to be immediate and enduring, constant and credible, persistent and transient, so also does reality sense, as content, combine the substance of what is real with the structural forms of reality in a permanent moment of recognition.

This point of view is similar to Whitehead's concept of process: an orderly system of modulated events in which both subject and object are immanent in each other [143]. Even as it passes away, each entity leaves traces and thus retains some of its immortal properties as an eternal object. Similarly, in the very act of psychoanalysis, and in the comprehensive, existential pact between analyst and patient, the nature of being and becoming emerges, through the persistent and transient properties of living moments. Fragments of experience pass away and may be swallowed up in an ocean of past time; but like relics recaptured from the deep, they may emerge later as fresh realities, bearing incrustations from the past. Somewhat similarly, Hartmann [54a] explained the irrational components in psychoanalysis as ways in which actual events can be given longitudinal rationality. Being, therefore, is not some metaphysical entity beyond the reach of reality sense. It is process caught in the act of becoming, so that every element, solid or vaporous, significant or trivial, enduring or evanescent, stands forth with organic meaning, as a single, irreducible event. Because it is itself a source of other convictions, the content of this event is equivalent to reality.

Reality Sense as Activity

The *fact* of being real requires a complementary *act of sensing* what is real. The myth of an abiding realm of "pure being," which survives the illusions and errors of our ways of perceiving it, has an everlasting appeal. Anyone who has found disappointment while searching for certainty, and who continues to seek reliable clues to an incontrovertible reality, is lured by his own wishes to believe in a realm of metaphysical perfection where beliefs are automatically correct and ideas are steadfastly true. Ontological acceptance and existential solitude conspire to produce an idealized version of themselves — an image of infallibility that could be true only of some complacent god who sees the inner structure of reality so clearly that he spends eternity contemplating self-evident truths about himself [71, 108].

The existential attitude is opposed to the position that bestows autonomy upon the common properties of different events and calls them "essences." Simply because he has many traits of other candidates, a compromise candidate is not an "ideal" candidate, nor does he represent the "essence" of political idealism. The existential attitude recognizes that there are truths and realities which are accepted without question, and that we tend to believe in the universal validity of what we ourselves believe. This reaction is inevitable, because we have no other choice but to reckon truth by our own standards and our own perceptions. In the analytic pact, for example, the analyst can appreciate what is real for his patient only by first being aware of the ways in which he himself discovers what is real. This point of view is, of course, based upon ontological acceptance. It is also based upon belief in the constancy, continuity, and credibility of nature, but without necessarily committing the believer to some remote, monolithic interpretation of what is, or must be, real.

Human activity endows events with meaning, and human activity puts a stamp of certainty upon the content of events. Long ago, Bergson [12] proposed that the process of analysis requires a prior act of intuition. Reality, he maintained, is perceived from within an event, and the validity of subsequent analysis depends upon the relation of separate factors to this initial experience of the whole. As a corollary, he also held that the process could not be reversed; full knowledge of many facts about an event will not lead to full comprehension of the event itself.

INTUITION
Polemics about the priority of induction or deduction, or about the relative importance of the whole and its parts, are idle pastimes because all experiment and exploration require at least some overall design which can be improved by knowledge of further details [35c]. I have, nevertheless, chosen the term *intuition* to describe *how* we sense what is real. Intuition, as Bergson, among others, described it, is an activity which is both self-evident and unitary. It seems to be an appropriate equivalent for *reality sense as activity* in that it complements *reality sense as content* — the simultaneous *what* of structure and substance that we call real.

Intuition [6] — and schools of thought called "intuitionism"

66

The Meaning of Reality Sense

[118] — has been so loosely used in the past that further use of this term requires unusual descriptive care. Intuition has been linked with many kinds of cognition, ranging from a modest awareness of something that had not previously been understood to spectacular flashes of foresight that transcend known processes. Although most of the discussion about intuition and its related ideas will be postponed until Chapter 6, some of its predominant features will be described here.

In the first place, intuition is not metaphysical, theological, or transcendent. In the second place, intuition does not make declarations about matters beyond human experience. It is a way to synthesize experiences of many kinds and, indeed, to simplify them. Intuition is the companion of insight, not just a device which circumvents knowledge. As Rapaport reminded us, schoolboys are often perplexed when they discover that the ludicrously self-evident theorems of geometry are difficult to prove. However, a cynic has added that whatever must be proved is not worth proving, since, if proof is needed, no one will believe it anyway. We can conclude — without proof, of course — that the purpose of proof is to be as self-evident as intuition.

Perception is not limited to what enters through perceptual channels, nor is consciousness identical with being aware of what enters. In simplest terms, as Klein [72] has shown, what is perceived is an active product of internal elaboration, and not a passive result of self-conscious reception. External "stimuli" are somewhat specious abstractions from the total process. A phantom limb is eloquent testimony in support of this fact. Whitehead claimed that the actual world is an activated world and that the "non-sensuous nexus of contemporary occasions" — intuition — determines the course of reality for both subject and object [143].

Psychoanalysis is situated squarely within this point of view. Freud's concept of the double origin of consciousness, and of psychodynamics itself, implies that consciousness is not just an awareness of something or other out in the world but a synthetic, creative activity, in which many perceptions are united for a purpose [46d, i]. The selective perception of a mother who is awakened by her child's crying but is not disturbed by much louder noises is an example of the purposeful activity of consciousness.

Like memory, judgment, thought, and perception — which are so familiar that they have become somewhat unitary, global faculties — intuition too is a well-known product of incompletely understood processes. It is incorrect to regard intuition merely as the active but unanalyzed phase of a process whose passive component is perception; intuition has distinguishing characteristics of its own.

Intuition is often defined as "immediate inference from minimal cues," but, at best, this only describes the *effect* of intuition [13b]. It tells us nothing about the nature of either intuition or inference, nor does it explain why inferences are brought out by some cues and not by others. Intuition is not a form of cursory conjecture or a thin kind of thinking which can be classified along with long shots and ragged guesses. To think of intuition simply as a way to envelop an event with an economy of examination is to describe it only as opposite to ample data, cautious inferences, and deliberate study.

Economy of effort is a deceptive quality. A scientist who knows the solution to a vexing problem upon awakening one morning is probably no less intuitive than a poet who spontaneously senses the inner affinity of existence through his emotions. Sometimes, if not invariably, intuition occurs after prolonged study and an abundance of cues. Psychoanalysis itself cannot proceed without many acts of intuition which piece together vast accumulations of data and observations [17]. Inferences are more or less general conclusions about the meaning and common properties of disconnected events. In a sense, an inference may be a formal expression of a series of subsidiary intuitions. Within the dimension of intrapersonal experience, however, intuition is how we designate instantaneous understanding of a familiar situation in a novel context. This occurs not just in the majestic company of geniuses but also in the mundane assembly of plain people. Anyone who spontaneously perceives a fresh meaning in a familiar event and acts upon it with an unquestioned sense of reality has made use of reality sense as an intuitive act.

Aside from its negative features, such as immediacy and economy, the intuitive act has at least four positive features: (1) equivalence, (2) equilibrium, (3) affirmation, and (4) emergence.

Equivalence. Intuition minimizes the difference between the being of activity and the being of things. For example, the intuitive act fuses the being of a flower with the immediate experience of sight and scent. The act of listening to music and the sound produced by the musician become a single event. Just as there is no difference, in daily living, between the act of breathing and the air we breathe, there is no struggle for this kind of enigmatic certainty. Whenever something "feels right," diversity becomes a single, infrangible fact. The apparatus and the act, the act and whatever is acted upon, are *equivalent*, if not wholly indistinguishable. Only when faltering, or impedance, forces a split is there discrepancy between the person who acts, his act, and what he acts upon. This root experience, which underlies both natural spontaneity and protracted frustration, leads to general concepts of continuity and discontinuity in nature.

Equilibrium. The aim of any biological process is to bring about some form of regulatory equilibrium, but in human activities inner equilibrium is recognized usually by a feeling of fulfillment, quiescence, mastery, or completion. Intuition seems to terminate at the very least in a relative harmony between an inciting cue and an adaptive response and at the most in a sense of consummation or achievement. What is the prompting cue that calls forth an intuitive act? It is seldom discovered, and this singular absence of a penultimate cue is what makes intuition seem both unexpected and remarkable. The sense of equilibrium associated with intuition is related to the degree of bafflement that precedes it. Whether an intuition is perceived as mundane or miraculous depends upon its contrast with tedious, stale, or futile acts that end nowhere, not upon its contrast with reason, logic, or punctilious investigation.

Affirmation. Intuition combines the *relational* experience of being with the *intentional* experience of becoming. In a single moment there is fusion of both the pertinent past and the purposeful future. Consequently, intuition can reconcile seeming contradictions and apparent opposites by reordering and affirming past events with respect to what is about to be. Its task is to *affirm* a relevant relation between the person who knows and all available components of what is known. If such affirmations do genuinely reorder and resolve problems, they will also provide refreshing and ironic contrasts between one mode of thought and another. Chapter 5 will show how psychoanalysis depends upon a constant flow of intuitive affirmations. Currents of thought, emotion, and behavior meet and mingle in an intuitive act; then, having shared a central meaning, they become prompting cues for new intuitions.

Emergence. Equivalence, equilibrium, and affirmation are characteristic not only of intuition. They may be found in almost any highly motivated act that culminates in a spontaneously gratifying, reordered viewpoint. The unique feature of intuition is the *emergence of novelty*. This can be either a novel meaning or a novel means of expression, whichever allows for a conviction of complete understanding. The quality of novelty has little to do with inductive inference [115b], although both may be expressed in similar verbal and nonverbal forms. The vehicle of intuition is whatever comfortably contains a fresh version of an old problem, meaning with a new twist, or a condensation of conflicting viewpoints.

Intuitive forms may be any means of communication and perception, ranging from terse formulas, to metaphorical imagery, to tangible artistic media [24b]. Ordinarily, neither dreams nor myths are considered examples of intuition, nor are they expected to conform literally with reality. But during sleep the dreamer believes in the reality of what he dreams, just as when awake he may act upon his sacred myths without recognizing them as mythical [73]. Short-lived belief in the reality of dreams, and lifelong acceptance of myths are both instances of reality sense as activity. In so far as dreams and myths create fresh meaning out of old ideas, familiar perceptions, and hackneyed formulas, or reconcile antithetical viewpoints, they are vehicles of intuition.

The Meaning of Reality Sense

Whether every dream or myth should be understood as an intuition is, of course, doubtful. Any psychoanalyst will attest that some dreams, from his viewpoint, seem hardly worth dreaming since, even after the most meticulous analysis, their inner significance seems banal, repetitious, or irrelevant. Because he recognizes that the very material of his work consists of analyzing the seemingly obvious, unimportant, or irrelevant in everyday life, he is naturally not satisfied with his own understanding. The "dream's navel," to use Freud's term, is still covered up. In contrast, the import of other dreams can be instantaneously grasped. With swift certainty the analyst understands them on their own metaphorical terms and relates them precisely to relevant issues in a far more comprehensive way than he could have if scrupulous associations from the patient had substantiated each conjecture. In waking life, too, a patient may perceive an immediate image of related events which can be more accurate than painstaking efforts at verbal formulation [13a]. Dreams compress time into a narrow moment and may condense a long history into a few panels of metaphor. Thus, the dreamer himself may do what the analyst only rarely achieves. He may bring perception, recollection, and meaning together in a novel interpretation of reality, even if it is only the reality of a dream. From the viewpoint of intuition the so-called manifest dream is not a mere sensuous husk which must be peeled away and discarded in order to get at the latent kernel. The analyst's understanding is strengthened when he can discover the singular, novel contribution which the dream *as a whole* makes to the dreamer's conception of what is real. The significant, emergent novelty which, the psychoanalyst believes, justifies the dream is not simply a remolding, or distortion, of daytime preoccupations and persistent problems. The dream is a fresh interpretation which residues of the night put upon waking reality. Both dreams and art will "distort" literal events, but they do much more. To overlook a dream's novel twists of creativity, and to perceive the products of dream work only as distortions, is like saying that genuine works of art are merely smears of paint. Whether in the form of dreams, myths, art forms, or verbal adumbrations, there is no codification for intuitive discovery, except that intuition flourishes in darkness and solitude and is destroyed by eager search perhaps as often as it is sacrificed to the cause of intellectual consistency or hallowed banality.

NONBEING

It is proper to conclude this discussion of the intrinsic meaning of reality sense with a note about nonbeing — the shadowy, aversive image of reality which is the negation of being, becoming, and intuition. Existentialists regard nonbeing as an alarming idea, even as a kind of spiritual plague which can lead to dread, despair, and death in torment [57, 121a]. Instead of a fire-and-brimstone notion of nonbeing, the paradigm of nonbeing is found in many abstract, desiccated philosophies or in the logical sophistries and metaphysical joustings of philosophers who are preoccupied with the sterile pursuit of the inconsequential and meaningless [71]. Although these turgid treatises seem to have no more reality than is discovered by deciphering the human equivalent of zero, they may unwittingly reveal the meaning of nonbeing more clearly than their words can explain [65]. If the immediate, living moment is negated by an absence of reality sense or by a pathological form of reality sense, then man surrenders his own existence and survives only as a categorical relic. Just as someone who is preoccupied will often be obtunded to events that surround him, whatever draws off the sense of reality for the present will foster states of unreality and depersonalization. Even in less clinical instances, many people exist only as categorical phantoms of compliance and convention surrounded by a manifold of doubt and negation. There are, of course, numerous situations in which one accepts and opts for a purely categorical status. Few people will feel depersonalized or unreal as they enter a voting booth, where their unique qualities are ignored. It is one thing to be in a categorical situation but quite another to perceive the image of reality solely as the reflection of group sanctions, standard ideas, and conventional expectations. This is the existential predicament wherein only nonbeing is real. Complaints of "not being myself today," or of "losing perspective," or of "not being with it" reflect feelings of nonbeing. In minor or major forms, nonbeing is a partial depersonalization in an unreal world, accompanied by little dreads and quiet despairs that appear and disappear almost unnoticed.

No truth is worth believing unless it is buttressed by an intuitive conviction that it is relevant to one's own reality. The organization man, who is scolded in print for surrendering autonomy to achieve institutional ambitions, is not a fresh phenomenon. Gaining the world for the Faustian price of one soul has never been considered good business. Similarly, when psychiatric patients protest that "people ought not to feel this way," they may be quite correct but, by saying so, they abnegate the substance of what they do feel in favor of the categorical shadows of "ought to feel" and nonbeing.

Nonbeing is more than a mere absence of intuition; it expresses an active anti-intuitive, anti-reality sense viewpoint. Like intuition in reverse, whatever is lacking in a situation becomes its positive perceptions. One dreads what is not there and despairs because this fact is recognized. For example, a shy person may enter a room filled with strangers, expecting that no one will greet him and that he will be shunned as an alien intruder. He is convinced that if they do, indeed, greet him, they will subsequently ignore him, or that he will certainly make a fool of himself and be ostracized anyway. What he assumes and perceives is that strangers are always and only strangers, not people. Hence, he can only define himself as a stranger, whose acceptance is as unlikely as is his ability to accept another stranger. Like an encounter between two categorical phantoms, the only possible relationship with these strangers is that of confirming the nonbeing he already dreads. By fragmenting his own image, as well as that of others, he brings about the banishment he fears — and perhaps also wants.

In general, the concept of nonbeing, imprecise though it is, is contrapuntal to being and becoming. It designates a defect in comprehending our own existential status. According to existentialists, it is a sickness brought about by discovering that being and becoming are neither *here* to be enjoyed in the act of living nor *there* to be sought and found in the plausible future. In this event reality sense gradually evaporates and the desiccated familiar world may even break into meaningless fragments. The world can become a series of images without reality. When being and meaning lose their root source in living experience, the world is transformed into a wound. Psychiatric disturbances which are induced by "sensory deprivation" experiments are, at most, only token encounters with nonbeing and alienation. When there is sharp reduction in perceptual input and suppression of expressive output, there can be neither emergent novelty nor fresh activity. In this predicament man is frequently thrown back to some other form of activity in which his reality was less uncertain [141a]. When sharp intuitive perception and decisive action are restricted, for internal or external reasons, man is left with only a meager relational residue. He may become another face in the crowd, another number in the telephone book, another impersonal cipher. He has lost his substance and ceases to be one who, by his own testimony, changes and remains the same.

Reality Sense as Judgment

Like intuitions, value judgments urge an unequivocal attitude toward some phase of reality as a whole. However, unlike intuitions, value judgments do not contribute to the intrinsic meaning of organic events. The value judgments of what is real and unreal are preconditions for any other judgments about acts, objects, and events. Just as certain statements are accepted as true when they seem self-evident, some events are accepted as real when they seem obvious. The value judgment of their reality is a means by which reality sense judges its own validity. Nevertheless, the judgment of reality is always made by an intrinsic observer who reports about an act, and not by an inside participant.

There are no partial judgments. To call something a little true, somewhat good, or slightly beautiful is not an honest value judgment but a grudging concession to outside pressure. Since our judgment of what is real and unreal is implied by every other judgment, reality sense puts a seal of certainty upon every variety of existence and experience. Without it we vacillate, and being in doubt then becomes almost a paradigm of despair.

In the end, truth is determined by the reality sense of its *criteria* [131]. Their constancy and credibility are necessary ad-

juncts to the reality sense of abiding *facts* and transient perceptions. Because the judgment of reality pervades the entire range
of human events, from the most casual, everyday encounters to
rigorous scientific demonstrations, and from fleeting, subjective
impressions to permanent principles, this section may seem to be
incongruously brief.

We use two meanings in our judgments about reality. One
meaning is the *value judgment* of events; the other is the *validation judgment* of statements about reality. Hence, judgments
about what is *real* should not be confused with what is *true* or, as
often happens, with what is pragmatically feasible, or *realistic*.
But although man more often prefers to be certain than merely
correct, he usually finds that reality sense requires the modulation
and corroboration offered by reality testing. Nevertheless, each
act of explaining and every explanation which reality testing calls
upon also impart reality sense to the events they purport to explain. Similarly, the reality sense adhering to diversified events
keeps various explanations "honest" and allows us to prefer one
hypothesis instead of another.

Reality Sense as Explanation

Explanations have two principal functions. As extrinsic components of organic meaning, appropriate explanations temper
and compromise the scope of absolute value judgments by limiting the conditions under which such judgments are made. The
second function performed by explanations is to augment the
reality sense of one set of events by establishing its relation to
other sets of events. This can be done because explanations operate on a more abstract level of experience than do any of the
events they encompass.

Reality sense as explanation is a necessary step in the transition from what is *accepted* as true to what can be *corroborated*
as true. It is a somewhat hybrid concept because it combines the
reality sense of explanation with the *explanation of reality sense*.
The first concept pertains to the psychological status of the act
called explaining. Why, indeed, do we explain anything? When
are we most likely to begin to explain? What makes one act of

explaining more credible than another? The second concept concerns the meaning and validity of different explanations of the process and the phenomenon of reality sense, including the subsidiary psychoanalytic theories upon which these explanations depend.

REALITY SENSE OF EXPLANATION

When life goes smoothly, no one asks the reason why. The awareness of "feeling right" is usually accepted as sufficient reason for things to happen as they do. This seemingly casual attitude stems from two convictions: that people do not behave haphazardly, but according to some inner plan; and that this plan may, if necessary, be understood.

The primary incentive to explain springs from the soil of personal experience, particularly when, in the act of living, we are confronted with discrepancy, disappointment, and discontinuity. Both *incentive* to explain and *faith* in harmonious existence depend upon a sense of reality for the constant, credible core of being which lies beneath the vicissitudes and accidents of everyday events. *The most convincing fact of reality is our own sense of being alive.* This fact stitches together objects, ideas, events, emotions, passions, principles, and perceptions into a cloak to shelter us against the rigors of other realities. Because each person is destined to reduce every experience to his own terms, he is also aware that, in his inner depths, there is an unceasing oscillation between the immediate *now* of contemporaneous events and whatever act he is *inclined* to do in the future. Consequently, explanations are not wholly derived from objects encountered in the world at large but are determined mostly by whatever acts upon man or is acted upon by man. In general, explanations provide a harmonious design which attaches one set of events to another; but, in the idiom of personal experience, explanations both relate and reconcile inner plans with outer events. In human behavior, explanations are expected to relate an inner *intention* with its completed act of *consummation*.

It is the unexpected event which becomes the unexplained event. Like the unimpeded act, fulfillment of an anticipation is assumed to be the way things are and is passed by without question. What motivates skillful or at least uniform behavior is considered to be merely "natural" until some other act emerges to interrupt this sequence of natural events. Thus our efforts to understand and to explain are prompted by deviant acts, attitudes, and events, or alien objects, which differ from what is "natural." For example, if I ask a friend why he went to a concert last week, my reason would be that I know he cares little for music and does not usually attend concerts. Now, if he were to answer that he went to the concert because he had bought a ticket, I would feel more rebuffed than informed — unless, of course, he usually sneaked into concert halls. Having a ticket is a prerequisite for attending a concert. It cannot be considered an explanation because it is part of the total act of attending a concert. My friend would, in effect, be telling me that he went to the concert because he went to the concert; in short, that it was none of my business. However, were my friend to tell me that, although it was unusual for him, he had wanted to hear a particular soloist, this statement of *intent*, or *wish to attend*, would be quite a satisfactory explanation. In all likelihood I would question him no further unless this statement of intent were, in itself, deviant or alien to his usual way of life.

Although the wish to hear a particular musician is fulfilled by attending the concert, the wish itself, or the statement of intent, is on two levels of experience. It is a *motive* for attending the concert; as an inner event related to a physical fact, it is part of the intrinsic meaning of the total event. On another level of experience the wish, or statement of intent, is an *explanation* for performing a relevant act. A motive is acceptable as an explanation *only* when it is relevant to several possible acts, not merely to the act which has been consummated. We know by experience that a wish is not always followed by a *rewarding act*, but, barring intrusion by some destructive force, a wish is always followed by a *relevant* act. Since an explanation encompasses different sets of events, a statement of intent alone will not account for any particular act.

Idea, Intention, and Inclination. For these reasons, when seeking any constant, credible explanation for human acts, we require a common sense of reality for both an immediate *now* of a present *intention* and an *inclination* toward some relevant, if unspecified, future consummation. This is found in the model of *voluntary action* — a concept which will be examined more fully in a later section (Chapter 7, p. 199). A truly voluntary act is, at best, a hypothetical entity, but it serves as an oversimplified model of psychological explanation, because the range of potential acts emanating from one's intention to perform this act is equivalent both to its *cause* and to its *source* of motivation. It is most important to recognize that the *idea* of the act as a whole, the *intention* which prompts it, and the *inclination* to perform it are identical in the so-called voluntary act. When the explanation of organic acts as a whole is concerned, it is not concatenation of external events alone but a sense of reality for a comprehensive inner design — idea, intention, and inclination — with respect to those external events that encourages belief in their common cause.

It is possible to believe in explanations, or to have confidence in explaining, only because we are already committed to believe that one event follows another with some degree of regularity, that no human act is utterly capricious, and that no level of human experience is completely determined by random collisions of alien events. The concept of *process* itself is based upon a mutual adjustment of forces within the organism and in the world. A more or less successful adjustment of such forces is called *adaptation;* a more or less regular adaptation, with a specific consequence, is called *cause-effect.*

Quite aside from the irrelevant question of whether or not any particular explanation is correct, the *credibility* of an explanation is derived, first, from the autochthonous, existential fact of personal immediacy and inclination and, second, from its analogy with the model of voluntary acts, with the resulting tendency to borrow some of the reality sense clinging to belief in such acts. In this way the wish stands apart from a potential consummation, yet both share a sense of reality for the act as a whole.

It is natural to seek more and more comprehensive explanations to appease the wish to explain. As thirst drives a man to seek a spring, the incentive to explain may lead us down a path of infinite regression by asking what explains an explanation, causes a cause, or motivates a motive. But there is an outpost of relevance and reality sense where reasons are accepted as irreducible, without further inquiry or interrogation. Beyond this point any explanation loses its cohesive impact and splits into component parts. These explanatory parts consist of a governing *idea*, or conceptual phase, an *intention*, or motivational phase, and an *inclination*, or causal phase. For example, some people try to explain their rash, deviant acts by appealing to some antecedent emotional aberration, such as "I was angry," "I thought I was in love," or "I was discouraged." Because bare affect is not a sufficient explanation, being angry, infatuated, and depressed are merely residues without meaning and only express a person's *inclination* to act as he did. The inclination needs to be substantiated with a prior *intention* in order to acquire meaning, and the act as a whole requires a governing *idea* which will be relevant, not only to the rash, deviant act, but to other related, potential acts.

Once the explanation-seeker passes the frontier of credibility, explanations become empty abstractions, with nothing but generality to recommend them. "Final causes," like "first causes," are the eschatology of nature. They exemplify the way in which explanations lose contact with the events they purport to explain. In the long run it makes no real difference whether ultimate philosophical entities are called matter, mind, spirit, substance, or any other congenial term that comes to mind. They are all verbal signs of inferences beyond direct experience and are attached to relevant events by only a tendril of reality sense.

Whatever we are passionately engaged in carries a conviction of reality. Routine acts lack the tang of sharp intention and inclination, yet preserve the shell of a governing idea. Without some encompassing concept, what we do may be both purposeless and preposterous. However, most human acts neither run dry nor run wild. Our actions seem to stand midway between the voluntary and the visceral and appear to be unified in some common emotional inclination.

The harmonies found in life may be distorted by conflicting

emotions or muted into dull monotony by inconsequential motives. When reality sense is at a low ebb, nothing is worth explaining, and no explanation is therefore relevant. In short, *the reality sense for acts of explanation depends upon matching our own sentiments with events in nature.* Consequently, we most eagerly seek explanations for those objects and events which participate in strongly motivated, vivid, and "hypercathected" acts [64b]. This does not mean, of course, that an explanation which shares a sense of reality with an event it explains will give rise to an identical emotion. After all, the explanation of reproduction, however vivid and convincing, is unlikely to evoke the feelings aroused by the reproductive act itself. Nevertheless, to have a feeling for something, in every case, is to endow it with reality.

Emotion. Emotion is to motivated acts as intuition is to cognitive acts. In the living moment of existential experience, the distinction we make between thought and emotion is largely one of convenience. It is even more difficult to distinguish sharply between emotion and intuition, from the viewpoint of intrapersonal experience. Some emotions are like crude intuitions, and some intuitions are like delicate emotions. Psychiatrists deal mainly with gross emotions and alien thoughts because they are easy to recognize and because patients complain about them. But these monophasic storms of emotion, such as anger, guilt, anxiety, and so forth, are relatively infrequent. For the most part, the sea of emotional experience is rippled by shifting currents that threaten no havoc and hence are scarcely noticed. Similarly, cognitive life is filled with inconspicuous intuitions in such profusion that their mass alone contributes to a deceptive calm. Only rarely is this calm broken by a surge of inspiration or the intrusion of a sudden insight.

Emotions do not make us angry here, anxious over there, or a little bit in love. The tendency of emotional life is to become diffused over consciousness, in much the same way that electrical stimulation spreads over the limbic lobe, activating and reactivating mutually related areas [104]. In fact, consciousness itself may be defined as the demand that reality makes upon the emotions, and intuition in conjunction with emotion may be regarded as related phases of the harmonious action of higher neurological processes.

Ideas are like solids which can be neatly separated from each other. Emotions are like gases that fill the vessel containing them. When emotions subside, no trace remains other than a lingering sense of reality for the vanished event. Although there is no memory of affect — the conscious aspect of emotion — psycho-analysis maintains that there are more or less fixed propensities which can be aroused by appropriate situations to evoke fresh emotions. Elliptical expressions such as "the unconscious sense of guilt" refer not to guilty feelings beyond awareness but to a latent disposition to carry out prohibited acts. Fluctuation of emotion itself may be the monitor of propensities to avoid, or to bring about, intended acts.

Affective Equivalence. These considerations lead to the principle of *affective equivalence.* It maintains that events attended by different affects may be acted upon in similar ways, and that wholly dissimilar actions, prompted even by different motives, may, under proper circumstances, give rise to equivalent emotion [113a]. For example, it was possible for a male patient to be chronically irritated by his employer and, for the same reason, to be compassionately concerned about his invalid wife. He was angry because his employer did not take better care of him but solicitous because his wife was unable to take care of him. He could control his anger toward his employer by per-functory compliance with minimal duties, but his latent anger and resentment toward his wife had been almost completely replaced by feelings of sympathy and tenderness. Despite his truculent compliance in one situation and altruistic dedication in the other, he brought to both relationships a similar wish to be taken care of, a disguised envy of his employer and his wife, and a bitterness that he was obliged to care for them, without reciprocity. In addition to the inner equivalence of these dissim-ilar events, the act of explaining depended upon recognizing similar motives and causes for his behavior and attitude in both instances [113b].

The process of dreaming illustrates even more clearly the

principle of affective equivalence. Dreams allow reality sense to hold different wishes, fears, scattered images, emotions, and random thoughts together in a confluence of events that extends far beyond the pressures of reason, logic, categories, and reality testing [46d]. Whenever a patient feels an uncanny, however enigmatic or illogical, relationship between his voluntary acts and the purposeless acts he must compulsively perform, he is responding to the affective equivalence of these separate acts in so far as they share a common base in reality sense [46p]. Affective equivalence accounts for the cohesive reality of metaphor, paradox, and conflict. Lady Macbeth, for instance, responded *as if* her wish to become queen were, in fact, equivalent to having murdered Duncan herself. The governing idea, inclination, and intention of every act she performed shared a mutual reality sense with every other act perpetrated in the conspiracy. Quite literally, she felt that she "had a hand in it."

The quasi-logical expression *as if* emphasizes the difference, and yet the similarity, between affective equivalence and literal equivalence [136]. It is a phrase widely used in psychoanalysis to designate "felt" relationships which, in turn, are often indications of affective equivalence.

The principle of affective equivalence is indispensable to psychoanalysis because it offers a way to link together all types and degrees of motives and emotions. Because it presupposes the abiding reality of psychodynamic processes, affective equivalence is useful both in understanding more or less contemporaneous events and in establishing an underlying longitudinal relationship of diversified acts on many levels of experience. For our present purposes, it is a concept which connects the reality sense of explanation with the explanation of reality sense.

EXPLANATION OF REALITY SENSE

Explanations in psychoanalysis, like the substance of analysis itself, arrange themselves according to different degrees of abstraction. Theoretically, since psychoanalysis always refers to a slice of subjective experience, every psychoanalytic concept ought to be so clearly expressed that theories based upon it could declare their own degree of relevance to clinical events and intrapersonal facts. However, psychoanalytic facts are indeterminate entities which frequently change according to the theories that interpret them, and psychoanalytic explanations tend to become less credible in proportion to their distance from direct experience. Although an explanation is relevant only to the extent that it bears a clear relation to the facts it explains, this somewhat self-evident truth is itself often overlooked. When vaporous speculations about dubious facts are invoked to explain specific clinical findings, their relevance is too remote and tenuous to be useful.

In some instances, disturbance of a person's normal appetite for food may be explained by a disease, such as diabetes mellitus, which affects carbohydrate metabolism. In turn, the pathological disorder called diabetes mellitus may be explained by a disorder of pituitary and pancreatic functions. The intervening steps may then be traced from endocrine imbalance to increased or decreased inclinations to eat. However, the patient's overall qualitative preference for one kind of food and his aversion to another kind cannot be ascribed wholly to endocrine imbalance, although it is possible that the carbohydrate content of certain foods may influence his preference. In other words, an explanation on one level of abstraction — such as increased blood sugar — may itself require explanation on a higher level of abstraction — such as disturbed pituitary and pancreatic balance.

These increasingly abstract explanations are less and less able to account for the clinical facts that occur in patients. Many familiar psychoanalytic concepts and theories are irrelevant and inadequate explanations for the events we find in psychoanalysis. This is why the significance of reality sense for the existential experience of psychoanalysis is our principal theme. There is nothing self-evident or intrinsically "real" about the psychoanalytic concepts which are presumed to be relevant to reality sense. Instead, like everything else, they too depend upon reality sense for their initial affirmation and, secondarily, upon reality testing for their indirect confirmation. The primitive community of acceptances and convictions, into which explanations and explanatory concepts later seek admission, is extended by means of affective equivalence and common emotional inclinations, in the midst of different kinds of experience. Bradley [19] said that metaphysics is the discovery of bad reasons for what is already believed by instinct, and even the most rational process, Ogden and Richards noted [103], needs instinctive interpretations. The flaw in rationalization, for example, is that the reasons mustered to support a conviction are not as persuasive as is the bare idea itself. In the beginning, and at the end, man is his own explanatory reference. He advocates explanations which are relevant to his emotional orientation and to his particular propensity to interpret reality in one way rather than another.

Psychoanalytic *interpretations* of what patients say, think, or do pertain for the most part to socially adaptive acts or motivated attitudes, but psychoanalytic *explanations* tend to be a relevant version of the economic viewpoint, set into the hypothesis of primary and secondary dynamic processes. Consequently, whatever their level of abstraction, psychoanalytic theories that purport to explain will tend to accept as real such concepts as the *dynamic unconscious, psychic energy*, and *affective equivalence* and to assume their relevance to motivation, behavior, and conscious emotional and intellectual experience.

Early in his career Freud accepted patients' reports of sexual seduction as literal facts, and these "facts" became the basis for his traumatic theory of neurosis [46a, b, c]. Later he discovered that the "facts" were phantasies produced by the neurosis and were not causes of the neurosis. Most accounts imply that Freud changed his mind when more clinical information became available, but Freud is silent about the kind of information he acquired. For our purpose, it is sufficient to note that he believed the stories of rape and seduction at one time but disbelieved them later. In fact, his early work disclosed some misgivings because, instead of citing confirmatory evidence for his conclusions, he appealed to the reader's personal prejudices and preferences. More recent studies [46l] intimate that the significant factors which induced Freud to give up the seduction theory of neurosis were experiences he underwent himself, and did not consist solely of additional information gathered from his patients. His father's death led to self-analysis, self-analysis led to analysis of dreams, analysis of dreams to dream theory, dream theory to the relation between neurosis and dreams; then, following some objectionable phantasies and dreams of his own, he arrived at a new conviction: the alleged seductions were phantasies, not unlike images occurring in dreams. That Freud was, in fact, influenced by fluctuations in his own sense of reality is further demonstrated by a lifelong tendency to "rediscover" his own work, periodically, in bursts of creativity and intuition.

Plato and Freud. The personal contribution by creative men to even their most abstract explanations and theories is often underestimated [120]. Although their explanations may apply to widely dissimilar fields and, of course, may be expressed in unfamiliar, technical vocabularies, their basic explanatory concepts may express a curiously similar sense of reality for certain explanatory images, as if there were an affinity of feelings, attitudes, and thoughts. After all, it is only natural to conclude that when thinkers try to account for the irrational in nature they are responding to a wish to find a congenial rationality for the irrational in their own nature. Thus their interpretation of nature is influenced by their inner design. For example, Plato propounded a perfectly rational, or rationally perfect, "World of Ideas." These pure Ideas, or essences, were the source of every value, the template of reality, and the highest purpose of human endeavor. He maintained that ordinary existence obscures the immanent perfection that abides in man, and that eros is love for the ideal, in whatever form this ideal occurs. He also seemed to recognize the futility of argumentation to defend his beliefs. Despite Socrates, and yet through Socrates, Plato "explained" himself by means of myth, analogy, appeal to emotions, and dialectical confrontations with paradox [129]. Furthermore, although the theory of Ideas is the cornerstone of Platonic philosophy, the Ideas themselves seem to have no positive attributes. Plato's Ideas are wholly imaginary forms of perfection, which were defined only as the negatives of existing objects and opinions. This fact implies that Plato became convinced about his idealized perceptions through the more mundane events, ideas, and customs in Athenian life. Since the scope of Plato's ideal world is not really conveyed by this negation of

every terrestrial quality, it is clear that his convictions and conclusions exceeded his capacity to describe and to designate. Consequently, Plato's gift to posterity is a monument to the search
for rationality amid the irrational forces in the world; his sense
of the inner equivalence of thoughts and things joined with his
own aspirations for order and perfection to produce the Platonic
philosophy. It is appropriate that the result of this quest should
be so characteristically inconclusive.

Plato and Freud, separated by almost 2,300 years, were concerned with vastly different ideas and events. It is significant
that, when their explanatory images are placed side by side, both
seem to have given their ideas a similar creative twist, as though
there had been a common irrational root which had proliferated
first in one form and then in another, but with analogous imagery. Of course, images are not explanations, but the *as if,*
affective equivalents of today may grow into the hypotheses of
tomorrow. Both Plato and Freud postulated (1) an eternal
source of energy, (2) a concept of universal motivation, and (3)
a set of permanent prototypes. What Plato termed the "World
of Ideas" Freud called "primary process." In other words, Freudian "eternal forms" consist of unconscious images, memory traces,
and undischarged quanta of psychic energy. By unceasing search
for objects offering perceptual identity with early gratification,
these psychic forms act as the vehicles for centrifugal discharge
of instinctual drives that are largely aggressive and erotic in
orientation. Analogously, Platonic "primary process" also consists of recollections of earlier states of perfection — incarnate
in man — which had migrated centripetally from the world of
essences, only to become obscured in the imperfections and errors
of the real world. By seeking and finding the fulfillment of eros,
the ideal embedded in man can again become manifest, just as
the fulfillment of instinctual derivatives enables man to overcome
his inner tension and conflict.

To continue the parallel, both Plato and Freud based their
concept of reality upon images of idealized pristine forms that
exist beyond direct encounter. Whether or not they called these
forms "Ideas" or "Instinct Representatives," they seem to con-
cur in the belief that eros is the sustaining force which inspires

man's adventures in desire and disappointment, against the relentless opposition of objects and things in the world. The fact that eros was thought of as idealized love in one instance and as sexualized energy in the other is secondary. More important, although neither primary process nor eternal forms can actually be experienced without many distortions, both Plato and Freud affirmed their belief that man has some innate knowledge, instinctual propensity, or idealized aim that constantly spurs him toward an ultimate consummation.

Libido and Libidinal Fields. A cautious retrenchment and reformulation of Freud's early concept of libido have gradually taken place in recent years. Originally, *libido* was the name given to "sexual energy." It was regarded as potentially, but not actually, quantifiable. Because Freud considered such energy capable of being invested in various objects, activities, organs, and apertures, libido became the source of the economic viewpoint. In turn, the economic viewpoint became the most widely acclaimed explanation of psychological events offered in the early years of psychoanalysis. Uncritical application of the libido theory became a kind of pantheism and almost every symptom and character trait was construed as representations of transmuted sexual energy.

It is purely a matter of conjecture whether libido is, in fact, an independent, pluripotential substance or is some kind of transformation that so-called psychic energy undergoes [30, 122]. Libido was, and remains, an explanatory concept, introduced only in order to delineate certain acts and organs according to their specific pleasurable sensitivity, or to qualify the emotional significance of certain kinds of experience. Since libido is never experienced directly, but only in postulated "forms," we may conclude that the referents for these diversified expressions of libidinal activity are fairly uniform clusters of affect within the orbit of intrapersonal experience. However, even in its most sweeping version, psychic energy alone cannot account for the exquisite variations in emotions or for the proliferative, subtle relationships between people. Thus, instead of concluding that libido "explains" the sense of reality, we may presume the reverse: that the sense of reality for constant and credible clusters of affect has given rise to the notion of a universal psychic energy.

As though they recognize that the common source of libido is to be found in reality sense, and in the secrets that the enigma of emotion holds, contemporary psychoanalysts [114] have replaced the earlier notion of libido with terms that qualify the entire range of emotional activity. They speak of libidinal development, libidinal objects, libidinal aims, and even of a process called libidinization. The issue is gradually centering around the mutual reality sense of ideas, objects, acts, perceptions, organs, and values contained within a field of experience called the libidinal field [140a]. Reality sense is by no means equivalent to specific emotions, but emotions can be experiences which modulate reality. Since whatever has reality sense belongs to a libidinal field, emotions circumscribe various inclinations to action and provide direction for acts which seek gratification within that field.

Examination of three well-known psychoanalytic principles — *repetition compulsion, pleasure principle,* and *constancy principle* — will confirm the hypothesis that they are related to three different aspects of emotion, called, respectively, *activity, affect,* and *direction.*

The *repetition compulsion* pertains to the periodicity of biological activity and acts, whether these are recurrent impulses, innate motivations, instinctual polarities, or refractory persistence of symptoms. The *pleasure principle* is no more than a generalization about the predominant affect that accompanies fulfillment of various appetites. The *constancy principle,* combining the principle of the "least action" with the "Nirvana" principle, has the adaptive restoration of equilibrium as its aim. It presumably governs efforts to gratify desire with the least expenditure of effort and energy. In a word, the constancy principle is the direction that motivated acts follow in order to reduce the emotion which produced them.

Since repetition compulsion, pleasure principal, and constancy principle refer to different aspects of the relationship between emotional inclinations and motivated acts, we can see that the reality principle [54b] — not to be confused with either reality sense or reality testing — refers to the obstacles and restrictions placed upon the objects, aims, organs, and functions within libidinal fields.

Pleasure and Reality Sense. Reality sense and reality testing are not ideas which can be merely subsumed within the concept of the reality principle; and they differ just as distinctly from the so-called pleasure principle. The sense of what is real has little to do with what is pleasurable. Pleasure may accompany fulfillment of wishes, relief from harassing emotions, and successful achievements. It may be part of whatever produces a sense of mastery or confidence, or a glow of effectiveness. However, in the existential events of life, pleasure is a circumscribed oasis on a bleak landscape. Its momentary quality appears when motivated acts are consummated, not an instant earlier or later. Pleasure pertains to the consequences of what we do, not to the sense of reality for the fact and act of doing it.

Like success and health, pleasure never sends a patient to a doctor. For whatever reason people seek psychoanalysis, the analyst will find himself looking for an explanation for their complaints and way of life by forging a link between how they feel, think, or act and some basic involvement with existence itself. These involvements are usually emotional, and they include grief, pain, anxiety, depression, and doubt. If, in formulating explanations, the analyst uses ideas such as psychic energy, libidinal fields, unconscious motivation, and so forth, it is because the galaxy of forces represented by psychodynamic psychology is derived from those deviant involvements with existence in which reality sense resides.

It is more accurate to conceive of an *un*pleasure principle that governs existence rather than a pleasure principle. Reality sense is enhanced by pain, intense wishes, fears, and emotional involvements of many kinds. The reality of perception and performance is cast in the image of desire, not in the fulfillment of it. Reality sense fluctuates, but it abides, throughout persistent pain and fleeting pleasure, to mark the way in which we contend with the world.

The Existential Core of Psychoanalysis

Time and Reality Sense

The sense of time is an inconspicuous yet indispensable companion of the sense of reality. Because psychoanalysis is committed to two views of man, it also maintains two corresponding views of time: *categorical time* and *existential time*.

Categorical time is measured by clocks and calendars. It is a way to separate, order, and number objects and events in the world according to their relative position on a continuum of space. As in the categorical view of himself, man is simply another member in the community of objects observed. He may be able to rearrange a few other objects or events, but he cannot modify time's relentless forward cadence.

Existential time refers to time experienced, rather than to time observed. It is primarily determined by qualitative fluctuations of reality sense, cycles of intrapersonal activity, discontinuities of perception, and alternating expansion and contraction of libidinal fields. From the viewpoint of intrapersonal experience, man is not a helpless bystander who observes the passing scene. In the same degree that he contributes to his own reality, he is an active determinant of existential time.

Existential time is the sense of reality for discontinuity, deviation, and flux, in our relation to the world. Thus, it has two aspects: *duration* and *sense of time elapsed*. The fact of being alive and the fluctuations of reality sense that accompany living acts enable us to keep our *ego identity* amid the oscillations of wish, fulfillment, desire, and disappointment. The sense of duration and constancy throughout the ebb and flow of time elapsed allows us to link the inner continuity of experience with outward perception of objects. *Ego identity* for ourselves is recognized by a constant awareness of *presence* for the world.

THE PARADOXES OF TIME

As a result of being simultaneously immersed in both existential and categorical time, we are confronted with many paradoxes. For example, we recognize that to die is the common fate of all organic life, but we cannot accept, or even imagine, the inevitable fact of our own subjective extinction. Reality testing, using the scales and sequences of categorical time, insists that because we, too, are objects and organisms we have a beginning and an end and cannot escape time's unilateral changes. In contrast, reality sense for our enduring existence, in spite of changes, creates an utterly incorrect feeling that we are exempt from time.

The paradoxes of time are part of psychoanalysis itself. They are produced by the incessant ambiguity of events which are set into existential time and yet are measured by categorical time. Existential time is *symmetrical* — the past and future are both contained in an immediate *now*. Fragments of yesterday, along with more remote residues, flow into the living presence of the world, and this confluence, in turn, directs the course of the future. On the other hand, psychoanalysis is interested in the past only because it has a functional relevance to the present and future. Whenever reality sense is strong or intuition is clear, the *now* fuses symmetrical images of time so that the past and future tend to interpret each other and we have the illusion of unlimited survival.

There are other paradoxes, less sobering and more familiar than that of survival or extinction, which are also based upon a confusion between measurement of categorical time and perception of existential time. We are familiar, for example, with the watched pot that never boils, the boring lecture that goes on endlessly, and the exciting weekend that is over almost as soon as it begins. In retrospect, the weekend seems to have been far longer than a few days; and, in contrast, other events which occurred many chronological years ago may seem to have happened only yesterday.

These paradoxes can be resolved by first understanding the relation of reality sense to the sense of time. Reality sense is most acute at moments of high intention and accelerated activity. When many different acts are crowded closely together, and then still other acts, strongly motivated and vigorously performed, follow so quickly that quiescence is incomplete, the result is a fusion of these separate acts into a single coalescent act whose reality sense, augmented by the sense of reality for every component act, is unusually vivid. These concordant moments produce an immediate *present* and *presence*, as though reality itself were on a timeless peak. Furthermore, while the present and presence persist, the sense of duration is brief. When at last the concordant moment ends, there is a feeling that elapsed time has been greatly increased.

In general, existential time can be judged "fast" or "slow" only in relation to categorical time [51]. The sense of time is perceived only at moments of *quiescence* following activity and is judged "long" or "short" according to the degree of activity that has occurred since the previous quiescent period. Thus, duration seems to be judged by the height of reality sense, while time elapsed is judged by contrast with previous activity. When there are only a few monotonous tasks to perform, quiescences are prolonged, duration seems unending, but the retrospective sense of time elapsed is diminished.

Reality sense is strongest when fulfillment is least. Between moments of activity and following fulfillment, reality sense is diminished, duration seems extensive, and the sense of time elapsed is prolonged. An analogy would be the familiar feeling of anticlimax which follows the completion of some devoutly desired, prolonged enterprise. At first the quiescence is experienced as relief. Then, because the reality sense of the inciting intention and purpose has become so faint, the entire enterprise, including its subsidiary acts, becomes alienated from the sense of duration and from the expenditure of time and energy devoted to just this single moment of reality. The time elapsed may seem great, but the concordant act itself may even acquire a halo of unreality.

Reality sense and time sense are both contingent upon peaks and plateaus of activity. A single strongly invested act that has high reality sense and a sharp inclination to quiescence is less likely to have an abiding value than will a number of less intense but more extended acts. According to this principle, the value of life depends more upon what we do with the time available than upon the length of time itself. Nevertheless, by his time sense alone, man is cast into a paradox. His reality is a function of his quest for fulfillment. But when it is found, his sense of

time deprives him of the reality that gave rise to the consummation, like Kronos consuming his sons. Man lives for his abiding
moments of reality but counts his days by the moments when
his sense of reality is least.

Time and Psychoanalysis

Psychoanalysis is no less committed to existential time than
to reality sense. In some respects psychoanalytic technique is
an effort to circumvent categorical time. The purpose of free
association — the fundamental rule of analysis — is to achieve
simultaneity of sentiments and ideas, not merely their *sequence*
in categorical time. There is no dead past in psychoanalysis, but
only events whose vestiges have not yet been evoked in one form
or another. Any psychic event occurs *now*, and, through its fundamental rule, psychoanalysis tries to establish a contemporaneous context for events which have been gathered from all
points along the historical continuum. It is more concerned with
emotional relevance and affective equivalence than with locating
events in their literal sequences. Psychoanalysis scrutinizes events
for their mutual relevance, as though they were soldiers dressed
in uniforms from widely divergent periods and different coun-
tries but all passing in review together. It is said that hysterical
patients suffer from reminiscences [20]. This is true only in so
far as the memories are still alive in the form of present suffering. Memories, as such, do not determine the living present, but
the emotional context of the present determines which events
will be recalled [113a]. Timeless facts, such as mathematical
formulas, may be retrieved when they are relevant to present
problems, not because they are decisive influences in our lives
that insist upon exercising some chronic effect. Psychoanalysis
attempts to revive traces of past events only because of their
emotional relevance in the present.

In most instances memories are disguised relics, so deeply
encrusted with succeeding events that they have become arti-
facts. In other cases the memory of an event may be more vivid
than the original event. Psychoanalysis certainly depends upon

memories, or at least upon reports about the past, but completely literal and historically accurate reconstruction of the past is neither possible nor, fortunately, necessary. It is necessary, however, to recognize the events which *endure* longer, not just those which occurred a very long time ago. The enduring events are discovered and rediscovered in many recurrent moments of existential time [37]. They survive by evoking fresh relevance and fresh reality sense for the organic meaning of the present. Thus, because related events tend to endow each other with a common reality sense, the memory of any single occurrence may have a sense of reality entirely different from that of the episode itself.

In Whitehead's theory of subjective forms [66a, b] the past is declared to be everywhere immanent in the present, and this immanence accounts for the dynamic properties of recalled experience. Whitehead emphasizes *actual entities* which pass away, leaving only traces of themselves in *eternal objects*. This philosophical hypothesis is quite compatible with psychoanalytic theory and practice, except that psychoanalysis is concerned with *activated* and *activating* entities that emerge from the categorical past to exert eternal and enduring effects during recurrent moments of existential time. These entities are not confined to recollections. Because memories are often deceptive substitutes for past events, to emphasize only the recovery of memories during analysis, and to downgrade contemporary issues, problems, and acts, is to construct a private pantheon of vanished occasions, where we pay tribute to our mistakes and to our wish for certainty. Memories are irrelevant in psychoanalysis if they are valued only as literal transcriptions. They are important mainly because they represent the cumulative influence of different decisive acts and involvements. In order to explain why certain trends persist, and why some ideas and inclinations recur so regularly, psychoanalysis has postulated concepts such as *primary process* and the *dynamic unconscious*. Whyte [145] has demonstrated that these explanatory ideas were not psychoanalytic innovations but novel applications of a long series of similar viewpoints toward mental events.

The Meaning of Reality Sense

Primary process is the primitive source of both reality sense and existential time. According to Freud, the primary process consisted of more or less amorphous images and traces of past events, whose representatives sought renewed fulfillment through acts of instinctual discharge [67a]. The original material of experience was transformed by unconscious, dynamic primary processes into fresh forms that gathered energy and combined with traces of former events to produce renewed activity. This material was then guided and refined by secondary processes until instinctual inclinations became realistically compatible with external circumstances [14a, b].

Primary processes function on a level of mental life where motive and emotion are not yet differentiated. The theory [113c] postulates that this is where the emotional linkage between subsequent experience is forged, and where the instigation for personal characteristics of style and belief arises.

Arguments about the priority of primary process over secondary processes are futile. Both are distinctive aspects of mental activity as a whole; they are not distinct geographical regions. As a rule, however, descriptions of primary process are those of *material transformations,* such as displacement, fragmentation, dilution, condensation, distortion, and attenuation. Descriptions of secondary processes are those of *functional transformations;* for the most part, they characterize ways in which the material is transmuted into different modes and methods of expression. If primary process is a mortar in which experience is pulverized into traces, to be reshaped for further use, then the dynamic unconscious turns it into a crucible for creating fresh versions on different levels of complexity.

Primary processes are said to be exempt from the conditions of logic, time, negation, part-whole distinction, and other qualities of secondary processes [46m]. This is not surprising because all of these qualities depend upon the functional distinctions brought about by secondary processes. For example, it is possible to contradict only interpretations and propositions, not the material on which the interpretations and propositions are based. Primary process must have characteristics other than just being the negation of secondary processes. Nevertheless, like Plato's eternal forms, the positive content of primary process can be understood only on the basis of its analogy with familiar events. Therefore, it is likely that primary processes include primitive, stereotyped action potentials, traces, intentions, and images. They can violate logic and resist negation and part-whole relation because these properties are familiar functional transformations that we call secondary processes. For the same reason, primary processes are absolved from an obligation to observe categorical time.

The primitive source of whatever underlies the naked experience of duration or the vacant sense of time elapsed seems to be the natural periodicity and visceral rhythms of sleeping and waking, hunger and satiation, inspiration and expiration, systole and diastole, excitation and quiescence. In a sense, sex and the seasons are the molds in which reality sense and time sense are formed. In any event, homeostasis is an active process, not a static accomplishment; it is a dynamic disequilibrium influenced by many different sources of activity. "Equilibrium" is a kind of fiction which is scarcely ever achieved without being promptly challenged by a multiplicity of new occasions and recurrent demands.

VERSIONS OF EXISTENTIAL TIME

The structural viewpoint in psychoanalysis is derived from different kinds of activity and so must include different versions of existential time. Id activities, for example, are distinguished by preconceptual resurgence and remission of visceral functions and stereotyped patterns of response. Their version of time is *periodic*. Ego activities are concerned with performing specific, practical tasks and bringing them to a finite conclusion. Their version of time is *discontinuous* and *interrupted*. Finally, superego activities are aimed at remote, teleological goals where fulfillment is, to say the least, doubtful. Their version of time is that of *protracted duration*.

The Meaning of Reality Sense

The psychoanalytic concept of *regression* [42] may be used to illustrate how a sharper distinction between categorical and existential time can clarify an otherwise confusing concept. Regression is usually defined — when it is defined at all — as a return to more primitive, relatively undifferentiated ego functions, accompanied by resurrection of problems that have already been solved more adequately than are the current problems which presumably prompt the regression. This definition is consistent with a concept of existential time. However, to define regression as the resurgence of unsolved but latent problems from the past, which have been activated by baffling present-day problems, also demands a concept of categorical time. As a result of this double definition, regression is a popular concept to invoke, but one whose ambiguity diminishes its value.

This dilemma can be resolved by recognizing that regression does not simply turn the clock back to a more or less successful categorical past. Whether a patient is regressed or not, any psychic event occurs in the present, never in the past or future. Regression occurs when a patient cannot act without conflict or intolerable anxiety in his immediate encounter with the world. As a result, he finds himself thrust *downward* through stratifications of existential events, rather than *backward* along a continuum of categorical time. By trying to find a stable sense of reality in his own depths, such a patient may be infantilized, but without restoration of his infancy. Some psychotic patients distort time by claiming to be younger than their chronological years [16]. The reported age may be what it was during the last period of relative health. Melancholic patients foresee no future, and schizophrenic patients cannot distinguish past or future from the immediacy of the present — a trait which corresponds to their concrete yet strangely allegorical interpretation of existence as a whole, and which has been called, erroneously, "primary process thinking."

Regression can thus be defined more precisely by heeding the kind of time experienced by regressed patients [22]. For those severely regressed, categorical time ceases, leaving only duration, primary process imagery, and periodic, stereotyped visceral and somatic acts. Regression in time sense will accompany regression from the level of abstract thinking to the level of concrete images [50] and from reality testing to unmodified reality sense.

THEORIES OF PSYCHOGENESIS

Theories of the psychogenesis of both symptoms and personality seldom distinguish between existential and categorical time. In the psychological field, cause and effect are simultaneous events, not sequential, as they are in a physical field. Psychic "causes," it has already been pointed out, are efforts to simplify heterogeneous events by means of a comprehensive explanation; they are not, as once was thought, isolated, external events that occurred earlier in categorical time. As in the fundamental rule of psychoanalysis, relevant theories of psychogenesis discover their causal residues within stratified samplings taken from moments of existential time, instead of in fragments from the disengaged chronological past.

A young man suffering from chronic depression and self-doubt reported that he had felt inherently defective ever since an undescended testicle had been removed when he was a small boy. This "defect" had interfered with his sexual adjustment, intellectual achievements, and professional advancement. According to his simplified genetic hypothesis, the orchidectomy had decisively influenced his attitudes and adjustment, even in areas where having one or two testicles was unimportant.

The abnormality which brought the patient to the psychiatrist was not the history of orchidectomy. It was his present-day complaint that he was always obliged to function from a position of weakness and vulnerability. He assumed that without the crucial operation his life and personality would have been substantially different.

There are many other theories of psychogenesis [52, 55] which, like this one, beg so much that they have little left to earn. From the viewpoint of categorical time, the patient's hypothesis was scarcely plausible since it assumed that his emotional responses in boyhood and in manhood were almost identical.

The Meaning of Reality Sense

From the viewpoint of existential time, however, the orchidectomy could be considered as though it were a *current situation* of weakness and defect, rather than a cause of every other attitude in which he felt vulnerable. The orchidectomy was not an acceptable explanation for the way he felt as a man but a paraphrase of his conviction that the events which spanned many years coexisted in an enduring presence.

At best, theories of psychogenesis and development offer a general context of meaning in which events in a person's life can be judged from the same perspective. The so-called anal character, for example, is supposed to be a person who has developed orderly, scrupulous, and parsimonious traits because of bowel difficulties in childhood [46e]. If these different events are just distributed along the continuum called categorical time, the hypothesis is impossible to substantiate. However, within a context of reality sense and existential time, the hypothesis refers not at all to a theory of development but to a group of patients who tend to deal with problems in almost identical ways. They are rigidly controlled, though prone to ambivalent relationships; they tend to be either doubtful or dogmatic, impulsive or restrained; and they respond to nontoilet situations the same way a child responds to learning how to restrain and to release bowel movements.

Before turning from philosophical considerations to more clinical issues, it is natural to wonder whether the existential viewpoint can offer a method by which psychoanalytic concepts can be more systematically derived and studied. Although this formidable task is beyond the purpose of the present book, succeeding sections will show that it is possible to define an idea clearly and yet preserve its link with the existential core of psychoanalysis, and that the central concepts of motivation and emotion are rooted in the subjective experience of reality itself. Further investigation of these still controversial problems may profit from closer attention to organic meaning and reality sense.

There is still another reason for pausing at this point. It is a way station where one phase of the investigation is terminated and another level of inquiry is approached. Now that its mean-

The Existential Core of Psychoanalysis

ing has been clarified, it is possible to follow the sense of reality into the domain of clinical psychoanalysis. This will allow us to examine the inner affinities of emotion, motivation, and organic meaning, particularly as they occur in the course of the psychoanalytic encounter. Nearly every concept which has been explained thus far is found over and over again in psychoanalytic work. After all, organic meaning is contained in motivated acts and purposeful behavior, and psychoanalysis can be more precisely defined as a means of studying motivation than as a method of treating emotional disorders. Reality sense and responsibility grow out of the same rootstock. The ensuing discussion of psychoanalysis will, therefore, only be a more explicit bridge between the sense of reality for the world and the sense of responsibility for oneself. Just as reality is not an irreducible ultimate that defies analysis, existence is more than merely "being in the world," as some existentialists claim. The most pervasive and persuasive fact in distinguishing between objects, people, and things is the *sense* of being alive, of activating and being activated by the changes and correlations that occur in the world.

5. Affirmation and Confirmation

THE PRECEDING CHAPTERS have laboriously expounded the case for reality sense. Its various meanings and processes, such as affective equivalence, organic meaning, intuition, and so forth, have repeatedly reminded us that the content of reality cannot be severed from the ways to comprehend it. Thus, the process of organic meaning relates the creative participation of the thinker to the texture of his thoughts and to objects in his world. Libidinal fields and affective equivalence are psychodynamic concepts that emphasize the inner unity of emotional inclinations, motivated activities, and explanations. The inherent principle is that no thinker can be separated from his thoughts without destroying the sense of reality they share, nor can the one who acts be arbitrarily isolated from whatever he acts upon.

To exist does not mean to exist in isolation. Ontological acceptance requires mutual substantiation between reality sense and reality testing. This can occur only in a world where there is coordinated action and shared reality sense between people. No man is an island, it is said, but we need not drown together in order to prove it. The abiding issue of how to remain distinct as unique entities and yet maintain comprehensive interchange with others is the basis of the distinction between *affirmation* and *confirmation*.

In the process of living, the thinker is frequently lost in the market place of thoughts and things, becoming simply another object to be known and dealt with accordingly. In contrast, if we strive to insure our own identity, we soon discover that, without objects to know, we scarcely can acknowledge our own existence. There is a root dualism, or a dualism of roots, which relates efforts to affirm ourselves with efforts to confirm the other one.

Both affirmation and confirmation are ways to get at the reality of others, as well as to testify to our own reality. Affirmation uses the full scope of reality sense, but without the reality testing and corroboration implicit in confirmation, affirmation would be only an idle sentiment. *Affirmation declares that what is real for me is real. Confirmation asserts that what is real is real for me.* Although affirmation pertains principally to the reality of the knower, of the knowing process, and of what is known, the process of confirmation establishes a responsive relation between various sets of known objects. Affirmation and confirmation are complementary concepts. Being sensitive to nuances of reality sense is not the same as having firm knowledge. Confirmation tempers the vagrant winds of affirmation by emphasizing the difference between private belief and public knowledge, or, in some instances, between what is real and what is true.

How difficult it is to surrender a belief in order to admit a new fact! The very spontaneity of affirmation, in the process of collecting synthetic judgments from here and there, manufactures certainty, harmony, and order out of presuppositions, random observations, easy inferences, and favorite sentiments, then fuses them into the oversimplified generalities and amalgams of everyday life. Affirmations thrive in the soil of their own brute certainty and unchallenged experience. Unless we try to communicate with another, or to persuade him, confirmation is rarely necessary. In fact, because proof and demonstration are too specialized for everyday use, most efforts to communicate and persuade only call upon other affirmations and appeal to some emotion or authority for their justification.

Irrational man believes only that of which he is already convinced. He affirms and reaffirms, out of his bones, out of his blood, out of his heritage, and out of his inner catalogue of beliefs. But, like intuition, affirmations seem to combine harmony and symmetry with a certainty that falls just short of novelty or discovery, as if each fact that is recognized, or each truth that is uttered, were about to be enunciated for the first time. Because affirmations tend to reflect existential facts, or at least facts of affective equivalence, they may make claims about events which have not occurred, and perhaps cannot occur, with the same unblinking certainty that they report immediate facts. With an urgency beyond all logic, affirmations may pose swift generalizations that no one is competent to validate.

The psychological process — affirmation — is often confused with the logical processes — induction and deduction. Although induction and deduction are theoretically easy to distinguish, in practice they are almost inseparable, and each can be regarded as a product of affirmation. It does not matter whether generalizations are affirmed as inductive reasoning or particular illustrations are affirmed as deductive reasoning; they both arise from an immediately present, here-and-now event. Rational affirmations are determined more by affective dispositions than by objective evidence, and seemingly irrational dispositions usually contain an inner design of logic and order.

Like any other human being, the psychoanalyst is rooted in dualism. He is forced to judge behavior according to its face value and manifest motives, yet at the same time he can understand the design of such behavior only by drawing inferences which take him beyond direct examination of himself and others. Acts are not random but are assumed to have a purpose, albeit unknown. Inferences about either the general or the particular presuppose some variety of data to make them feasible. Generalizations must be presumed to indicate pertinent events.

However, affirmations do not escape challenge. Truth always hurts when it invades a serene sphere of certainty and disrupts the harmony of accepted beliefs. The unruffled continuity of dogmatic affirmation constantly encounters the obstacles and counterthrusts of deviant facts and disappointing acts. There are always facts which will confound staunchly held rules and transform grand intuitions into egregious errors.

Affirmations are the original data of psychoanalysis and the content of psychoanalytic hours because they are explicit clusters of reality sense, not because they are particularly true. If the resulting reality is strange or distorted, it is still possible, through reality testing and confirmation, to find its inner rationality and justification. In no sense is confirmation an assent to the validity of what is affirmed. In its most elementary meaning, to confirm is to resonate the affirmations of another person, even though this primitive response is only an acknowledgment of his unique presence and of the reality of his affirmations.

In his actual practice the psychoanalyst is concerned more with organic meaning than with objective truth. When he investigates impersonal facts, it is only to formulate working hypotheses for organic events. This is, of course, not the unambiguous psychoanalysis of the lecture platform, textbook, seminar, or panel. It is the psychoanalysis that originates in a here-and-now encounter. The past is largely unknown and, at best, can be reached only through still other affirmations and working hypotheses. Hence the analyst must find his way through intuition, quiet appraisals of fact, and a judicious mixture of both affirmation and confirmation. It is a lonely enterprise, this encounter, and in many respects an impossible task. But, for that matter, so is living itself.

The Psychoanalytic Encounter

Psychoanalysis is periodically accused of being doctrinaire, reductionistic, impersonal, or talmudic. Less extreme criticism suggests that the study of psychodynamics tends to blunt one's natural appreciation of the patient as a person. Too much emphasis upon categorical rules, it is claimed, ignores the crucial existential elements which transcend rules. However, rules and principles are not incompatible with intrapersonal events. Even though events will elude whatever web of rules is spun to capture them, the pursuit cannot be given up. From one point of view algebra can be regarded as an unusually elegant system for dealing with unknowns. Although it lacks the symbolic precision and abstract purity of algebra, psychoanalysis, too, seeks a way to contend with other kinds of unknowns.

Psychoanalysis is not a delusion, practiced by the fanatical and perpetrated upon the gullible; nor is it a mere recital of psychodynamic litanies. Its basic fact is the *encounter*, which belongs to living experience itself, apart from whatever hypotheses, formulations, or theories ensue. It is an effort to meet the patient as a unique being, with respect to himself, his world, and other people. A patient ostensibly enters analysis because of some non-medical sickness, but if his sickness has turned him into a categorical nonentity, then the person without his sickness must receive major attention. It may be said that the difference between categorical and existential elements is finally understood when a patient realizes that *who* he is differs from *what* he is, and that the *truth* about himself differs from the *facts* of himself. *The encounter is the fact of being in analysis for the purpose of the analysis of being.*

The term *encounter* began as a useful expression, but, by overuse and abuse it is now, too often, merely flourished as a tendentious cliché. The same thing has happened to *repression, unconscious, defense mechanism, commitment, sublimation,* and that more than prevalent cliché *the human condition.* Just as too frequent handling soils a fabric, loose handling has admittedly damaged the scientific significance of the encounter by turning its name into cant. However, there is no other equivalent term to designate the analytic adventure that begins when the independent existence of both patient and analyst is accepted. By affirming their mutual reality as human beings, patient and analyst also acknowledge a mutual enterprise.

The Existential Core of Psychoanalysis

It is quite possible to look upon the analytic encounter as an entirely intellectual and technical exercise, the way a boy may play with a prism and a ray of light and pretend that he is an objective scientist. Similarly, it is also possible to glorify the analytic encounter into some kind of supermundane mystery accessible only to the initiated. Neither approach is correct. The analyst is not a technician, nor is he a high priest. As he was leaving at the end of analysis, a patient once said, "Whatever we may have talked about — my parents, my love life, my phantasies, my fears, et cetera — it was the 'et cetera' that mattered most."

The full reality sense of the encounter can be found only in the encounter itself, despite analysis of its component parts. After all, the being of another person is always met head on, not in books about books about books. However, there are different ways to meet reality. Scholars who seclude themselves to contemplate the world meet existence just as frankly as those "practical people" who briskly go about their self-righteous business.

The truly elusive element in the encounter, hidden in a forest of technical minutiae and theoretical underbrush, is the analyst himself. Some analysts tacitly avoid this issue by taking a categorical view of themselves. They rely upon the sketchy guidance offered by metapsychological theories and manuals of analytic technique, like sailors who stow aboard a large supply of maps before starting on a long voyage. Other analysts realize that, even with the most accurate maps, they must travel upon the surface of seas that extend in all directions, and that their equipment is both fragile and faulty. Landmarks may be reassuring, but they are not destinations.

The human mind is like an irrational number: it can be symbolized, talked about, and even used, but it cannot be exhaustively analyzed into fundamental units. Every method designed to study the mind seems to create its own system of integers in the process. Psychoanalysis has never overlooked the *Erlebnis*, or sense of living reality, which lies beyond definitions or categories. Rank and Sachs [112] recognized, early in its history, that psychoanalysis could not be confined to the clinic, office, or podium. More recently, Kris [78] demonstrated how strictly psychoanalytic issues could be sharpened by separating them from pure psychopathology. Analysis is filled with irrational beliefs, refractory attitudes, and intractable convictions that defy understanding, let alone explanation. In such an atmosphere dogmatism cannot survive, and significant issues cannot be indefinitely avoided. Psychoanalysis illustrates, only too well at times, the principle which maintains that natural events undergo some deformation in the course of describing them, and that, consequently, generalizations and conclusions are not equivalent to the events they are based upon. The inevitable dualism between the thinker and the product of his thinking reminds us that the very instrument of analytic thought may ultimately prove to be an inappropriate means of understanding its own intrinsic workings. A razor cannot cut itself, regardless of how sharp it is. Nevertheless, we do not recommend capitulation, nor should we forsake the search for the inner logic of irrational events. A reticent and reluctant patient once complained that there was really no incentive to talk with his analyst because he had heard that, after all, analysts understand only about 30 percent of what patients tell them. Without disputing this, I told him that, even if it were true, we still could not be sure which 30 percent it would be.

THE CHANGING IMAGE OF THE ANALYST

It is inevitable that the theory, technique, and issues of analysis are decisively influenced by the people who practice it [132a, b]. The analyst's image of himself — his self-affirmation — must include some convictions about the validity of what he does and about his own participation in the analytic encounter. A surgeon's technique is the resultant of his scientific knowledge and clinical experience. A psychoanalyst's technique is all of this, but his knowledge and clinical information are themselves influenced by his personal orientation. He, too, has acceptances and unspoken axioms which act upon his style of response and upon what he responds to. His enthusiasms and reservations about certain clinical events may be much more influential than the formal body of principles he professes. In fact, his explicit theoretical viewpoint is modified both by his innate predisposition and by the particular image he has of himself.

The image of the psychoanalyst as a shadowy, anonymous,

forbidding figure first developed during the period when neurosis was believed to be the result of conflict between impersonal instincts and an equally unyielding reality. According to this theory, when reality dammed up these drives, anxiety developed. Furthermore, if reality became adamant, or injurious, during a particularly vulnerable period, the whole course of personality development would be altered. The patient was an impersonal, double pawn of instinct from within and reality from without. The goal of psychoanalysis at this time was to release the psychic energy that was bound up in neurotic symptoms. The theory maintained that patients fell sick because of their inability to achieve instinctual gratification. The therapy maintained that patients could get well if psychic energy could be released through interpretive intervention into unconscious conflict.

Although some analysts tried to cut the Gordian knot of conflict by offering token gratifications, the prototype analyst was as impersonal, relentless, and coercive as the reality that frustrated the patient at every turn. Because neurosis was a product of the opposition of instinct and reality, the analyst, too, in his efforts to cure, became a similarly fearsome, forceful, and frustrating adversary. Always, the analytic encounter was one of impersonality, and the analyst was a "blank screen" that represented the indifference of reality and the insistence of instinct.

As Alexander [1a] pointed out in his writings at this period of psychoanalytic development, the patient had only two choices: to give up his symptoms or to keep them because of his affinity for obsolete, unattainable aims. In a parallel fashion, the patient could either accept his analyst's interpretations or remain bound to his anachronistic attachments. Although the patient may have sought to bring about a truce between reality and instincts through his symptoms, his analyst was wholly uncompromising and looked upon any such efforts to hinder the analysis as unmitigated "resistance."

With the discovery of transference, the analyst's image was no longer only an impersonal, frustrating reality. He was also the target of emotional attachments — largely irrational — and the object of instinctual vicissitudes. Still later, the emphasis placed upon conquest of monolithic resistance was modified by a growing appreciation that ego functions influenced the acceptance or repudiation of interpretations and ideas [46k]. Hindrances, then, were not entirely the product of recalcitrant instincts.

As each theoretical change took place, there were also changes in the analytic encounter, in the image of the analyst, and in psychoanalytic technique. We may presume that changes in explicit theory appeared last of all. When Freud announced [46i] that the mental apparatus consisted of id, ego, and superego, it was a somewhat belated acknowledgment that, in relation to his patient, the analyst is variously an agent of instincts, a countermanding reality, a replica of childhood values, and, in general, an evocative source.

It is said that patients like those described in early psychoanalytic case histories no longer exist. Psychoanalytic theory changes, and so does analytic data. We may conclude that analysts also change, even though their abiding purpose — to seek the source of conflict — remains the same. Aside from the distortions of transference, no analyst can easily overlook his contribution to the reality of the analytic encounter [49]. By means of affirmation and confirmation, his involvement is part of the analytic work itself; it is not a contaminant of the pure field of psychoanalysis.

THE TRAINING ANALYSIS

The training analysis has also remolded the image of the analyst. Instead of being an anonymous practitioner of unfamiliar skills or a dedicated acolyte who transmits immutable truths, the modern psychoanalyst is usually quite aware of his own unique characteristics and recognizes the creative contributions he makes to the analytic encounter. Despite criticisms of the institution of psychoanalytic institutes, the training analysis acknowledges the edict of the Delphic oracle, "Know thyself" — even if it hurts. If today's analyst cannot always satisfy the directive "Physician, heal thyself," he can at least be better equipped not to deceive himself. According to the cliché, a training analysis seeks to eliminate "blind spots" in the potential analyst. This is an impossible aim, since blind spots never can become points of clear vision. The training analysis improves his self-perception and therefore enables him to influence patients simply by being who he is and understanding who he is. His authentic reality is not an extraneous factor if he realizes how he also is influenced in the analytic encounter. As a fallible human being, any analyst may ignore some of his patient's conflicts and exaggerate others. To preclude this kind of distorted perception, and self-perception, is only a negative result of the training analysis. Its positive accomplishment is to nurture his own reality as a constructive component of the encounter.

Psychoanalytic Communication

The principal reason for entering into analysis, instead of some other form of therapy, is the wish to understand and to be understood. Suffering, of itself, is not enough incentive if there is no hope of being able to communicate. This wish to be understood is not a search for sympathy, nor is it an offer to exchange information. It reflects a belief that communication will illuminate and dispel the shadows which obscure inner life.

Like the term *encounter*, *communication* has also suffered from overuse and aggrandizement in recent years. Although not without specific value, the growing use of tape recorders has steadily tended to reshape communication into a monotonous tracing, as if what a person says has one and only one meaning for all to share. The guiding principle of taped interviews seems to be that, if it is good to have an outside judge of interview content, two judges checking on each other are better, and ten judges, or even a jury, are better still. Sometimes the patient's unique meaning is sacrificed to establish a common meaning. This kind of communication separates people instead of bringing them together. To be is to be different. The paradox of communication is that this singular difference only rarely can be shared with another person. Yet in psychoanalysis it is this special and unique quality of meaning which serves as the common denominator of communication. There are, admittedly, many matters within experience that are beyond language. When an aphasic patient gropes for a word, only to recognize it immediately when he hears it, communication has filled a personal void.

Affirmation and Confirmation

When the sanction of conventional communication makes security possible only at the price of conformity and allows truth to survive only in solitude, the result is not encounter but isolation. Psychoanalytic communication seeks to overcome this. It pays greater attention to overtones of meaning and encourages complete candor. Psychoanalytic communication need not always be verbal, nor must similar statements always convey the same kind of communication. A statement intended to be supportive, for example, may have an opposite effect when spoken impatiently or at the wrong time. In other instances, a fairly explicit interpretation may be received by the patient as if it were wholly supportive, or critical, when neither response was intended by the analyst. Effective transmission of meaning does not depend upon finely honed declarations, elegant phrases, or impassioned exhortations. A fragmentary comment may offer a clue for a fresh viewpoint. More often, fleeting phrases may awaken images and ideas that painstaking propositions have failed to arouse. It is more difficult to evoke significant communication than it is to reduce meaning to a dry ritual of disinterested utterances. Unless communication is a unique contribution to the reality of the moment, it is wholly possible to "work through" endlessly what is already clear; both participants are equally bored and have departed long before they officially decide to terminate the relationship.

KINDS OF ANALYTIC COMMUNICATION

Communication is whatever can awaken a sense of reality in the analytic encounter. Its relevance to the meanings, motives, moods, and modes that permeate a patient's existence must be recognized by both the analyst and the patient. In general, there are two kinds of analytic communication: (1) *propositions that interpret meanings* and (2) *evocations that encourage intuitions.* In both, the aim is the same — to recover meaning out of a chaotic field of silence and sound and to transmit it to someone. When the flow of speech runs from the patient to the analyst, it is usually called *free association.* When the flow of speech runs from the analyst to the patient, it is usually called *interpretation.* However, free association and interpretation are only the extremes of analytic communication. What the most loquacious patient says is but a dipperful from the stream of thoughts and feelings coursing through him; and what the most astute analyst offers by way of interpretation is usually imprecise and incomplete. Still, unlike conventional communication, in which the speaker may use the listener as a sounding board for declamatory music and the listener may find in another's words only the clarity of his own convictions, psychoanalysis gives both analyst and patient the hope that their words will activate a wider range of meaning in each other.

When an analyst confirms his patient's affirmations, he does not merely restate the obvious, parrot his agreement, or even respond promptly. He transmits meanings and evokes responses through interpretations and intuitions. As a rule, he tries to translate amorphous emotion into guiding thoughts and to transform stilted verbalisms into emotional language. As strategically as possible, he gently sets his interpretations into the patient's orbit of understanding. Whatever influence he exerts is not accomplished by skyrockets of insight or thunderheads of character transformation. In fact, although he may not know how to measure his influence, he has learned to distrust the "complete cure," the testimonial, the conversion to "bigger than life" well-being. Patients who assent too quickly to the analyst's interpretations are often looking for approval, not understanding. Conversely, patients who habitually dispute the analyst's observations may, indeed, understand but feel obliged to fend off the influence of another. A strongly rejected interpretation is more likely to be remembered and considered than one which is readily accepted. Just as the plausibility of ideas is determined by their attachment to principles and perceptions of high reality sense, so also is the genuine influence of interpretations more dependent upon their evocative properties than upon tests for validity.

FORMS OF CONFIRMATION

Confirmation occurs in two forms. If the response is brought about by propositional meanings, confirmation is *corroboration*. If the response is to evoke intuition, confirmation is *concurrence*. Corroboration does not mean scientific proof, nor does concurrence mean explicit acknowledgment or assent. Concurrence indicates that a message has been received which we are not inclined to dispute. Corroboration attracts other affirmations which imply that the meaning is valid as a general principle.

These two forms of confirmation are important distinctions between psychoanalysis as a *clinical practice* and psychoanalysis as a *scientific discipline.* Because they refer to highly personal, unsharable events, interpretations are often both tentative and ambiguous. In the course of further work, interpretations are usually modified or dropped entirely, not because they have been invalidated but because they do not adequately cover clinical facts. Refinement of a proposition, with respect to its scope or precision, is not the same as corroboration of a hypothesis on scientific grounds. In any case, to maintain that psychoanalytic interpretations are corroborated during the course of analysis is about as absurd as to claim that all physicians use only substantiated scientific principles and never rely upon empirical judgments.

In practice, analysts go to work as they see fit, knowing that affirmation and confirmation depend upon community of belief, rather than upon scrupulous corroboration. Since we have no reason to believe in the infallibility of analysts or of the analytic method, analytic propositions are at best only approximations which have a limited range of meaning. Few interpretations hit the bull's-eye of conflict with unwavering accuracy. We cannot even be sure that there is a correlation between "correct," or "relevant," interpretations and the intrapsychic agencies that effectively influence patients. There is, moreover, the embarrassing possibility that the change in a patient produces his retrospective insight, and not that insight invariably produces change. A banal proposition may be quite correct but irrelevant. Other interpretations, seemingly incorrect, may be so evocative as to be exquisitely relevant.

ACCURACY AND RELEVANCE

Most interpretations are incomplete, not incorrect. In fact, it would be something of an accomplishment to conjure up a totally incorrect interpretation. Because the purpose of analytic communication is to evoke further meanings, whether through propositions or intuitions, accuracy is less important than relevance. Affirmations are precise when their meaning is clear. Only confirmations can be correct or incorrect when, as a result of concurrence and corroboration, they are logically and empirically true or false. Hence, were any analyst to restrict himself only to propositions which could be corroborated, he would do so because of fear of making a mistake, not because of scientific purity. He would be like the fictional student who found the cerebellum so complicated that he wondered how people manage to walk at all.

In the never ending war between rules and realities, theory and technique lag far behind practice, but practice, in turn, is influenced by latent theory. Malinoski's dictum [103] that grammar is a product of language, and language is a product of action, is particularly pertinent in psychoanalysis. In the absence of absolute knowledge, there is sometimes a pedantic tendency to exaggerate tactical maneuvers and to confuse them with operations for getting at the truth. After all, when divorced from the individual encounter, analytic technique is anti-intuitive. It assumes the validity of certain analytic operations but ignores the significance of analytic communication as a bilateral process.

Authentic analytic technique is a product of the encounter since it combines both skill and knowledge with communication. The distinction between pedantic tactical maneuvers and authentic analytic technique can be clarified by answering three disingenuous questions: What do we try to do in psychoanalysis? How do we try to do it? Do we do it? The first question refers to our theories and aims; the second, to our operational methods; the third, to our validations.

Patients soon learn that they do not enter analysis in order to purchase ready-made solutions to their problems. Also, young analysts quickly learn that, in the actual encounter with patients, to adhere overscrupulously to punctilious propositions is about as appropriate as it would be to substitute recipes for food. If science demands rigorous definitions and intellectual precision, then psychoanalysis is not "scientific." However, the truly germinal ideas that influence people are never carefully pruned and planted in tidy tracts. In evoking an emotional response, an ill-defined idea often is more effective than a self-conscious intellectual statement. Facts of experience are usually more persuasive than the rococo theories which are designed to explain them. In short, reality sense seems to be carried more effectively by the evocative property of analytic communication than by the information transmitted.

THE AESTHETICS OF MENTAL LIFE

Truth and beauty are not, of course, synonymous, and good poetry and mythology make bad science. Metaphors, analogies, and emotive language, however, can arouse more comprehensive intimations about reality than can be elicited by astringent propositions, despite their exactitude. The sense of reality depends upon the inner harmonies of affective equivalence, the unity of libidinal fields, the symmetry of existential time, the spontaneous simplicity of motivated acts, and the ultimate translation of secondary differences into primary process identity. Much of what passes for a *science of mind* is actually an *aesthetics of mental life*. Those psychoanalysts who have a theoretical bent look for both systems and symmetries because it is emotionally disquieting and logically indefensible to study only a part of the mind, unless there is an implicit whole to which this part can be referred. Furthermore, propositions which appeal to an entire field of reality sense are more likely to be confirmed than those which offer only cool facts and logical precision. Freud's theory of dreams, for example, has logical and operational shortcomings that are apparent to all but the most uncritical devotees. Nevertheless, there is a great value in his interpretations because of his adroit recognition that dreams, as metaphors of the night, bind the fleeting residues of the day to vanished relics of the past and, by a strange union of opposites, disclose the concealed wishes and fears of the future. According to logical standards of waking life, dreams are senseless, but mankind has never ceased to wonder about them and has never been convinced that they are wholly haphazard events. Man's abiding interest in dreams is not necessarily due to the inner rationality of primary process; it is derived from his native, intuitive appreciation of the aesthetics of mental life.

The Existential Core of Psychoanalysis

In a curious conspiracy of nature and art, many significant scientific contributions, such as Maxwell's electromagnetic equations, are both accurate and artistic. They demonstrate that a comprehensive hypothesis can be a beautiful thing and that scientific discovery itself is often indistinguishable from artistic creation. In contrast, when heterogeneous events are briskly summarized and condensed into a succinct slogan, it becomes an oversimplified labor-saving device that violates the aesthetics of mental life and tends to discourage the intuitive act.

To encourage conditions that will favor intuition, psychoanalytic communication must depend upon the private meaning of language, rather than upon its ordinary significance [76, 98]. The objective is to bring together opposing impulses, antithetical wishes, and contradictory attitudes into a fresh, appealing viewpoint. By harmonizing the differences and similarities of events, intuitions will enhance the sense of reality that persists throughout change. Moreover, these insights will make full use of aesthetic principles and, because they arise spontaneously from within, will differ from categorical interpretations. With each new affirmation, *propositions that interpret meanings* are likely to become more and more abstract. In contrast, *evocations that encourage intuitions* are likely to become more and more concrete, because fresh experiences are continuously being sorted into clusters of reality sense. As this back-and-forth flow between reality sense and reality testing continues, the inner identity of successive problems mingles with the longitudinal similarities of previous perceptions and principles.

It is not surprising to discover that analytic communication is difficult to report. Taken out of context, it seems to be a mixture of evocative enigmas and downright dogmatism. Because people themselves are living amalgams of antithetical compulsions and irrational constraints, it follows that psychoanalysis is required to operate in an area somewhere between unambiguous propositions and unanswered riddles. Caught between these opposites, analysts often peer into the darkness of conflict through the windows of metaphor and paradox, because they are always nearby.

116

Metaphor, Paradox, and Conflict

Brutus declares that

> There is a tide in the affairs of men,
> Which, taken at the flood, leads on to fortune;
> Omitted, all the voyage of their life
> Is bound in shallows and in miseries.
> — *Julius Caesar*, Act IV, Scene III

The literal meaning of this quotation is of no consequence. Its appeal lies in the evocative force and metaphorical meaning of poetic language, not in the literal, homely truth it contains. Fortune is not a port of call, life is not an ocean voyage, and what is true of seas and sailing is not generally applicable to human affairs. However, to declare without qualification that all human embarkations are identical transcends literal meaning and generates a feeling of universal relevance in a way that a more precise proposition would certainly fail to do.

Metaphor is the natural agent of intuition. Two events may be quite different, but intuition can unite them and form a new version which encompasses both, and which yields a sense of reality possessed independently by neither. In metaphor, as well as in intuition, transitory events are joined to more enduring ideas. In fact, the more incongruous the conjecture, the more persuasive the affirmation. Its reality sense not only will be generated long before suitable reality testing is available but will usually persist in defiance of reality testing. The so-called big lie will survive the attack of small, separate truths. The evocative force of a stirring metaphor, which is a kind of lie, tends to survive the dissuasive qualifications and negations urged upon it by literal truth.

Metaphor is a device for tersely expressing the affective equivalence of certain symbols, thoughts, and objects. Since its purpose is to arouse action, not to formalize meaning, its literal absurdity only enchances its evocative powers. However, if a metaphor is scrutinized too closely, its evocative power fails, the way a joke loses its point if its meaning is explained.

117

The Existential Core of Psychoanalysis

Common language would collapse without metaphor [38a, b]. Poetry, metaphysics, and metapsychology use metaphor as much as mythology does, although overuse and abuse of metaphor tend to make it more difficult to detect [11]. As a method of expressing an unverifiable intuition, or as a preliminary exercise in scientific description, metaphor is indispensable. But mythology is no substitute for science, and ripe metaphors, however evocative, should not be mistaken for precise knowledge. The persistent use of metaphor is an indication of scientific failure. Though science may begin with metaphorical description, it must gradually be relinquished. Sleep may knit up the raveled sleeve of care, but only as a metaphor. Knowledge about the neurophysiology of sleeping is not furthered by evocative or elliptical statements about what sleep does or does not do for fretful people. How long has it been since a poem was written about mathematics?

Metaphors have two valuable properties. In addition to their evocative and aesthetic appeal, they also have the capacity to declare, in an elliptical form, what cannot be expressed in unambiguous propositions. Like reality sense, metaphors and intuitions do not hedge and qualify. In fact, there are no negative metaphors. Long before knowledge can build a bridge between different kinds of events, metaphor and intuition will perform a *tour de force* by leaping across the gap. When we speak about soft lights, sweet music, hard looks, and dark moods, we are communicating exactly what we mean. We are able to do so *because* the distinctions we customarily make between one perceptual mode and another have been violated [34], not *in spite of* this fact.

In the preceding paragraph the point was made far more clearly in metaphorical terms than it could have been by tedious explanation. Obviously, knowledge builds no bridges, and neither metaphor nor intuition does any leaping across gaps. Most word meanings are rooted in perceptual events, a fact which endows words with their initial incrustations of reality sense. During subsequent changes and derivations, this perceptual link will connect even the technical meaning of words to their original organic meaning. For example, the modern term for prejudice, *bias*, originated as a term in bowling and later became used in sewing. Bowling, sewing, and prejudice have only one thing in common

— a term which denotes a slanted act. The original prototype of bias was solely the perception of an event that involved oblique action. Although the bias of prejudice has a secondary literal meaning of its own, it still retains metaphorical relations with its bowling predecessor.

Freud noted the antithetical meaning of primal words [46f], and recognized their relation to repression. Other words are naturally ambiguous, and still others survive only as negatives of their original meaning [46j]. We have already seen how objective meaning is distilled from organic meaning. Just as different kinds of experience cohere because of shared reality sense, it is also apparent that metaphorical meaning, through its relation to a common perceptual event, antedates more literal, specialized meanings. By mutual participation in a libidinal field of perceptions, passions, or principles the metaphorical conjunction of a familiar word with a dissimilar event occurs before they are separate objects.

METAPHOR AND PSYCHOANALYSIS

The stilted clinical language of medical and surgical histories, including psychiatric records, is a residue of metaphorical language. In the transactions between physician and patient, however, metaphors are more informative than the explicit propositions that later appear in the written record. By complaining that her husband gets under her skin with his snide comments and eats her up inside, a woman tells more about her marriage than if she were merely to report bare facts about her daily life. For this reason, if the doctor suspects that the woman has more specific ideas about her marriage than she can express in ordinary terms, he may follow her metaphorical lead and speak as if the metaphor were literally true.

The imprecision and incompleteness of psychoanalytic interpretations has already been emphasized. The terms *exact interpretations* and *inexact interpretations* are themselves metaphors, not literal facts. Many interpretations begin with comments such as "It looks as if . . . ," or "This reminds me of . . . ," which are designed to single out the properties shared by dissimilar events.

The Existential Core of Psychoanalysis

Dream Metaphors. Dream work is metaphor in action. Dreams express abstruse ideas in concrete terms just as surely as ordinary language expresses abstruse events in terms that arise from direct experience. So-called dream symbols are today recognized as special condensations of images with significance only for the individual patient, and not as arcane indications of universal relevance. What a dream "means" depends primarily upon organic meaning and metaphor.

The typical dream metaphor arises from the affinity of ordinary, everyday events for the unconventional, unexpected, incongruous, anachronistic, or outright impossible. In spite of a dream's manifest absurdity as a literal event, its metaphor allows for disclosure of conflicts as well as for their resolution. Dream *interpretations* are secondary elaborations of metaphorical meanings according to waking standards. It is not uncommon, for example, for a patient to dream that he is standing naked in a crowd of passers-by. Moreover, despite his nakedness, he feels no shame, and although he is surrounded by people, no one seems to notice. This incongruity reflects the dreamer's anxiety, but it also offers a consolation. Because the metaphor links guilt with shame, it simultaneously points out that private guilt is not public shame and, therefore, that the dreamer's transgressions will not be exposed. The image of the naked dreamer and the disinterested crowd also alludes to a more poignant fact of existence—that beyond a certain point no one notices, and no one really cares who stands naked and alone. This is the invisible nakedness.

There is a gradual transition from the implicit metaphors of ordinary language to dream metaphors, and from dream metaphors, to the explicit metaphors of delirium and schizophrenia. For example, a man who had a mitral valvotomy for rheumatic heart disease knew that the surgeon probed the heart with a blade attached to his finger. After the operation his chest pain continued. He referred to it in increasingly metaphorical language. "I have pain" became "The pain is crushing my chest," and this changed to "A hand is crushing me." Within a few days he became so agitated that, exhausted and combative, he screamed, "I've been fingered by the syndicate! The doctors are spies, and they're going to kill me!" When Goldstein [50] described schizophrenic language as less abstract and more concrete than ordinary language, he implied that schizophrenic patients not only will take their metaphors literally but will often use language which has private, organic meaning. Schizophrenic communication is therefore difficult to understand without a special talent for deciphering metaphorical allusions.

Problems with Metaphors.   Because metaphor is so essential to communication, it can also be a source of danger and deception. Sometimes the reality sense of certain ideas leads an analyst to advocate one interpretation instead of another, simply because he favors a particular metaphor and not another. Most analysts realize that such phrases as "castration anxiety," "penis envy," "anal sadism," and so forth, are not to be taken quite as literally as they once were. To interpret any cleft as a symbol of a vagina is probably not more unreasonable than to make dogmatic conjectures about what patients are "really" saying in the metaphors they use [130]. The ease with which we can slip from one extreme viewpoint to another may inadvertently lead to exclusive reliance upon interpretations of metaphors and subjective impressions. One result of this is that we become hierophants in a communion of ill-defined emotions. A more common result is that we reify personal preferences into rational principles by giving them elegant names that emit an impressive aura but refer to nothing in particular. Mystics and rationalists are curiously alike; one makes pronouncements about matters far beyond human knowledge, and the other selects a certain factor within a complex situation and declares, with sweeping oversimplification, that it is the significant factor.

These are all crucial problems for the psychoanalyst because he operates at that interface of existence where knowledge and aesthetics, metaphor and science, emotions and thoughts mingle, then emerge as conflicts of emotion and paradoxes of thought. He needs forbearance toward his own theories, lest he scorn or bow down before them. He must recognize that, even when certainty seems to prevail, psychoanalysis can progress only by fomenting and tolerating doubt. Since primary processes underlie our awareness of the inner relations of events, and intuition affirms the unity of opposites, the source of certainty is also the source of uncertainty. Stern adherence to logic and reason can breed the same mystical faith in rationality that logic and reason are supposed to eliminate. Corroboration is readily confused with concurrence, when psychological issues are concerned, and may therefore be only a rationalist's way to reaffirm what was unquestioned in the first place. Rationality may simply be how we justify our own inclinations, while absurdity may be how we describe the way someone else understands the fundamental units which seem to hold existence together. The most outrageous paradox of all is that rationality itself depends upon irrational assumptions which cannot be reduced to simpler ideas, and upon cognitive processes which cannot be absolutely corroborated.

The psychoanalyst cannot be an objective scientist in his work, nor can he be a kind of poet of the mind. He formulates propositions and interprets meanings, but he also evokes intuitions and traces the paths of emotions through thickets of circumstances. In order to uncover common themes among endless variations, he is forced to encompass complexities with metaphorical adumbrations.

Kinds of Metaphors. There are two kinds of metaphors which are useful in psychoanalysis. One is the metaphor of language—*the linguistic metaphor,* which communicates ideas and emotions. It is a word or phrase that acquires special meaning by being attached to some perceptual reality or familiar concept. An ambitious man who described his work as "A raging beast I must beat down every day, before it lets me alone" used a linguistic metaphor, since he assumed that his listener was already familiar with the idea of raging beasts. A mature woman called herself "the little match girl," although she neither sold matches nor underestimated her age. By comparing her private feelings with how a little girl feels when others have what she can only yearn for, she communicated a metaphorical meaning similar to the literal feeling of being "out in the cold."

The second kind of metaphor is that of content—the *iconic metaphor.* It is a condensed image of the ideas, feelings, and events of different eras that converge into a single, focused entity. Screen memories, dream images, and key clusters of affective equivalents are iconic metaphors and, like linguistic metaphors, are not literal transcriptions of historical events. Dramas and allegories frequently use iconic metaphors to portray collective experience; in ordinary speech, iconic metaphors fill out the bare meanings of literal truth. For example, it is literally true that Christmas Day falls on December 25. Any tangible reference to Christmas will not pertain to just a day of the month but may become an iconic metaphor. On any other day a fir tree is only an evergreen tree, but on December 25 it becomes a metaphorical condensation of every collective incident and idea associated with the holiday of Christmas.

During the first few hours of psychoanalysis a curious phenomenon occurs. Almost all the essential ideas, conflicts, defenses, and relationships which subsequently will be exposed in greater detail are represented in condensed form. It is as if a symphony orchestra were accelerating its performance, so that every note runs into another note and only an occasional clear phrase emerges. This does not mean that future analysis only spins out the obvious or that the task of analysis is to decode an obstinate message. It means that the patient's style of life, body of values, and pattern of emotional response present themselves early in analysis as a mosaic of linguistic and iconic metaphors. What subsequently occurs is neither extensive retilling of old soil nor daily harvest of new biographical products. However, rarely does completely fresh information emerge; most of the labor consists of detailed amplification of typical events.

Key Events. What makes some events *typical* and others *exceptional?* The living facts and iconic metaphors which characterize a person's style of confronting, and being confronted by, reality are revealed in key experiences apparently as typical for that person as his signature, voice, and fingerprints. Furthermore, when an analyst talks about "traumatic experience," "precipitating events," or "screen memories," he designates a patient's change in attitude, or manner of response, with respect to some key experience. At the instant of its occurrence, this key experience, whether it is damaging or not, is strongly augmented by its emotional affinity with related experiences. A precipitating event is an iconic metaphor that denotes a cluster of events closely associated with an emergence of conflict. Screen memories, too, combine signal characteristics of different events into a concrescence of metaphors.

The key events which an analyst studies are unlikely to be historically accurate; nevertheless they share some emotional inclination, governing idea, or comprehensive motivation. Typical events put a special stamp of individuality upon a patient's world. Like grains of sand, they may be the nodulus for later accretions of significant reality.

This viewpoint is completely consistent with the previously described concept that reality sense is an organic process combining content and activity (see Chapter 4). Metaphor is to language what intuition is to knowledge; being is process caught in the act of becoming something different, but, by doing so, it accentuates the meaning it retains. The psychoanalytic process, then, is a way to discover these representative habits of meeting existence.

Couch Data. Let us pause to examine a few implications. If patients do not really report historical events, and if metaphor subtly replaces literal truth, how do these circumstances influence the validity of the couch data so painstakingly collected day after day? How can unreliable couch data become scientific data?

In the first place, couch data cannot be understood apart from some context of meaning. In the second place, couch data, even though held together by affective equivalence instead of literal truth, are still subject to discriminative judgment. Breuer and Freud [20] recognized that "mnemic symbols" could represent a number of emotionally related events and that metaphors were necessary to depict the realities of mental life. Patients suffer from those reminiscences that survive in the present and that can be set forth as representative modes of meeting experience. The accuracy of reminiscences also suffers, because of association with symptoms and related events. A painful leg, for example, can represent other distressing events and can, metaphorically, "stand for" painful memories. A fear of crossing streets may be related to fears about other "transgressions." The sense of reality that was carried by the metaphorical demonology of early psychoanalytic studies has sustained the investigative spirit, just as the discovery of affective clusters of key experiences gave psychoanalysis its original thrust. A lively metaphor commands attention, but it is fragile. When handled as a literal fact, it dies. A dead metaphor is a cliché, just as a dead truth is a banality.

PARADOX

There is nothing noteworthy about a genuine tautology. That "A is A" is a dull but necessary truth. The force of a metaphor, however, is generated by ignoring the differences between two events and declaring them identical. Because it contains a refutation of the identity it affirms, a metaphor is a spurious tautology. If a metaphor implies that one A differs from another A and at the same time claims that "A is A," it declares, in effect, that two opposing ideas, A and not A, are true, and are true together. The common expression "Business is business" looks and sounds like a genuine tautology, even more than most metaphors do. When used to justify dubious practices, it means that legitimate and ruthless acts are identical because they both occur in business, and that any business practice is therefore legitimate. Although no one doubts that ruthless acts do occur, and that the same man can be ethical at times and ruthless at other times, no one who really cares would accept these two contrary ideas as self-justifying or identical. The phrase, therefore, is a spurious tautology — a metaphor which has great appeal to businessmen who ignore customary rules of conduct. In fact, its terse redundancy allows the metaphor to pose in the guise of a necessary truth.

In the strict, logical sense, paradox depends upon (1) self-applying definitions, (2) false assumptions of existence, and (3) promiscuous use of negation. In the loose, psychological sense, paradox depends upon two ideas, or truths, each of which can be accepted as real, or true, but not when they occur together in the same context or proposition.

A metaphor is a capsule paradox, whether expressed in perceptual images or in a spurious tautology. Metaphors borrow the sense of reality belonging to one event to augment the reality sense of another. Paradoxes heighten the sense of reality by opposing one truth with another. By being pitted against each other, inconsistent statements become stronger than either would be alone. Metaphors are the inaccurate, gentle concessions we make to facilitate communication, but the purpose of paradox is to jolt us into thought.

Paradoxes are usually made up of antithetical truths, but ideas which are merely irrelevant banalities sometimes become paradoxical when put side by side. For example, it is decidedly banal to say, "The sea is blue" or "The night is dark." Since the sea is not blue at night, and night is not dark when the sea is blue, what happens when these two statements are joined? The compound statement "The sea is blue and the night is dark" is now a paradox. Fresh truths can stand by themselves, but banalities can often be roused by setting them in opposition and stirring life into them, like two inert chemicals that ignite on contact. Although the bare proposition "The sea is blue and the night is dark" may not be very exciting, a curious investigator might be puzzled enough to find some context in which dark nights and blue seas could occur together. Scientific study is frequently spurred by such humdrum events, or casual paradoxes, even though neither idea awakens much interest by itself.

The evocative property of some paradoxes can be effectively used to transport ideas from the realm of banal truth into the domain of the aesthetic. If solemnly uttered, "The sea is blue and the night is dark" seems to take on great portent because it is now being used as a metaphor. It is possible to intone that the sea stretches out before us in a patina of blue that covers untold depths and that the darkness of night illuminates boundless depths of the universe. With a little imagination, a listener may even conclude that what matters is not the improbability of dark nights and blue seas but their identity. Blue seas and dark nights together become opaque windows against which we see reflections of our own finite vision of the world. The paradox then urges us to meditate upon the depths of existence, whether in the sea, in the sky, or in the solitudes and surfaces we find in ourselves.

Affirmation and Confirmation

Reality Sense of Paradox. The reality sense of paradox, not its logic, has significance for psychoanalysis. Its evocative power reminds us anew that affirmations can be existentially true yet logically false, and that experience can be real even before statements about it are either true or false. However, paradox would not be worth discussing were it simply a metaphysical mystery or a trick of linguistic legerdemain. Metaphor and paradox pertain to the realities on the threshold of thought which are still beyond any formulation other than in concrete language and dualistic conceptions.

In general, dissociations of reality sense and reality testing may be attributed to the companion concepts of the *relativity of the real* and the *dualistic character of thought* [140a]. These dissociations frequently produce a conditional, yet existential, set of truths known to us as paradox. That indeterminate factor which falls somewhere between what is real and what is true may be called a *modulated existential*. Since the reality of being depends upon both the reality of change and the articulation of the real and the unreal, the concept of the modulated existential is an effort to capture whatever is only evanescently real and transiently true in the unending process of coming to be and passing away. Despite the sting of reality sense and the endurance of existential time, a fringe of nonbeing rings each moment of experience. Living and dying, anxiety and conflict, ignorance and anguish are grim reminders that existence is no unequivocal fact, that paradoxes offer reality, and that reality cannot be counted on to offer either certainty or care.

Reality sense is not at fault when many of our statements turn out to be paradoxical or absurd. The modulated existential is predicated on paradox, and paradox depends upon the modulated existential for its validity. Paradoxes may sometimes seem like jokes, but only if we take them very seriously. A woman who says that she reads only books that express her own beliefs, but must first read them in order to find out what she believes is certainly not talking nonsense. Unwittingly, she acknowledges the truth that any argument is convincing, provided one already believes it. A man who promises to give up religion for Lent is no more absurd than one who declares that the humble shall be renowned, and the renowned humble; or one who claims that the whole of his knowledge is that he knows nothing. In any instance of paradox, people make use of the modulated existential in order to preserve and to convey their perception of reality. Curious emotional affinities catch up banality and puzzlement, knowledge and sentiment, and shape them into paradoxes. Although they beggar confirmation and at times can scarcely be affirmed, most paradoxes arouse reflections and reveries.

Use of Paradox in Psychoanalysis.   Psychoanalysis starts with paradox and is sustained by paradox. There is paradox in the patient, in the analyst, in the analytic process, and in analytic communication. A patient may be able to eat everything but rare meat, go anywhere except into a crowded department store, or valorously fight a war but be afraid to meet friends on the street. These puzzling events are paradoxes before they are symptoms. If a man who can climb mountains with enthusiasm is afraid to go up a stepladder, only a very naïve person would conclude that his trouble is with climbing. Many people are obliged to live with similar paradoxes; they scarcely question their source yet resist efforts to probe whatever conflicts accompany them.

In his lifetime a psychoanalyst sees only a handful of patients, most of whom represent a highly selected fraction of humanity. Yet, knowing this, he is still convinced that his meager efforts and dubious results justify inferences transcending the piquancy of time, place, and person. His plight is like that of a man who stands in a railway station, noting the arrival and departure of trains, without even knowing where they come from or where they go; and with only this sketchy information he tries to understand how a locomotive works.

During the analytic process itself a patient is asked to lie down and to suspend critical judgment of his thoughts, in order to evaluate his thoughts more effectively. He is encouraged toward an orderless recollection of the past, so that the future can be managed systematically. He is urged to examine distorted perceptions that may help him to clarify his viewpoints. In turn, the analyst helps his patient to cast him in a variety of roles, each of which is explicitly declined. He deliberately withholds aid or succor, for the benefit of his patient. In order to illuminate the basic reality of both himself and his patient, an analyst exposes self-deception and disguise wherever they are found.

Psychoanalytic communication will use propositions that interpret meanings, and evocations that encourage intuitions. Evocative metaphors are often used but beyond this analysts will also frequently employ paradox, in a deliberate effort to jolt people into intuitive thought. Indeed, without paradox, as without metaphor, analytic communication would be highly artificial. Even an analytic banality such as "Part of you is angry and part of you is afraid" is a paradox because emotions cannot be separated like parts of the body. Furthermore, because he is most likely to uncover conflicts in his patients by detecting paradoxes in their statements or behavior, it is not unusual for an analyst to test his own understanding by the introduction of paradoxical expressions. For example, let us postulate a patient who habitually becomes angry and then is afraid of being destructive, or of being destroyed as a consequence of his anger. Sometimes he is first afraid, then becomes angry at people who make him afraid, or even at himself for being so vulnerable to fear. Let us also hear him report how often he brings about the very opposite of what he claims to want; how he antagonizes people whose friendship he wants, and rebuffs people who actually approach him openly and in a friendly manner. This is a typical paradox for psychoanalytic investigation, and one which lends itself to formulation.

Many patients cannot help expressing themselves in paradox. One man insisted that feeling well depressed him; a strongly inhibited patient promised that beginning next week he intended to act more impulsively; a highly dependent man, speaking about his indifferent mother, said, "I don't want to cut the thread, even if it is attached to nothing." Each of these slight paradoxes expresses a sober truth. Sometimes psychosis itself is not as baffling as the strange paradoxes and cryptic metaphors of psychotic communication.

Any paradox may conceal a common factor which, when understood, discloses a point of consonance. It is our inability to discover this point beyond paradox that produces a sharp dichotomy between the normal and abnormal, or the sane and insane. As we examine, study, question, and analyze, reality sense alone determines that point of rationality where we say, *beyond here* there is only madness.

CONFLICT

Much of the day-by-day, routine work of analysis consists of eliciting, recognizing, explaining, and resolving paradoxes. However, paradox-finding is not an end in itself. It is important only because paradoxes may be guides to latent conflicts and to the antithetical wishes which feed into conflict.

What metaphor is to language, and paradox is to thought, conflict is to emotions. Metaphor, as already noted, is a singularly apt device for expressing the inner equivalence of essentially unrelated facts. As a capsule paradox, it simultaneously conveys both similarity and difference. Paradox is an explicit way to elicit the incompatibility of truths, and this exposure is a first step in resolving their differences. However, although resolution of paradox is a sturdy intellectual exercise, psychoanalysis uses it to get at a more evocative factor: conflict and its component emotions.

Antithetical trends are inherent in every natural process. Any set of concepts allows for bipolar ideas. One process seems to require another process which can reverse it. Time's own discontinuity only emphasizes the uninterrupted symmetry of past and future. Affirmation in one direction necessitates affirmation in an opposite direction, whether these disjunctive affirmations are, for example, war and peace, religion and science, love and hate, anode and cathode, attraction and repulsion, growth and decay, anabolism and catabolism, or any other parallel concepts.

Without error there would be no truth. Without surprise, to interrupt the periodicity of events, there would be no incentive to discover the principles of nature. Without contradiction there would be no knowledge. The established order always needs the challenge of the exception, the aberrant, the absurd, or the meaningless. Exceptional events, by violating a system that works too well, help to reform that system. Exceptions elicit the antithetical processes within a system, and these processes, too, will be violated, until a harmony of complementary opposites is again established.

Psychoanalytic theory can be described as a system of concepts and formulations that attempts to account for ways in which wishes are mitigated, fulfilled, transfigured, and frustrated, and for ways in which antagonistic wishes generate conflict. Patients consult analysts because of the conflict they encounter in the process of fulfilling wishes, even if their presenting complaints are usually fears, avoidances, inhibitions, or just repudiated or inaccessible wishes. Discussion of the *theory* of conflict will be postponed until a later section (Chapter 7, p. 207). We are now concerned only with the intrapersonal *experience* of conflict — the antithesis of motivated acts — in which every stable fact seems lost in anguish and doubt, so that the future exists only as a hopeless perpetuation of the insoluble present.

Beyond Paradox. The psychoanalyst can use neither the art of the novelist nor the symbols of the scientist to describe the living fact of being in conflict. Consequently he is obliged to depict conflict according to its physiological or psychological results, or as a semi-mythical struggle between metapsychological titans — ego, id, and superego. But to interpret conflict as an opposition between ego and id, with superego as a potential, sometime ally of both, is neither an explanation, a formulation, nor even an adequate account of what it feels like to be in conflict [42, 101].

To be *in* conflict means to *be* that conflict, just as to feel loss means to be that loss. Paradoxes can be tolerated without distress and usually can be resolved without much difficulty. Dilemmas are perplexing, but decision eliminates them without complication. Conflict, however, is brought about when two strong appetites have incompatible consummations, so that neither can be satisfied without pain or penalty [140b]. *Conflict is a stark existential fact*, not a conceptual plausibility. People may have inconsistent ideas incarnate and yet be free of significant conflict. The point beyond paradox may disclose a consonance that resolves intellectual incompatibility, but it may also expose a persistent conflict of tangled and antagonistic wishes and fears transcending mere plausibility.

Where is the point beyond paradox in the man who is angry, then afraid; afraid, then angry; who provokes potential friends and rebuffs actual friends? Plausibilities drift through his analyst's mind: perhaps he believes others intend to exploit his friendship; perhaps he despairs about getting the love and esteem he wants; perhaps he drives people away before they can disappoint him; perhaps he incites people and repels friends lest they make demands upon him which correspond with his demands upon them; perhaps he seeks retribution for some earlier deception or disappointment. Speculations know few boundaries, and the domain of "perhaps" is almost as limitless as those phantasies that imagine, "What if . . . ?"

The reality of conflict depends entirely upon the reality sense of its sources, not upon the validity of more or less plausible interpretations. To some extent, however, these trial hypotheses are necessary. Threads of wishes and fears may be patiently teased out of the common texture of events, but the warp of their many sources never comes to an abrupt end. One putative source, or trial hypothesis, tends to become continuous with another, and only emphasis of one phase over another makes possible any distinction between them. Where, then, does analysis come to a halt? Sooner or later, analytic inquiry passes beyond the horizon of facts and observations into shadowy regions where theory offers no guidance, where even paradox yields no clue to hidden conflict. When this happens, the analyst's own fluctuation between doubt and certainty begins to reflect his patient's inner conflict. He then asks himself what it is like to *be* a person who wants friendship and yet finds it threatening; who is menaced by innocent acts and yet scarcely recognizes his own antagonism in them; who squanders his life away as a resentful outcast and yet holds self-preservation as his governing value. By thus becoming forced into a grim analogy between himself and his patient, the analyst's subsequent insight will be somewhat supported by the primitive ontological acceptance that, however incomplete and tentative, any interpretation may be relevant. His efforts are designed more to focus his sense of reality upon the patient's experience of conflict, and to confirm the patient's despair, than to formulate conflict in theoretical terms. This in itself lends some measure of certainty to his continued efforts to understand.

With conviction borne by the belief that a sense of reality for the patient himself is relevant to the patient's conflicts, the analyst again seeks the meaning of the patient's paradoxical offending of potential friends. The common denominator of this paradox is whatever enables the patient to protect himself against his fear of being damaged, to satisfy his wish to have friends, and to control those sentiments which he has attributed to others. To accomplish these ends, he is forced to limit relationships. He does this by constantly probing and provoking others and by shunning people who transgress the limits he has imposed. Had he merely wanted to protect himself from potential enemies, the patient might have discouraged everyone by being aloof and unresponsive. For a short time, and under restricted circumstances, he could tolerate friendship with people he did not particularly like or admire. Then, to forestall pain, disappointment, anger, or fear, he could readily withdraw, on his own terms, by prompting an attack or by alienating people, and thereby justify the belief that solitude was preferable to friendship. It is true that a man with his hand in his pocket may be about to shoot, but we do not provoke such a man, nor do we shoot him simply because his hand is concealed. While searching for some hidden menace in friendly people, the patient came upon his own wishes to be destructive and to exploit others — an image which he had concealed behind a bland, somewhat affable exterior. In this way, provocation of potential friends avoided an attack upon them.

Doubt and Certainty. We must recognize, of course, that even the most sensitive perception of the patient as a human being will not, by itself, clarify many pertinent problems. Reality sense needs to be crystallized into organic meanings, and these, in turn, into relevant interpretations and working hypotheses. *Doubt* and *certainty* are two phases of reality sense which have constant value as ways to appraise clinical events and tentative hypotheses [154]. For example, Freud [46d] explicitly used doubt and certainty to challenge his own interpretation of a particularly baffling dream — "R. was my uncle." After completing an initial interpretation, he writes, "I felt that I had not yet finished dealing with it. . . . what my dream expressed was only my wish that it might be so," for he had noted that his warm and friendly feeling toward R. in the dream was quite different from his actual attitude. Freud then forced himself to pursue the dream analysis against strong inner opposition. He was sure about some parts but dubious about other parts of the dream. Finally, his sense of reality completed the analysis when he discovered a more convincing reason — a specific conflict about academic ambitions — for the dream's reversal of his actual attitude toward R.

Doubt and certainty in themselves merely serve as indicators of the state of reality sense. Neither one nor the other is an actual check on the objective validity of reality or truth. However, we may wonder how doubt and certainty finally achieve a satisfactory equilibrium. At what point in his interpretive efforts did Freud approve and accept his own insight into his dream and declare, "*This* is correct"? It is this sense of completion that fuses intuition and content, interrupting the exploration of the "perhaps" with the conviction of having attained "insight." This will be the theme of Chapter 6.

6. *Intuition and Insight*

IN ORDER TO RESOLVE PARADOX and to clarify conflict, psychoanalysis rests its case upon intuition and insight. One evening, while Freud was feverishly writing what is today the "Project for a Scientific Psychology," he reported [67a]:

> . . . I was hard at work, tormented with just that amount of pain that seems to be the best state to make my brain function, the barriers were suddenly lifted, the veil drawn aside, and I had a clear vision from the details of the neurosis to the conditions that make consciousness possible. Everything seemed to connect up, the whole worked well together, and one had the impression that the Thing was now really a machine and would soon go by itself. The three systems of neurones, the free and bound state of Quantity, the primary and secondary processes, the main tendency and the compromise tendency

of the nervous system, the two biological laws of attention and defense, the indications of quality, reality and thought, the position of the psychosexual group, the sexual determinant of repression, and finally the necessary conditions for consciousness as a function of perception: all that was perfectly clear, and still is. Naturally, I don't know how to contain myself for pleasure.

Unfortunately Freud's enthusiastic intuition waned, and this synthesis of his insights was never offered for publication. Nevertheless, it was the design for all of his future work, even though the comprehensive presentation in its original form did not again appear.

The moment of intuition is sometimes like poetic inspiration. As it acquires authority, Kris [78] contends, inspiration seems to detach itself from the person out of whom it arose. It is like revealed truth, and its originator is exempt from responsibility, criticism, and doubt. Like a breath of life, inspiration seems to exercise a demonic influence. The creator escapes fate; he is freed from shackles of determinism, cant, and convention.

Intuition need not occur only at moments of lofty inspiration [90a]. Self-evident truths can appear wherever peaks of understanding suddenly emerge upon the dreary plains of tedium. Whenever an old set of facts is seen from a fresh viewpoint, and it is possible to declare that *this* is real, *this* makes sense, and *this* is true, intuition and insight are simultaneously affirmed.

The relation of intuition to insight is the same as the relation of process to product. Intuition always produces insight, but insight can result from many other processes. Any perception of object meaning is an insight. The mechanic's understanding of an automobile, for example, is one of the tools of his trade; but an engineer's intuition is more than a tool. It not only enables him to do his job effectively but can expand his range of understanding into completely new fields of reality.

The familiar psychoanalytic distinction between "emotional insight" and "intellectual insight" refers to different *attitudes* toward things thought of, rather than to an *explanation* of those attitudes. Intellectual insight deals with categorical meanings within a conceptual field; emotional insight gathers together the varied organic meanings within a libidinal field. Intellectual insight is an object-centered comprehension of facts; emotional insight is a subject-centered act of intuition.

THE ANALYTIC METHOD AND THE AESTHETIC METHOD

The world teems with insight; our problem is to discover which bits of insight to discard and which to preserve above all others. The challenge is always that of reconciling opposites, whether in the field of science, art, or practical affairs; in the idiom of language, perception, thought, emotion, or action; or in the special domain of metaphor, paradox, and conflict. There are two ways to effect this reconciliation. One, the *analytic method*, is to find a common element, which is something like finding a divisor for different sums of integers. The other, the *aesthetic method*, uses intuition and reality sense in order to capitalize upon paradox and to bring about fresh interpretations of reality. The analytic method necessarily bleaches out reality sense, but its facts can be carefully arranged in sequences and hierarchies. In contrast, the aesthetic method produces clusters of understanding which flow together because of their common sense of reality. Each method complements the other, just as intuitive acts and objective facts, together, expand the range of truth.

Traditional textbooks cite the familiar syllogism "All men are mortal. Socrates is a man. Therefore, Socrates is mortal." This barren bit of logical truth has been perpetuated because of the structure of its sentences, not because of Socrates, the man. The same analytic insight into man's meaning could be applied to any man; reduced to a bare statement, it asserts that any man is mortal.

But there are other meanings in this syllogism, related to Socrates himself, which cannot be reduced to a redundant statement or an axiomatic truth. The stark conclusion that any man is mortal has been drained of intuitive possibilities; it will probably defy the aesthetic method because its inherent paradoxes are missing. For example, the banal truth which remains tells us nothing about the act of personal death that you and I will face one day, and nothing about the agonies and pleasures of existence and extinction.

Is it still possible to find some lingering paradox within this dormant syllogism? Except for conceding the mortality which Socrates shared with other men, the analytic method has ignored the reality of Socrates. Unlike most men, Socrates loved wisdom more than life and preferred death to life without meaning.

The life and teachings of Socrates are a paradigm of paradox. He knew only that he knew nothing; he taught by asking questions. He punctured pretense, inconsistency, and deception wherever he found them. Yet he maintained that all men are capable of knowing the truth and acting upon it. His death, which he chose in order to perpetuate his belief in the ultimate equivalence of what is true and what is good, points beyond its own paradox. His "mortality" signifies more for us than the plain fact that he died. It evokes an intuitive affirmation that wisdom is worth more than an unexamined life, that knowledge exists in order to challenge itself, and that intellectual pretense is a most pernicious form of corruption. Whether or not we of this generation can fully accept his affirmation, we can at least understand that the death of Socrates accented his act of living. Thus, the bleak syllogism about the mortality of Socrates still preserves traces of his unique life, his death, and his style of coming to terms with paradox. If this intuition generates fresh insight, it is because the syllogism contains its own paradox: Socrates, the immortal, lives on as an example of mortality. If the original syllogism is now read backward — Socrates is mortal; Socrates is a man; All men are mortal — the syllogism will become a kind of epitaph, and a synecdoche.

INSIGHT AND CONFLICT

There are no axiomatic truths in psychoanalysis. Even more paradoxically, the analytic method needs strong support from the aesthetic method. Consequently, many so-called insights contain paradoxes upon paradoxes, involuted upon themselves. Illumination in any one area, like a bright light from a small lantern, creates darkness in another. Furthermore, although it is ordinarily assumed that insight is the major tool of psychoanalysis, the fact is that insight will not in and of itself resolve conflict. Resolution of this particular paradox depends upon knowing that insight cannot be imparted by an analyst, or by anyone else. Whatever kind of coding process analytic information entails, we can be sure that analytic observations, questions, and confrontations are intended only to encourage fresh intuitions in the patient.

Insight in psychoanalysis often seems to be the *result* of a resolved conflict, not the *cause* of its resolution. In any case, it is a by-product which can scarcely be planned, just as recovery from neurosis, or remission of symptoms, can only be sought, not predicted. A favorable prognosis for the outcome of psychoanalysis does not depend solely upon a putative capacity for insight. If this were the case, suitable patients could not be recognized until the analytic work was completed! As a rule, much of the insight derived from analysis occurs long after the formal work has been terminated. Most analyses begin with conflict and paradox; then, after an undetermined lapse of time, when conflicts are reduced and the patients' habitual means of contending with life are less incapacitating, we allow our patients to settle for more or less conflict-free ambiguities.

If insight is a by-product of psychoanalysis, and a patient is expected to achieve it by himself, what, then, do analysts "analyze"? The length and breadth of analysis is devoted to understanding conflict. Since neither insight nor intuition is able to function in the presence of conflict, one of the tasks of analysis is to discover the specific motivations that determine a patient's wishes and fears [82a, b]. Psychoanalytic theory is based upon the premise that there is a finite set of appetites which seek appropriate consummation. However, there is a broad gap between the psychoanalytic theory of unconscious motivations and the ordinary reasons we give for our actions [107]. What we usually call "wishes" are inferences drawn from purposeful acts. If an act is thought to be successful, its motive is assumed to be identical with the immediate objective attained; if an act is a failure, we tend to believe that its motive is related to some obstructing force [144]. Because conflict brings opposing potential acts together, we are obliged to assume that the inciting motives for these acts are antithetical wishes.

Antagonistic wishes that fail to be fulfilled enhance reality sense. This is why, even when paradoxical motives have not yet been revealed, heightened or inappropriate affect is a clue to conflict. Unfulfilled desires, it has already been pointed out, seem to underscore reality more emphatically than do wishes that find quiet consummation. The analyst who observes conflict must make full use of his intuition in order to identify the inciting wishes and to understand what has obstructed their fulfillment. These obstacles could include a stronger wish in another direction, a concomitant fear within the intended objective, an intrinsic inability to perform the intended act, and an objective which is actually impossible to attain.

POSTULATES OF PSYCHOANALYSIS

When we extend our conjectures backward, beyond the point of intuition, to try to discover "original" motives, we seek motives of motives of motives. Like searchers for a psychological Garden of Eden, we soon become lost in thickets of surmise. Nevertheless, whenever we search, as analysts must, for common sources of dissimilar acts or for different motives of similar acts, the psychoanalytic method and its theory compel us to postulate that (1) a patient's spontaneous associations and reports are reliable indicators of the way in which wishes find their devious expressions; (2) the thinking process and its product — thoughts — arise from common sources and follow similar nervous pathways; and (3) the wellspring of thought, emotion, and action endows every act with purpose, every emotion with imagery, and every thought with intelligible symbolic form. With these extravagant assumptions clinical analysis attempts to discover the integrating factors for a manifold of different events. To facilitate the quest, reality sense, as both the content of experience and the activity by which reality is comprehended, is an indispensable link between intuition and insight. *Psychodynamic theory, in brief, is a grammar of conflict.* Intuition of the divisive attitudes concealed within the solitary experience of conflict is necessarily the precursor of subsequent insights, formulations, theories, and hypotheses.

Questions and Answers

Even though his sense of reality and his perception of the aesthetics of mental life carry the analyst beyond the point of paradox, affirmation alone will not sustain understanding. Flashes of insight must be stabilized by the more constant beams of confirmation and corroboration before reasonable people can discuss their observations with a measure of order and clarity.

Our most diligent formulations fail to encompass the reality embedded in quite ordinary events. Analysts may rightfully wonder how any mere mortal can glean meaning out of the masses of data that sweep before him hour after hour. Evanescent significance and uncertain conclusions recurrently nag him with the notion that, after all, careful psychoanalysis may be no more than pictures painted inside a paper bag. Nevertheless, unless he is prepared to declare that psychoanalysis offers nothing more than an opportunity for verbal catharsis, he must guide the flood of communication into channels that can be identified and classified as acceptable knowledge.

Any analyst who proudly proclaims that "everything fits" has hacked away at some observations to make them coincide with his theories and has conveniently ignored others. There is an inaccurate platitude which describes an analyst as one who "hovers" over a vast panorama of psychic events, alertly waiting for the crucial issue to come into view. Meanwhile he is supposedly sustained by well-established principles, unambiguous facts, and reliable ways to acquire fresh observations. Unfortunately, he is seldom borne aloft; he more often beats his wings against the cage of his limited understanding.

What does an analyst do as he listens, observes, postulates, and investigates? Above all, he carries on an unending, silent self-interrogation. What does this mean? How is it related to what happened yesterday? There is some fear now, but of what? Maybe it isn't fear at all. Shall I interrupt and ask about it, or wait and see? So it goes on, as he tries to interlace interpretations and propositions with evocations and insights. Then, during long stretches of intervening silence, he turns to the task of extracting significant questions from the multitude of answers his patients unwittingly present [140c]. The technical problem of when and how to comment is merely secondary to this antecedent search for relevant questions.

An analyst questions himself, but he tries to avoid direct interrogation of patients. Whenever he asks about some specific fact, he risks sacrificing incipient novelty to get information which may emerge later without inquiry. As a result, lest evocation or intuition be thwarted, most analytic questions are not meant to be directly answered. They are simply open-end inducements to still further affirmations. Open-end questions have no answers. If the patient knew the answers, he would not have to be asked.

The intellectual scaffolding of scientific theory depends upon the mutual relevance of question and answer. Not only do genuine questions have answers, but some answers are relevant and others are not. Whether from couch or microscope, raw data and uninterpreted observations *become* relevant facts and ideas only when they are the answers to appropriate questions. Collingwood [31] insisted that there are no "right" answers until we know the question for which the answer is correct. Only by seeking new questions for familiar observations can fresh thoughts clarify nature. In psychoanalytic investigation there is not only a *question of meaning* but a *question of being* and a *being who questions* [79].

As an analyst diligently tries to distinguish between clinical facts and the questions he asks about those facts, he is bound to realize that psychoanalysis is burdened by a plethora of answers for which no pertinent questions have ever been formulated. Furthermore, because no question can cover every aspect of an event, some clinical facts must be left uninterpreted and some potential questions must be discarded.

Some psychoanalytic questions can be answered by couch data alone. Usually these are empirical questions relating to the analysis of individual patients. But other, quite proper analytic questions, such as those related to character formation, cannot be answered simply by collecting couch data from individual analyses. Still other questions, which are phrased as analytic issues, cannot be properly answered by psychoanalysis at all because there is no *operational* link between the question and plausible couch data. For example, it is conceivable that psychoanalysis can throw light upon problems in the fields of religion, anthropology, politics, law, and so forth, but this will depend upon a formulation of genuine, relevant questions within those fields, and not upon extensions, analogies, and "applications" of psychoanalytic concepts.

OPEN-END QUESTIONS

Open-end questions which guide a patient to still another affirmation are just as real and relevant as are more prosaic requests for information, even though they have no specific answers. Although open-end comments may be expressed in metaphorical language and may even seem irrelevant, they encourage reaffirmation of ideas that might otherwise be overlooked. Mere breadth of generality is not a substitute for genuine questions, nor is accumulation of data itself likely to produce significant answers. Just as a fact plucked from its context is no longer a fact, an irrelevant question may distort the meaning of any observation [106a].

In addition to the specific meaning of questions, the relevance of open-end questions in analysis is also determined by *who* questions and *what* he questions. The question of relevance and the relevance of questions are both based upon the image of reality held by the questioner, who, by his questioning, gathers information in order to act, or to establish an attitude appropriate to some action. In this context, patients are even more active questioners than are their analysts. *Relevance* always refers to a guided, motivated activity. At first it depends upon private, organic meaning; later it acquires a more public, objective meaning that applies to a variety of acts. Relevant questions about today's weather, for example, are primarily related to some private course of action, such as staying indoors, traveling, wearing heavy clothes, and so forth. These questions use organic meaning, and when today's weather is described as bright, cloudy, wet, or warm, these are conclusions based on the relevance of different perceptions to individual activities. More scientific, public appraisal of

143

today's weather, by means of quantifying instruments, secondarily standardizes personal judgments by emphasis upon the common properties of different potential acts.

To ask a question is to ask for a guide to action. Consequently, relevance has two preconditions: (1) a common *context of action* and (2) an explicit relationship between *objects of thought* and the *properties of objects* acted upon. Questions which are verbally alike may have different relevance, and even different meanings, because of different contexts of action, objects of thought, or properties of objects acted upon. But open-end questions allow knowledge to grow, and new items of reality are formed when one relevant context is linked with another.

PSEUDOQUESTIONS

Just as some statements appear to have meaning but do not, there are questions which seem to be genuine but are not. Pseudoquestions pose as genuine questions because of their verbal and grammatical similarity. However, a genuine question leads to a significant proposition whereas a pseudoquestion does not. A significant proposition is one that can be judged true or false by some relevant act or test. The contribution that relevant answers make to genuine questions is to turn them into significant propositions.

As a rule, relevant answers should offer more to questions than the agreement and disagreement conferred by "yes" and "no." In many situations, of course, explicit assent, or reaffirmation of an assumption, is desirable; rhetorical questions and numerous mundane inquiries are like this. Because these queries contain implicit propositions which can be tested, they are genuine questions. There are other, equally familiar questions which seem to make sense and yet are pseudoquestions. Is life worth living? Should children be punished? Is there free will? Do contradictory ideas exist together in the unconscious? These are pseudoquestions because they are unanswerable. Many pseudoquestions of this type call for a categorical "yes" or "no," but others are so elliptical or ambiguous that there is no way to convert them into significant propositions.

Pseudoquestions have several common features: (1) A categorical answer is demanded for an unstipulated context; (2) the relevant issue is presumed to be a real issue; and (3) no operation is indicated which tests the relevance of the answer to an activity intended by the question. In other words, pseudoquestions are either unwarranted generalizations or formulations that are too loose to make a distinction between right and wrong answers possible.

Sometimes pseudoquestions may be salvaged by rephrasing, by more explicit stipulation, by more accurate definitions, by analysis of the question into component, genuine questions, or by exposure of the fictitious entities which pseudoquestions often assume to be real. For example, the pseudoquestion "Does free will influence our acts?" assumes the existence of something called "free will," then asks for explicit confirmation or dissent. However, if we reformulate the question and ask, instead, "What are the factors that limit choice between alternatives?" the new version will be a genuine question, although a difficult one. The pseudoquestion "Do contradictory ideas exist together in the unconscious?" assumes that opposing ideas coexist in recognizable form in the depths of a netherworld, beyond consciousness. We may formulate a genuine question by asking, "How can two contradictory ideas both be repressed?"

SIGNIFICANT PROPOSITIONS

There is no reason to believe that intuitions are evoked more readily by genuine questions, valid propositions, or unambiguous interpretations than by any other form of communication. The purpose of formulating genuine questions and seeking relevant answers in psychoanalysis is that significant propositions are *mediating instruments* between affirmations on the existential level and general hypotheses on the categorical level.

Psychoanalysis is cluttered with generalities. Not only are different levels of observation melded by different kinds of language, but there is often too little recognition of the differences between facts and conjectures, affirmations and hypotheses, questions and propositions. Consequently, it is impossible to determine, in many instances, which questions have been answered and what significant propositions have produced the generality. Declarations like "The infant's longing for oral gratification provides the basis for a primitive type of identification" may be meaningless. Even before this can be ascertained, it is doubtful that the mass of verbiage can be sorted out into the genuine, relevant questions which presumably gave rise to it. Does the phrase "longing for oral gratification" simply mean hunger? Is the term "identification" unambiguous without reference to some person, act, or object which participates in the identification? Answers to such questions will help determine whether the original declaration can be factored into subsidiary generalizations and relevant component questions. In this case an empirical hypothesis like "Infants thrive on breast milk" can probably be combined with genuine questions about the significance of breast feeding for hungry infants, as well as with genuine questions about factors that may influence different kinds of early identification. This reformulation will eliminate a sweeping, ambiguous declaration which, if it has any meaning whatsoever, is a portentous assumption.

In the language of logic a question is a propositional function [28]. That is, when combined with a logical value or appropriate answer, propositional functions become propositions, and, in effect, questions become hypotheses. This step allows psychoanalytic observation to rise above its empirical data to another level of discourse. It allows us to examine the relevance of other questions that can be asked about the propositions themselves, without caring whether the secondary questions are relevant to the questioner or to the original objects questioned. At this stage of discourse organic meaning is replaced by objective meaning, and reality testing takes over from reality sense.

Hypotheses and Pseudohypotheses

There are many relevant, intelligent psychoanalytic insights, patiently and painstakingly forged in the heat of long analyses, which can be used as ways to understand other patients and their conflicts. Nevertheless, these insights are in a kind of limbo. They are appropriate for their clinical purpose but are unable to join with other insights and propositions to become hypotheses with wider scientific application. The step beyond relevant questions brings us to the level of significant empirical propositions. Beyond this level, however, higher-order reality testing and scientific evaluation require unambiguous hypotheses that can be detached from aggregates of organic meaning.

Couch data and empirical propositions affirm realities and clarify paradox and conflict. But lest we become intoxicated with a vision of psychoanalysis as the "science of man," let us be sobered by the reminder that any individual psychoanalysis will not confirm theories about mental processes [111a, b]. Furthermore, although intuitions can be highly gratifying, they can also be wrong. An analyst who depends exclusively upon his vagrant intuitions, without having some rational formulation of what he thinks, forfeits the existential value of intuition. Perforce, every analyst — intuitive or rational — puts his bench mark on his work. Those propositions, interpretations, and insights which he submits for confirmation are likely to be recognized more as indications of the priestly or prophetic tradition than as empirical or rational hypotheses.

Affirmation and confirmation are complementary processes in so far as they operate within the psychoanalytic encounter. The existential attitude in psychoanalysis does not advocate reliance upon pure subjectivity, nor does use of traditional viewpoints mean reliance upon "revealed truths." However, when analytic propositions advance beyond the metaphors and intuitions of the actual encounter and move into the domain of objective meaning and hypotheses, significant propositions tend, naturally, to become less existential and more rational. They are not as concerned with the ideas and insights of individual analyses and are more concerned with the technicalities and abstractions about psychoanalysis in general. Thus, the methods used in psychoanalytic practice and in psychoanalytic research are quite different [60b]. The affirmations, insights, and interpretations that propel clinical analysis are only potential sources of hypotheses. To declare that every analysis is "research" is to avoid recognizing that we have no way to validate psychoanalytic hypotheses except through clinical practice. The perception of reality in the course of practice is to the validation of an analytic hypothesis as recognition of the sound of the milkman in the morning is to knowledge of the dairy industry.

VALIDATION AND ANALYSIS

Confirmation is a process which includes secondary corroboration as well as existential reaffirmation and concurrence. While secondary corroboration refers to reality testing within the scope of an individual analysis, there is an extended meaning of corroboration which refers to significant propositions and hypotheses outside the analytic encounter itself. This is called *validation*; its task is to distinguish between genuine hypotheses and pseudohypotheses.

No hypothesis is ever proved beyond dispute. The paradox of a genuine hypothesis is that it only provides for invalidating instances; it is not proved by a valid instance. However, by allowing for its own shortcomings, and for false cases, a genuine hypothesis can be repeatedly modified and improved [109]. Thus, one small exception can do more to advance a genuine theory than can a host of instances which seem to corroborate the theory. In contrast, just as the pseudoquestion has no relevant answer, the pseudohypothesis has no false case. It can be stretched to encompass every exception and be molded to fit any anomaly.

Validation begins at the point where affirmations become hypotheses and organic meanings become fixed, objective meanings. It moves *forward* by finding successive instances which invalidate each hypothesis — and each modified version of that hypothesis as well — until a refined, yet relevant, theory emerges. The method of *analysis* begins at approximately the same point but moves *backward* as it traces affirmations, ideas, and attitudes which produce paradox and conflict. Just as validation makes greater use of reality testing, analysis depends upon a sense of reality for whatever can contribute to some final understanding. These methods study *hypotheses* in two ways. *Validation tests conclusions; analysis examines premises.*

The difference between "research," or the validation of analytic hypotheses, and the practice of psychoanalysis may be illustrated by examining a fairly uncomplicated interpretation that was offered to a 40-year-old business executive during the course of his analysis. He was told, "You seem to feel guilty whenever you are successful."

What makes this particular interpretation worthwhile? Had he been told that he seemed to rejoice whenever he was successful, the remark would have been both banal and redundant, since success and rejoicing usually are found together. Had he been informed that he seemed to feel guilty whenever he failed, it would have been scarcely more interesting. The significance lies in the paradox that success leads to guilt. One aspect of the interpretation is an affirmation about the mutual relevance of guilty feelings and successful acts. The second aspect of the interpretation is a *hypothesis*, which proposes that if he succeeds, he will feel guilty. The first aspect is subject to further analysis; the second, to validation. If the patient understands that success is followed by guilty feelings but that not every feeling of guilt must be preceded by a success, then validation is deceptively simple. A single instance in which he succeeds without feeling guilty will puncture the entire hypothesis. However, by progressively restricting the conditions under which the success-guilt hypothesis can be upheld, new versions of the hypothesis will be stronger, and fewer invalidating instances will be found.

The method of psychoanalysis is more arduous and less definite. Validation — actually, the method of invalidation — requires only that a hypothesis be clearly stated, because it assumes that its precursors and premises have been reliably understood. The analytic method, or *affirmation in depth*, examines just such assumptions. Like the process of stratification in existential time, which it closely resembles, analysis rejects the concept of a final end point. That there is always a moment which precedes every other moment, or an event which influences succeeding events, is less important than the existential simultaneity and affective equivalence of episodes and occasions that are widely separated in time and space. Consequently, analysis sets out to learn everything possible about this man, whose success is complicated by guilt. At the beginning it was ascertained that he wanted psychoanalysis in order to understand his unexplained periods of guilt and depression. It was also learned that for several years he had felt increasingly uncertain about his competence, despite many achievements, wide recognition, and financial success. At the outset of his business career success had aroused him to future accomplishments, but recently success had left only apathy, which had changed into depression and guilt.

In tracing the success-guilt paradox the patient reported that, following the death of an older sister, his parents had insisted that he and his twin brother look after each other, sharing their possessions as well as their lives. As he grew older, and the innate differences between the boys became more apparent, he resented having to curtail his interests and activities simply because his brother could not participate. Finally he escaped into a business career far from home while his brother faltered in a variety of undistinguished jobs.

The conclusion that success, in itself, made him feel guilty was not immediately evident, although it was always clear that his symptoms of recurrent depression and guilt neutralized the pleasure he derived from meeting a challenging problem successfully. The natural unfolding of thoughts and attitudes over the months of analysis helped to establish an inner rationale for many seemingly unrelated feelings and acts. There were numerous exceptions to the success-guilt paradox. Indeed, the success-guilt paradox was itself an exception, not the rule. He usually fulfilled his business obligations successfully and, if not triumphant, at least he enjoyed his own competence. It was finally discovered that pangs of self-rebuke were likely to be felt whenever he bested a business rival in a particularly close competition. It then was possible to ask these relevant questions: Was his depression and self-rebuke related to violation of his parents' directive to share equally with his brother? Was his guilt about besting a rival also related to an earlier guilt about wanting to eliminate the hindrance of his brother?

Theoretically, in order to analyze a conflict, the analyst could examine every situation in which the patient felt guilty and every success which failed to gratify him. The task would then be to establish a transition of emotion from the initial blunting of pleasure to the final form of conflict, in which he found himself gradually losing confidence as well as feeling guilty and triumphant simultaneously. In actual practice, however, this kind of systematic dissection is unlikely. Analytic tributaries are inexhaustible, just as the "complete analysis" is a myth. We are limited to *typical* events and, at best, to vivid intimations of original emotions. This means that, once again, we depend upon the clues available within clusters of reality sense.

An invalidating example of a hypothesis means that two acceptable truths are unacceptable together. In order to validate a genuine hypothesis in the presence of this paradox, we must limit the rule to allow for the exception. Since validation is primarily concerned with conclusions, the rule will be limited to respecifying the conditions under which it will hold. In this example the rule is *not* the interpretation "Success leads to guilt"; the simultaneous occurrence of success and guilt constitutes the *exception*. The *rule* is that success is followed by pleasure. One limiting condition for this rule would be to add the proviso "unless the success violates the parental directive to share everything with your brother"! The exception can easily be expressed as an analytic hypothesis and, as already seen, can be readily invalidated. To leave the problem of validation in this form, however, would tell us no more than we knew at the outset, when the patient reported that sometimes success pleased him, sometimes it did not, and recently it made him feel guilty.

To analyze an interpretation we must examine the *premises* of a hypothesis to discover how the reality sense of both the rule and the exception generate conflict. There are, of course, innumerable rules, or acceptances, and exceptions to be found in anyone's life. In this patient the analytic task was to find relevant contexts within which success and guilt not only were affective equivalents but shared the same organic meaning. Intuition of these contexts responds to the reality sense, or quality, of the rules and their exceptions, not simply to the overall understanding that we live by some rules and violate others. It is this *quality* of certain rules and exceptions that stimulates analytic inquiry and even spurs the analytic process.

Once again, it is apparent that psychoanalysis loses its own unique quality and principal source of conviction when it tries to establish itself solely as a method of "research." This does not mean that genuine hypotheses are superfluous; indeed, because psychoanalysis is saturated with rules, exceptions, and implicit hypotheses on many different levels of experience, clear formulations are mandatory if pseudohypotheses are to be recognized. Pseudohypotheses allow for no invalidating instances; they must therefore overlook exceptions, bypass paradox, and, in effect, exclude the very event they presumably wish to explain — conflict.

Validation and Intuitive Judgments

According to the ontological acceptance, we believe that our thoughts about reality are both relevant and correct. Our propensity toward certain thoughts or actions seems to be the result of intertwining intuition and emotion (cf. Chapter 4, p. 80). What we spontaneously know and feel not only influences what we actually do but will even create fresh reality to do it in. Convergent tributaries of reality sense contribute to a sense of certainty, just as divergent tributaries bring about a sense of doubt. To contend with conflict, intuition reconciles divisive emotions as often as it encompasses paradoxical ideas.

Intuition and rationality together master problems and control aberrant facts. Fresh ideas, alien beliefs, false cases of established theories, and exceptions to conventional rules are some of the strange, disturbing events that transgress accepted viewpoints. Yet these aberrant events insist upon having their reality accounted for. Thus, an aberrant fact is both the inverse of intuition and the incentive for further explanation.

Sometimes, in our rational attempts to sustain hypotheses and establish truth, we allow the sense of reality to bleed away. The difference between what can be understood and what exists often puts us at the rim of reality, with our faces turned toward nonbeing. When both intuitive judgments and rational validation fail to solve pressing problems, doubt and despair arise.

Every discipline of thought and action is threaded by a common problem: how can exceptions be reconciled with established rules? Unexplained symptoms in an otherwise healthy body first appear as baffling exceptions to customary ways of feelings. A responsive, responsible physician can sometimes relieve and support troubled patients because he can comprehend aberrant thoughts or feelings and reconcile them with more acceptable principles. If exceptions can be at least recognized as unfamiliar forms of events that are already understood, they are less intimidating. This is the kind of support a frightened citizenry gets when told that a series of baffling crimes is "under investigation." The priest, shaman, policeman, physician, or parent is respected and revered as a powerful agent when he can restore alien, threatening events to their proper, reasonable, acceptable context. If he fails, or shows himself to be weak or untrustworthy, it is almost impossible to forgive him, and people will transfer their faith and trust to some other magical source. There is true *despair* when every available means of mastery, test, or validation falters. When principles themselves are inadequate guides, or authoritative sources of certainty are abruptly depleted, there is no choice but to deny the reality of the aberrant fact. If this too is impossible, experience as a whole becomes unreal, because certainty itself will then be determined by the alien event.

When there is no external source of appeal, how do we judge the reality of the rule and the reality of its exception? An illegal act violates established law, but it does not demand that the law be changed. An incorrect answer to an algebra problem does not insist that the mathematical rules are wrong. There are, however, some aberrant facts and acts of such high reality sense that the established rules they transgress are challenged. In *The Rebel* Camus [23a] described acts of rebellion which have significance strong enough to defeat an entire moral order. These "metaphysical crimes" are extreme examples of what goes on less conspicuously when we contend with ordinary problems. A person who speaks of an "experienced" physician means one with a wide range of rules to call upon in difficult and exceptional situations; hence there will be fewer aberrant facts and acts to undermine his comprehension.

How is this discussion pertinent to psychoanalytic validation? When object meaning is unambiguous, the methods of logical consistency, correspondence with public data, and accurate predictions will verify scientific propositions and invalidate equally clear-cut hypotheses. However, as we have seen, it is more difficult to validate psychoanalytic premises than to invalidate scientific conclusions.

Like affirmations in any other sphere, intuitive judgments are sometimes unreliable even when they are the premises of more objective conclusions. In their daily encounter with fresh tributaries and unanticipated byways, psychoanalytic intuitions often become less certain, and what seemed real and true on one day may be mere banality on the next. Although intuition cries out with its own validity at the moment of its birth, its sense of reality depends upon component beliefs. In the analytic encounter, intuitive judgments are also products of the affirmations of both analyst and patient. For example, the patient may believe that he feels guilty whenever he violates a parental directive to share everything with his twin brother; the analyst may hold yet another component belief — that *this* directive explains the aberrant event in which his patient's success is followed by guilt. The reality sense of each component belief will determine the comprehensiveness of intuitive judgment.

LOGICAL AND INTUITIVE JUDGMENTS

Intuitive judgments are like newspaper headlines that feature a dominant theme on one day but relegate it to an inconspicuous column on the days that follow. In order to account for the variations in reality and relevance shown by different affirmations from day to day, it is necessary to distinguish between logical judgments, intuitive judgments, and intuition itself. Intuition deals with only one value — the judgment of real or unreal. Intuitive judgments are concerned not only with the evanescent value of what is real or unreal but with the relevance of other values as well. In instances where truth and reality are the sole issues, logical judgments of truth imply that everything *false* has been *excluded*. By rejecting qualifications such as "if" or "unless," intuitive judgments affirm that aberrant facts, exceptions, false cases, and qualifications have been *included*. Logical judgments limit the scope of a proposition, but intuitive judgments broaden it.

The fact is that intuitive judgments can be neither validated nor invalidated. Genuine hypotheses can only be invalidated;

pseudohypotheses are largely meaningless; and intuitive affirmations can be confirmed only by appealing to another intuitive affirmation. But how can the second affirmation be judged except by appealing to another judgment? This leads to an infinite regress of still other judgments, none of which can be proved and all of which may vanish without a trace. To remind us that we deal only with feelings of certainty, instead of validity, it is more appropriate to speak of *certification* of intuitive judgments.

CERTIFICATION

There are two kinds of certification — certification *by* intuitive judgment, and certification *of* intuitive judgment. Certification *of* intuitive judgment refers to the existential source of affective equivalence, which can establish a common ground for both intuition and emotion and can thereby create an inner identity between different kinds of events and propositions. As a result of both kinds of certification, intuitions and insights share a kinship that survives fluctuation, modification, and obsolescence.

Intuitive certification tells us that "good" reasons are seldom correct, that "correct" reasons may not be complete, and that "logical" reasons often have little else to recommend them. At one extreme, when we make unequivocal judgments about reality, without niceties of thought or proper protocols of reason, what is "correct" is often irrelevant, and only the subjective spirit of persuasiveness is important. At the other extreme, of course, rationality and scientific method are not concerned with the persuasiveness of statements, but only with being correct.

In psychoanalysis persuasive exceptions are sometimes confused with "correct," universal truths. For example, because some criminals want to be caught to relieve their guilty feelings, all crime does not necessarily follow this pattern. Some people are "wrecked by success," but, as Freud indicated, these are "exceptions"; many more are wrecked by failure. There are so few patients in any psychiatric series, and even fewer in psychoanalytic series, that hazard inheres in every generalization. This hazard does not arise because psychoanalysts are particularly prone to logical errors, but because certainty of belief and intuitively certified judgments tend to influence other kinds of judgment. As preachers and political candidates well know, people are swayed more by intuitive judgment than by reason and facts. Indeed, as a hypothesis gains in plausibility, it usually loses its intuitive flair. In contrast, crude generalities often arouse strong intuitive certification.

"GOOD" AND "BAD" INTUITIONS

A feeling of triumph is characteristically the initial quality of an intuition. It may be assumed that this quality is produced by emergence of a fresh viewpoint which encompasses and contains every previous exception and aberrant fact. If still further exceptions then appear, the intuition loses its charm and certainty, and its affirmation is debased. A compromise candidate for public office is less likely to offend and more likely to be elected because fewer people take exception to him. Like the compromise candidate, a debased affirmation may be better prepared to withstand the rigors of campaigning through many trials and tests. The unquestioned fact of incorrect insights discredits intuition no more than false propositions discredit logic. Critics who minimize intuition by calling it a product of irrational passions, and who reject the crudity of first-order affirmations, fail to recognize that the primary function of intuition is to include the aberrant fact and exceptional event unconditionally. Whether an intuition really includes or merely overlooks exceptions is probably the difference between a "good" intuition and a "bad" one. Conversely, even though a proper function of secondary processes is to negate and to modify its own affirmations, systematic attempts to exclude exceptions by qualifying the premises of hypotheses are anti-intuitive.

THE EXCEPTION AND THE RULE

It is not true, of course, that the exception proves anything, including the rule. However, by forcing the rule to change its scope in order to accommodate an aberrant fact, the exception *evokes* the rule. The aberrant fact makes a claim upon reality sense which is equal to the principle it violates; therefore, as its convictions converge, it demands and gets an intuitive resolution, without exceptions.

Intuition and Insight

The *rule of the exception*, not the exception to the rule, monitors our efforts to master the alien world that thrusts against us. When an affirmation yields readily to fresh doubts and emerges as another certainty, the plausible becomes the possible, the possible becomes the probable, and the probable becomes the actual. Confirmation and reality testing may do the world's work, but without the scanning and selectivity of intuitive judgments, which affirm and then vanish, there would be neither a reality to test nor a judgment to confirm.

Both psychoanalysis and experimental science are based upon the self-justifying value of truth and the liberating value of reality. Whenever ignorance and nonbeing are not faced up to, they take over. Fear of despair, in science and in psychoanalysis, produces dogmatism as a by-product of capitulation to the categorical attitude. This is reflected in the ways we heed exceptions and assimilate aberrant facts.

What begins as a genuine insight may become fossilized and worshiped, as though it were a fetish, if succeeding exceptions are ignored. Then again, some facts are overlooked because a set of relevant rules has not yet caught up with them. Many more exceptions are casually dismissed as erroneous or trivial. Often, in the history of science, discoveries turn out to be rediscoveries, and old errors reappear as new truths.

The experimental method, usually thought of as the paradigm of rationality, is the *strategy of finding exceptions*. At its nonrational core it is indebted to the primitive struggle for certainty and control with which man is confronted when he tries to solve the problems presented by nature. An experiment is an adventure within the rules of reality testing. It is a partially controlled event which, in effect, sets a trap to ensnare the exception. Unfortunately, psychoanalysis has no experimental method. However valiantly its protagonists argue that psychoanalysis is like other sciences that have no experimental methods, such as astronomy and geology, there are remarkably few constants in psychoanalysis. For the most part, psychoanalysts are forced to deal with aggregates of variables.

The only way to test psychoanalytic propositions — those affirmations which become the protases of every other psychoanalytic proposition — is to certify intuitive judgments according to the principle that *resolution of the exception forces refinement of the rule*. This process has three successive phases: (1) translation of affective equivalents into formal concepts, (2) convergence of intuitive judgments into foci of reality sense, and (3) formulation of propositions which can accommodate both acceptances and exceptions. For example, the man with the paradox of success and guilt lived according to the implicit rules that successful men are jubilant, that parents ought to be obeyed, and that no man should compete with his brother. Conflict developed when he found himself between the rules, where he discovered that success made him feel guilty and depressed. The aberrant fact could not be understood, or reconciled with his implicit rules, until it became clear that vanquished business rivals were affective equivalents of his brother, with whom he was forbidden to compete. By stipulating the conditions under which certain exceptions could be tolerated, this reinterpretation preserved his conventional rules.

In the face of so many variables, and with so few constants, psychoanalysts may not know whether a clinical event is an exception to some rule, an exception to still another exception, or a true case of some yet undiscovered rule. Consequently, the analyst can only guess at the answers to many relevant questions, such as why this patient is so reluctant to violate parental decrees. Does his reluctance have anything to do with his sister's death or with the phantasy of his brother's death? Why is it so difficult for him to admit resentment or rivalry with his brother?

To discover any patient's dominant rules, it is necessary to have an approximate understanding of his style of life, acceptances, nuclear beliefs, relevant values, and the ways in which he reconciles what he wants with what he does. The analyst must strive to suspend both doubt and certainty, acknowledge the relativity of what is real, gather up negations and affirmations, and, finally, attest only to the inner uniformity of discrete events. He will fail if he adopts values other than *real* or *unreal*, or passes judgment on the intrinsic merit of his patient's rules, or tacitly advocates still other rules for the patient to follow. If he steadfastly believes in a centralized program of motivation and meaning, he will discover that there are no categorical imperatives which everyone is forced to observe, but that there are only existential interrogatives which everyone must ask of himself.

Intuition and Prediction

In the absence of experimental methods, psychoanalytic investigators have turned to prediction as a means of validation. After all, clinical interpretations are not only thinly disguised rules but guides for predicting the future. For example, the success-guilt hypothesis implies that, in an appropriate situation, the patient will once again feel guilty after a success. If the analyst were sanguine enough to expect that owing to the magic of confrontation the patient's conflict will automatically disappear, he will also predict that, once his patient has been told about the rule, it will no longer apply!

An umpire, despite his thorough knowledge of baseball, cannot foretell what will happen during a game. However, he knows what rule will apply in any circumstance. A psychoanalyst, lacking an equivocal set of rules, is less fortunate. He must develop fresh empirical rules for every patient. Even when some previously established rule is applicable, he cannot be sure that there are no other equally pertinent rules. Nevertheless, an analyst is obliged to assume that (1) the past guides the future in a statistically determinate, and indeterminate, way; (2) general rules are possible; (3) some rules are more relevant than others; and (4) there is a reasonable, but finite, range of expected events.

With so many possible interpretations of psychic events, it is not surprising that the wish to be correct — which is quite different from the wish to validate a hypothesis — leads some analysts to cherish the grand surmise and, in effect, to play the long shot to win. At the other extreme, some analysts offer such cautious interpretations that they seem to have the umbrella ambiguity of diplomatic statements. Whatever happens, these analysts are always correct. Still others, the more dogmatic analysts, do not hesitate to predict because every assertion they make about the past or future falls within their system and so cannot be wrong. While all three of these viewpoints may lead to different kinds of predictions, and even correct predictions, they share a common consequence — the fatal stultification of reality sense.

Benjamin [10a, b] has shown how imprecisely the concept of prediction has been used. Even intuition has been confused with making predictions that are at once astute and remote. Actually, the usefulness of prediction as a way to validate psychoanalytic hypotheses has been exaggerated, not because prediction itself is an unreliable method but because prediction as a method asks too much of psychoanalysis. Engel [39] observed that physicians will have notions about the relevance of psychological factors in certain "psychosomatic" diseases without having specific knowledge of what makes these factors relevant. Both misguided predictions and accurate predictions result from both correct and incorrect interpretations because there is a greater range of possible events than of existing rules.

DISCIPLINED AND UNDISCIPLINED STATEMENTS ABOUT THE FUTURE

Although psychoanalytic theory, as Rapaport [113c] conceded, is based upon postdiction, and upon a tendency to exclude observations which do not fall within the theory, predictions are not inconsistent with postdictive postulates. However, instead of striving in vain to develop consistent criteria for prediction, it is more useful to recognize that predictability consists of *disciplined* and *undisciplined statements about the future*. The task is, then, to discover what factors give rise to each.

The difference between disciplined and undisciplined statements about the future depends upon knowing which interpretations, rules, or hypotheses are relevant to the putative future events, as well as what kinds of future events will exemplify the rules. For example, the success-guilt rule excludes all disciplined statements about the future except those that refer to the patient's guilty feelings after a success. The rule does not permit predictions about what would happen if he should fail, or if his brother should suddenly become a success and thus remove part of the deterrent to his feeling of satisfaction. However relevant, these conjectures are undisciplined, and they remain so until further information and rules become available. We do not know, for instance, why the patient was so competitive from the start, or why, if success was followed by increasing guilt, he continued to pile success upon success.

The psychoanalytic tradition of psychic determinism [67b] has predisposed investigators to confuse predictability with disciplined statements about the future and to ignore the contribution of undisciplined statements. Consequently, they assume that any hypothesis can be proved or disproved by accurate predictions of future events and that any future event can be predicted by proving or disproving enough hypotheses. Even if we overlook the principle that hypotheses can only be invalidated and thus become, at best, more or less plausible, there are several objections to this assumption. First, psychic determinism is scarcely a hypothesis; it is more like a declaration of faith in the ultimate mechanism of mental events. Second, the course of future events is not determined in a laboratory, where an investigator can manipulate significant factors and so derive different results. We are often right for the wrong reasons, and wrong for the right reasons, and even if we know which factors or rules are relevant, we seldom know what makes them relevant. Third, within any reasonable range of expectations, there will be some relevant events that cannot be anticipated, despite extensive knowledge of whatever rules apply. Fourth, psychoanalysts can do no more than predict the meaning which several kinds of potential events will share. No analyst can predict the precise events themselves, nor, by knowing relevant rules, can he conjure them into existence.

In the presence of these and other objections, we can now recognize that the implicit predictions contained within most psychoanalytic propositions tend to be undisciplined statements. They are more akin to reality sense and intuition than they are to reality testing and validation.

There are two senses in which intuition seems to offer disciplined statements about the future, and there is a third sense in which undisciplined anticipation contributes to our naturalistic attitude toward prediction and causality. In the first sense, intuition seems to predict future events because of the *timelessness* of reality sense. In the second sense, affirmations seem to predict future events because of their *deductive corollaries*.

The Existential Core of Psychoanalysis

When reality sense is high, time sense is low (cf. Chapter 4, p. 92), and, at the moment of affirmation, intuition puts no time limit on itself. Affirmations may even be accepted as visions of "higher realities," especially when they are unmodulated by reality testing. These sonorous truths regularly appear in writings about aesthetics and religion, but such "eternal truths" are not a part of psychoanalysis. Indeed, were psychoanalytic concepts "revelations," we would not need to validate or refine our insights.

Affirmations about the future condition of a thoroughly understood system are deductive corollaries more often than they are predictions. If "eternal truths" are prototypes of undisciplined predictions, deductive corollaries are prototypes of overdisciplined predictions. They are related to intuition only in so far as complete understanding of a complex system allows an expert to group together novel facts and expected events and to draw conclusions which seem "exceptional." A neurologist, for example, knows enough about spinal reflexes and stretched muscles to be certain that if he strikes the patellar tendon the leg will extend. Medical diagnosis is based upon such deductive corollaries. Abnormal findings indicate that the intact system has faltered and can no longer sustain deductive expectations. The aberrant fact of a leg that does not extend when the patellar tendon is struck is a deviant fact which the neurologist takes into account in his diagnostic affirmation. As a rule, everyday statements about the future refer not to anticipated *deviations* but to redundant *deductions* that are based upon habitual behavior. Because there is so little to arouse interest, and scarcely any novelty, these "predictions" are no more surprising or challenging than are predictions that a burning log will be hot and will ultimately become ashes.

FUTURE AND PAST

In a third sense, anticipation is so clearly a property of being alive that we seem to have faith in our ability to assert something — disciplined or undisciplined — about the future, just as we can make assertions about the past. The value of intuitions is that they are both real *and* transient. Significant intuitions are not expected to strike a fixed pose. An intuition either is here in full bloom or quickly withers. Whether their specific insights are destined to survive or not, intuitions always must give way to fresh intuitions. Although disciplined statements about the future confine predictability to the stringencies of reality testing, the relativity of the real reminds us that reality is not a lignified absolute. Reality testing, furthermore, means both testing *of* reality and testing *with* reality. Undisciplined statements about the future share their reality sense with statements about the past. Both contribute to a naturalistic attitude toward *prediction*, which pertains to the future, and *causality*, which reflects the past. From a naturalistic viewpoint the concept of *cause* is an extension of a wish to have nature respond with the same swift certainty that we recognize in voluntary acts. The natural act of *predicting* is derived from a wish to control nature as it unfolds in the process of becoming. Thus, by confusing their wishes and deeds with the interpretation of nature, men persuade themselves that their interests are fused with those of the world. However, like reality itself, prediction of the future and rational assessment of the past are possible only when we allow for the unexpected. If a theory is closed to false cases, exceptions, surprises, and aberrant facts, it is beyond reality. Only when there is room for error is there room for truth. This must be our consolation as we turn to face the naked necessity of *responsibility* for our own actions.

7. Responsibility and Reality Sense

THE SENSE OF RESPONSIBILITY is to the self what the sense of reality is to the world. Man's paradoxical efforts to control nature combine his primitive awareness of vulnerability with his capacity to determine, and even to foretell, the consequences of his individual acts. The incongruity between what man chooses and what fact exacts is a paradox of responsibility which began with The Fall and still persists as a problem to each generation. To believe in responsibility is to discover that moments of mastery are also moments in which complete extinction can just as readily take place. In one sense responsibility defies reality, but in another sense responsibility embodies reality.

The sweep of stars across the heavens, the ebb and flow of life, the fragile imbalance of imponderables upon which survival depends — these do not encourage belief in the power of human responsibility. Yet, through some inner alchemy and despite his vulnerability, we find man claiming unrestricted power and perception, wisdom and decision, understanding and control, far beyond his frail capacities. Nevertheless, with few questions, he accepts the sense of responsibility and the fact of responsibility as equivalents. Because this unlikely belief occurs within his natural predicament of illusion and despair, it suggests that men do not possess responsibility — they are possessed by it.

Psychiatrists ought to be the first to doubt and to question the reality of responsibility; they should also be the first to affirm and to answer these questions: What is meant by responsibility? Why do we persist in caring about it? What difference does it make? Is choice merely another deception to conceal our compulsions? Is freedom a fact or an illusion?

The sense of reality declares that *this* is real — and not like anything else. The sense of responsibility affirms that *I* am real — and not like anyone else. To feel responsibility is to have a sense of reality for an inner capacity both to respond to the world and to effectuate responses in the world. Responsibility, therefore, combines a sense of being alive with a comprehensive, uncompromising feeling of mastery. However, this undisputed sense of responsibility often clashes with the overpowering reality of the world it challenges. The result is conflict, and defeat means that personal responsibility is transformed into an urgent, helpless anonymity. When man is in the extreme form of conflict, he can neither protest nor consent. There is no appeal from a world that thrusts him this way and that, reducing him to a brute obligation to follow laws that govern masses and principles that guide tropisms.

According to popular, conservative opinion, psychoanalysis is committed to an inflexible, optionless psychic determinism [81]. Quite the contrary is true. Indeed, the reality of unconscious processes and of motives beyond awareness helps to create the sense of reality for responsibility. Psychoanalysis cannot even pretend to answer many relevant questions about responsibility simply by affirming its reality. Although it can distinguish acts which are truly responsible from those which are merely purposeful, moral, or ethical, psychoanalysis cannot, for example, judge who should be punished for his acts, or what acts he should be punished for. However, although psychoanalysis is silent about strictly legal issues, in some respects it has more practical relevance for these issues than do many of the abstruse generalities produced by other reflections about responsibility [127].

In the following discussion it will be possible to consider only five phases of responsibility: (1) the organic meaning of responsibility, (2) the psychoanalytic meaning of responsibility, (3) responsibility and superego, (4) the nature of the responsible act, and (5) responsibility as a source of conflict.

Organic Meaning of Responsibility

Just as I must be aware of my own existence to be able to experience the reality of anyone else, anyone who makes judgments about responsibility in himself, or in others, must first be aware of his own status, and of the status of others, as unique facts of existence. Beyond this bare sense of reality, he must further affirm that he has a measure of control over himself and what he does. Above all, he must believe that what he does is worth doing and that the changes he effects are for the better.

The difference between the existential and categorical views of man, let us recall, is the difference between *being* and *being something*. It is also the difference between being someone unique, or deviant — at least an exception — and being someone who shares every attribute with someone else. The existential view emphasizes the *I* of man; the categorical view of man is that he is an *object*. The two views contain two different concepts of responsibility. The existential attitude produces the concept of *subjective responsibility.*

Objective responsibility pertains to man's responsiveness — the way he responds, as an object, to the impersonal forces that act upon him. These forces can arise from within, in the form of more or less stereotyped "instinctual" drives, or can be imposed from outside, as more or less fixed social sanctions. In either case, men are expected to yield to or comply with these inexorable forces as long as their response falls within the range of accepted behavior. Thus, men of responsibility are taken for granted when they follow the rules. When their conduct is deviant, however, and rules are broken, they are blamed, and are called abnormal, rebellious, or even criminal; but if their conduct surpasses mere obedience, these exemplary acts are praised and even called heroic because such idealized responses seem to justify the standards themselves.

Objective responsibility acknowledges the independent reality of another person, but it is likely to disregard his subjective experience as an *I*. Because it is an outside judgment about the deviant behavior of someone else, objective responsibility is concerned with culpability or irresponsibility and not with those factors which help a man to feel responsible for himself. Objective responsibility is, therefore, the *deterministic* side of responsibility.

Objective responsibility allows for a common set of values and, through its rules, encourages the control and appraisal of human action by means of reality testing. Nevertheless, because individual men are primarily objects which are acted upon, they are judged according to their acts, particularly their violations. The common law itself seems to have evolved by discriminating between different kinds of offenses and the varied conditions under which these violations come about. As a result, the altered circumstances in which men are held culpable have indirectly produced the so-called mitigating factor. An increased respect for the manifold ways in which men can respond has tempered the attitude toward violations that in earlier times led to drastic punishments and, a fortiori, has heightened rather than diminished responsibility.

Subjective responsibility, which is our major concern here, accords primacy to man as the initiator of acts instead of to man as an object acted upon. It recognizes the reality of choice, freedom, consciousness, motivation, and the capacity to control the consequences of purposeful action. These realities are a man's private property, and he cannot barter, share, or surrender them. Subjective responsibility corresponds closely with the sense of reality for what we are and what we do. Existentialists call this *authenticity;* psychoanalysts call it *identity.* It is, therefore, the *voluntaristic* side of responsibility.

DISTINCTION BETWEEN MIND AND BODY

The traditional split between *mind* and *body* — those habits of thought which practice dogmatic dualism while they profess militant monism — has blurred the distinction between the two kinds of responsibility. It has often been pointed out that the distinction between mind and body is largely one of methods and assumptions, not one of substance. The concept of mind is also a *personification* of all those mental functions which actively influence motivated behavior [119]. In contrast, body is conceived of as a highly personal, nearby example of an object acted upon. Inevitably, to the extent that we are obliged to conform, to obey, and to avoid blame, the concept of mind commits us to subjective responsibility, while the concept of body confines us to objective responsibility. Under the weight of lifelong directives and prohibitions, these extrinsic sanctions amalgamate the human objects acted upon. The contribution made by subjective responsibility to the full meaning of being an autonomous human being has been relegated to a more intangible, even mystical, domain, owing to the pressures of both experimental science and social standards.

Subjective and objective responsibility exercise corrective control upon each other. If, for example, we are to use freedom fully, then some degree of basic conformity and obedience to law is mandatory. Similarly, obedience and conformity, as well as our inclination toward certain values, are determined more by our reality sense for what we are than by what is forbidden. Most men are honest, let us say, simply because they have no appetite for dishonesty, not because there are laws that expressly forbid it. Nevertheless, in many instances subjective responsibility seems to be in conflict with standards of objective responsibility. Unless there were strong inclinations toward forbidden acts, no laws would be necessary. In some respects social values are the antithesis of certain primitive fears, just as laws may be an effort by the community to curtail its own persistent wishes. The common purpose of these restrictive and corrective agencies is to forestall social and personal disaster — an objective shared by both kinds of responsibility — because a "strong inclination" can no more justify itself than can the dehumanizing conformity required by unjust laws.

When man feels that he is the *cause* of what happens, he also feels *subjective responsibility*. When he feels that he is the acted-upon *result* of what happens, he also feels *objective responsibility*. This is the consequence of the distinction between mind and body, and between the existential and categorical views of man. An excess of conformity may destroy subjective responsibility, but the inherent correctives imposed by custom and reality testing tend to leaven any misguided confidence in subjective responsibility that its own reality sense creates. Subjective responsibility and the creative side of consciousness are the existential roots of narcissism in its rawest form. By discovering an affective equivalence between subjective responsibility and creative capacity, some men are convinced that, because they can act effectively upon other people and things, they can also control them. To be sure, reality sense does enable us to appreciate the creative contribution we make to reality, just as reality testing allows us to test our own reality. However, unbridled narcissism is hardly equivalent to subjective responsibility, inasmuch as narcissism is an *uncorrected* belief in man's ability to control the course of nature, or even to destroy the world. Fortunately, unbridled narcissism is a state found only in a few psychotics, mystics, fanatics, and romantics and in the sealed-up phantasies of many others. The significant ingredient distinguishing subjective responsibility from mere self-seeking power, quite apart from what does and does not violate laws or customs, is that responsible man seeks a standard of excellence, called the *ego ideal* [46i]. To this end, subjective and objective responsibility, in their most enlightened forms, together take a stand against any kind of unregulated force, such as blind dedication to the control of human freedom or helpless compliance with uncompromising tyranny.

The Existential Core of Psychoanalysis

"HARD" AND "SOFT" DETERMINISM

James recognized these two kinds of responsibility by making a distinction between "hard" and "soft" determinism [64b]. In general, hard determinists feel directed by forces beyond themselves and believe that their capacity to control events is insignificant. Life to them becomes a process of adaptive compliance — "realistic adjustment" — to glorified impersonal and inflexible principles and regulations. Soft determinists use their admittedly limited but significant internal powers to modify and master surrounding circumstances, thereby directly influencing the course of local events, if not of nature as a whole. Gradations between hardness and softness of determinism link the polarities of extreme objective and subjective responsibility. Whether people tend to favor a hard or a soft determinism depends upon the comparative power they believe natural forces, social sanctions, or personal ego ideals have to direct responsible conduct.

ORIENTATIONS TOWARD RESPONSIBILITY

When we believe in the reality of freedom and choice, and in some measure of conscious control, nature is not thereby transformed into a showcase for the demonstration of our personal values. Scientific objectivity and enlightened impersonality are not only feasible but enhanced by a strong sense of subjective responsibility. The feeling of freedom carries its own justification with no less validity than does the triumphant self-evidence of intuition. This does not mean, of course, that we are free to choose indiscriminately — a notion frequently termed *indeterminism*. It does mean that the apparent opposition between freedom and fate is more likely to arise from our personal orientation toward subjective and objective responsibility than from different theories about man and nature.

There is no basic incompatibility between subjective and objective responsibility in psychoanalysis, despite conflicts found in certain masochistic, paranoid, and melancholic patients. The only genuine question of responsibility is how each kind shall be used. When a psychoanalyst talks about responsibility, however, he means subjective responsibility. His orientation is based upon the significance of the ego ideal for motivated acts. When a judge talks about responsibility, he means objective responsibility, because his orientation is based upon the significance of society's prevailing standards of conformity for the culpability of motivated acts.

An analyst and a judge may differ in their primary orientation toward responsibility, but neither can ignore his own involvement in both kinds of responsibility and in various value systems. Because being responsible in both ways is a prerequisite to judging others, reality requires that the *dedication* of subjective responsibility be integrated with the *conformity* of objective responsibility. One must not be confused with the other. Thus, people who conceal their own untutored propensities under a robe of self-awarded authority are no more responsible than those who sacrifice their own creative ideas on the altar of conformity. However intriguing the sound, subjective murmurings of our viscera, stirring in response to biological forces, are not the music of the universe. The sense of responsibility, anchored in both the unique existence and common condition of man, keeps us from becoming either involuted advocates of our personal predispositions or infallible adherents to entrenched dogma.

Although these distinctions seem simple, each kind of responsibility is often mistaken for the other. The well-known aphorism "To understand all is to forgive all," aside from its ambiguous humanitarian appeal, suggests that no one, when his complete background is understood, can be blamed or held responsible. It also implies that forgiveness is a function of information and that, as biographical knowledge increases, understanding grows, rancor diminishes, and offenses are condoned to the vanishing point. This is a typical example of the confusion between the operant conditions of subjective responsibility and the mitigating circumstances of objective responsibility. As a result, the meaning of both responsibility and forgiveness is undermined. If the aphorism means that a sufficient number of extenuating circumstances will exempt an offender from subjective as well as objective responsibility, then it becomes possible neither to forgive him nor to hold him accountable.

Objective responsibility makes no distinction between a man

and his acts. Therefore, knowledge about him is only indirectly related to his reality as an existential fact. Subjective responsibility, by emphasizing the primacy of the existential fact of man, regards what he does as somewhat secondary to what he is, so that forgiveness is not likely to be wholly influenced by accumulating categorical information. Forgiveness is an existential transaction that occurs between two autonomous human beings, regardless of which way they define themselves as categorical entities. Punishment has characteristics of both the existential and the categorical, but, like guilt, one kind of punishment is derived from the existential attitude while another kind is simply equivalent to an official record of code violations. One significance of everyday subjective responsibility — which differs from mere knowledge about another person — is that we spontaneously assume that the person has worth, consciousness, values, and capacity and thus take him at face value, however ill advised this acceptance may turn out to be.

Legal guilt differs from personal guilt. One is a sanction which permits the community to punish acts that violate its laws; the other is an awareness of being a person whose very existence shatters an ego ideal. Myth and tragedy have celebrated this conflict between different versions of responsibility, different types of guilt, different forms of forgiveness and punishment by depicting man's vain and valiant struggles to free himself from the tentacles of fate and tradition. The struggle usually ends in death — the price of freedom.

AUTONOMOUS MAN

The psychoanalytic encounter includes both subjective and objective responsibility. It emphasizes *autonomous man*, within whom there are categorical factors to influence him as an object and existential factors to endow his acts with a sense of reality and worth. The salient distinction between the exercise of subjective responsibility and judgment of another person's objective responsibility is that the capacity of autonomous man to judge himself exceeds his capacity to judge the other one.

The categorical fiction that complete knowledge of another person is possible conceals a theory of hard determinism which is inimical to responsibility. Nevertheless, in the field of medicine this viewpoint is tacitly endorsed. Because we tend to ascribe hard determinism to the actions of objects and things, but not to people like ourselves, physicians often think of sick people as if they were equivalent to their disease [15]. Thus the patient either is held culpable for all of his acts or is completely exempted as if he were a passive object.

Medicine is stimulated by its incomplete knowledge about disease. Trying to discover the scope of individual behavior that is consonant with responsible conduct presents an even greater challenge. This is particularly significant when the categorical walls of disease entities, laboratory tests, statistics, and so forth, break down, in which case both physician and patient are stripped of their respective roles and cease to be objects. They meet only on an existential plane, each confronting the meaningless suffering of the other. The physician tacitly blames the patient for being sick, and the patient demands more and more from his physician. This is the penalty imposed upon the physician who implicitly promises to exempt the patient from subjective responsibility — a promise which no doctor can keep without being false to his own responsibility. Suffering is brought about by abrupt confrontation with different kinds of responsibility. When a patient can no longer expect miraculous intervention by his physician, he is thrust back upon his own subjective responsibility and must heal himself. When a physician can no longer expect miraculous responsiveness from his patient, and when the patient turns to him with complaints that cannot be comprehended, the physician's subjective responsibility is damaged. He is then faced with his own guilt and with the task of forgiving the patient who has caused him to suffer.

Psychoanalysts are not exempt from this existential confrontation. There is no analytic "neutrality," only enlightened impartiality. Existential forgiveness is an act that restores the subjective responsibility of the one who forgives as well as the one who is forgiven.

The ontological acceptance is that what we think corresponds to what exists. The idea of personal responsibility extends this acceptance to include the belief that we can create reality in the image of our ego ideal. The existential significance of responsibility defines man as a unique, self-consciously autonomous being who has a strong sense of reality for himself and for the world he helps to create. His conviction that he is in control of what he does is counterregulated by another system of controls which insists upon conformity as a condition for freedom. Autonomy is temporary at best because it is constantly challenged by circumstances. Autonomous man accepts failure as inevitable, but he also understands that failure — or for that matter the fall of man — is brought about by inexorable forces within himself as well as by invincible forces beyond comprehension. Thus, the organic meaning of responsibility is more than freedom or culpability in any narrow theological or legalistic sense. It is that quality of reality sense which allows us to choose, control, and consummate our intended acts with a high level of self-esteem. It is a state of being and becoming for the sake of an idealized and probably inaccessible existence.

Psychoanalytic Meaning of Responsibility

The meaning of responsibility in psychoanalysis is more practical than theoretical. It does not depend upon resolution of the ancient philosophical antithesis between "free will" and "determinism" [62]. Knight [74] has shown that these two ideas are based upon different kinds of experience; they can no more be compared than can the joy of flying be compared with the law of gravity. Actually, the contrasting concepts of an unrestricted free will and an inexorable determinism are both incompatible with the idea of responsibility. At the heart of responsibility are the capacity to respond and bring about responses, and the ability to choose and carry out one form of conduct instead of another. Utter freedom to choose at random from an unlimited range of potential acts and a strict causal necessity that permits no choice destroy responsibility equally. The only difference between free will and determinism is that freedom assumes the primacy of the self, and determinism puts priority on impersonal, alien forces.

A man who carries out his intended acts with full consciousness and confidence usually feels that he is acting with purpose and through choice. Nevertheless, from a wholly impersonal viewpoint, there is no way to prove that his behavior is not completely governed by causal forces beyond his choice, consciousness, and control, regardless of the delicacy and foresight with which he acts. Psychoanalysis cannot settle the problem of choice and necessity in mental life. After all, this may be a pseudoproblem, unanswerable by any science. The psychoanalytic meaning of responsibility is not concerned with the *sources* of specific human actions; it is concerned with the human potential for different kinds of reflective behavior. It is the *uncertainty*, not the *origin*, of these acts that encourages belief in the reality of responsible choice.

From time to time people claim that psychoanalysis teaches an absolute psychic determinism, to the extent that every human act is preordained by unconscious necessity [60*a*]. Not surprisingly, this criticism is often made by people who also believe that impartial self-inquiry is dangerous. They seem to sense that psychoanalysis tries to come face to face with something that they themselves do not have under complete, conscious control. But this does not mean that psychoanalysis *advocates* surrender of conscious control, or that, if the demonic in man is confronted, a horde of demons will be unleashed. Even were such criticism of "Freudianism" valid, it would indicate that so-called unconscious forces are not rigidly determined but wholly chaotic. This kind of criticism, far from being based upon a concern for determinism or responsibility, is based upon a fear of freedom.

The reality of psychodynamic processes and unconscious motivation does not support the notion of unflinching psychic determinism [149]. Processes are not people, and it is not possible to understand people by cataloguing the processes that go on within them. The dynamic unconscious is embedded in a person, not the reverse. People use the contributions of the dynamic unconscious, rather than merely responding passively. There are unique dimensions of existence in which each person exists alone, not only influenced by his unconscious processes but committed to responsible activity and able to exercise a measure of control.

Psychoanalysis needs a concept of responsibility. To assert that psychoanalysis negates the reality of choice or the fact of responsibility is no more correct than to claim that it opposes human values or destroys emotional relationships. There are automatic and obligatory postural mechanisms that are controlled by the midbrain and cerebellum, but this does not imply that all purposeful movements can be reduced to mere efforts to maintain equilibrium. Indeed, few motivated acts could be performed without the silent, postural guarantee of automatic activity. Just as this is a more or less unconscious component of ordinary physical acts, so also does the unconscious contribution toward meanings and motives help to make purposeful, responsible acts possible.

Psychoanalysis recognizes that to feel responsibility for everything is no less a deception than to feel responsibility for nothing. There can be no pride in human achievements unless we know that man must operate within a narrow range of possible responses simply to survive, and that there is a healthy integration of unformulated processes that underlies both brute survival and creative acts. Through its tiny peephole into motives and behavior, psychoanalysis can investigate only some of the factors that contribute to relatively harmonious conduct and some of the factors that restrict choice and responsibility.

THINKING

Whenever anyone starts to think, he wrecks part of his world. He deliberately introduces ideas which violate familiar rules and challenge accepted principles. In the sense that he transgresses his own code, or conventions, he is culpable. Thinking is said to be "trial action." But what is put on trial? Who is put on trial? Rediscovery of what is already known is not thinking; it is corroboration by an appeal to custom, and stale custom can destroy whatever unique meaning is contributed to reality. Some aberrant facts alter the structure of the world and thereby force a drastic revision of prevailing rules. Our own unique responses may be strong enough to shatter our conventional image of the world or the conventional world's image of us. Both may go on trial.

Thinking is one kind of trial, in which different images of the world are impartially challenged and compared. If we discover an irreconcilable difference between our private sense of subjective responsibility and our power to alter our responses to external events, this may be the starting point for another kind of trial — a trial of crisis and decision. If the form of responsible choice we call decision cannot be reached, thinking itself may catapult us into conflict. When reality testing is impaired, we may not be able to contend with the problems reality presents. But there are other, more crucial occasions when the defectiveness of the reality we test is abruptly exposed, like some wound that fails to heal. In the heat of its fever even the barest distinction between the self and the world may be lost. New ways and new signs, whose meaning is unclear, seem to take the place of long-hallowed landmarks and familiar guides.

Aberrant facts can both disrupt the familiar world and help to put it together. The aberrant facts that are called medical symptoms are signs of the body's efforts to heal itself. Psychiatric symptoms may represent the way the mind treats its wounds. In both instances these new facts of experience put *reality* on trial, and, as a result, reality may be revised in order to reconstruct a world in which personal responsibility makes sense. A schizophrenic patient once told me, "You people think I am crazy. If I sat where you are, I would think so, too. But I am not sitting there. I am over here. I *am* crazy and you people *are* reading my mind!" We do not know what forces people to become schizophrenic. This man did not merely retain a shred of sanity; he became insane in order to preserve a measure of responsibility in the midst of a defective reality.

We cannot visualize the psychic spectrum that will include the diverse ways in which subjective responsibility is challenged by reality. Nevertheless, the way a man manages to come to terms with his aberrant thoughts and anomalous feelings may make the difference between a creative thinker and a schizophrenic. Every person alters reality in some respect. For an autonomous man responsibility means that, within the scope of the ego ideal, he offers a unique contribution to reality, and to the living reality of another person. In response, he himself is reaffirmed.

The Existential Core of Psychoanalysis

Psychoanalysis uses the concept of responsibility to liberate the singular existential quality in man [43]. If the notion of insight is not the reliable index of mental health that it was once thought to be, at least insight implies that subjective responsibility is feasible, and that there is still room for conscious choice. These are not alternatives, for there is no freedom without responsibility, no choice without the limitations and obligations of unconscious processes. Genuine freedom is freedom for achievement, not freedom from obligation.

If all this is true, why did psychoanalysis originally pretend that the determinants of an act invariably produce the act? Psychic determinism is not a theory; it is an article of faith in the ultimate precision of nature. However, in order to foretell even its most banal events, human nature requires such generous latitude that we cannot conceal our uncertainty behind a fine name like "psychic determinism." Conversely, we may also ask why, if choice, responsibility, crisis, and decision are so significant, early psychoanalytic theory had so little use for them and seemed to accept determinism as an undisputed fact.

There are several possible reasons why psychoanalysis during its early years emphasized deterministic factors instead of more humanistic ideas. First, in the late nineteenth century a scientific psychology had to conform with other sciences by postulating a rigid system of causality to account for thought, perception, emotion, and action. In his *Project*, Freud, aided by the neurophysiology of his day, attempted to describe mental events in terms of consciousness. Finally he had to capitulate, and thereafter he regarded all mental life as if it were not only entirely unconscious, but free of any neurological substrate! Another reason why psychoanalysis could not rely upon such concepts as choice and responsibility was that consciousness and control had, unfortunately, become associated with the moralistic platitudes of psychiatrists like Dejerine and Dubois, who dealt with neurotic conditions by delivering psychological sermons, which they made more palatable by appealing to dubious physiological analogies.

Responsibility and Reality Sense

The discovery of the dynamic unconscious exploded the self-righteous dogma that neurotic patients were moral defectives suffering from some form of "weakness." Responsibility and choice, among other similar ideas, were too redolently moralistic, too tainted with vapid quasi religion, to be useful as impartial ways to elicit the causes of psychic conflict. The exciting possibilities of exploring the uncharted domain of unconscious motivation and of clarifying the mystery of mental operations held out a sense of reality and purpose that more familiar pursuits could not challenge.

It is unfortunate — too mild a word of regret — that psychoanalysis lost touch with its neurological antecedents. Although Freud could find no way to make it explicit in his clinical work, his implicit structural and dynamic orientation was derived from neurology [110]. Furthermore, as he struggled to maintain a purely psychological viewpoint, he became more and more immersed in the kind of imagery that is consistent with a *four-dimensional neurology*. Even after the oversimplified theory of sexual trauma as the cause of neurosis had been modified, Freud clung to the hypothesis that the occurrence of sexual excitement in a particularly vulnerable organism at a crucial period of life could induce lasting neurotic symptoms — or, at least, lasting until disturbing memories could be exorcised. It is certainly true that we have no better theory today, although our theories are much more complicated. The purpose of psychoanalytic theory seemingly remains as it was then: to reduce psychic conflict to the status of medical disease, and to trace anomalous emotional responses back to crucial interpersonal or impersonal events. This persistent tendency can be maintained only by tacitly excluding both neurophysiological factors and what have been called issues of responsibility, though neither can, in fact, be put aside.

The followers of a great innovator are rarely innovators themselves. Through reaffirmation, repetition, and rewriting, the postulates of psychoanalysis became the creed of many of the first generation of analysts. The early analytic practitioner dispensed insights in much the same way that his medical counterpart dispensed pills from his own formulary. These were, putatively, insights into the "unconscious," a region of such intrigue and mystery that its relevance to conscious experience became more and more doubtful.

When the dynamic unconscious and primary processes are thought of as separate institutions of the mind — of paramount significance and, at the same time, far from everyday experience — there is a concomitant tendency to downgrade consciousness, as well as to minimize notions such as responsibility, choice, manifest ideas, and so forth, which seem not to be derived from unconscious factors. As a result, the patient himself becomes a kind of vehicle for psychopathology [142a, b]. The existential interface between him and his fellow man where consciousness and responsibility meet is, of course, taken for granted, but for this reason it is also ignored.

It is an interesting paradox that analytic patients are often assumed to be passive conveyors of unconscious "material" while lying on the couch but are thought of as thoroughly reasonable, utterly conscious and responsible human beings when they are on their feet. In some clinical respects the manifest person who is the patient is like an alien intruder standing in his own way — and certainly in the way of the analyst, who tries to see through or around his defenses into the recondite regions of unconscious motivations. Even so, no analyst can maintain a consistently clinical attitude in which mental events are mere "specimens." Issues are brought up, perhaps peripheral to the intrinsic "material" of the session, which make it absurd to ascribe to the patient anything other than purposeful, conscious, voluntary, and responsible aims. Moreover, while the myth of psychic determinism seems to exonerate the patient from any active collaboration in his impulses, phantasies, and dreams, it is tacitly held that he has some control over those facets of his personality which are likely to bring him in contact with the public.

This dichotomous attitude is gradually changing. The fiction of "analytic detachment," like the metaphor of the inconspicuous mirror, is disappearing. The pious ambiguities of earlier practice have become somewhat more reasonable and realistic. The contemporary concept of the *therapeutic alliance* [96], for example, presumes that patients want to be analyzed and are able to express relatively unmonitored verbal reports of what they think. The key idea is that patients and analysts collaborate in a mutual enterprise, rather than that a "healthy ego" is helping to analyze an "unhealthy ego." The only assumption made by the therapeutic alliance is that the patient is prepared to use his subjective responsibility to help him understand that phase of himself which is constrained by conflict. This is a more practical concept than the one which insists upon a sharp distinction between "sick" and "well," "mature" and "immature," or between any other value-laden judgments. It is the *person* who uses his responsibility; responsibility is not a function of a separate department within him.

ANOMALIES OF RESPONSIBILITY

Responsibility is so imminently real that, at every phase of analysis, issues concerning it are, indeed, as relevant as are the factors compromising the patient's autonomy as a participant in reality. To understand the nature of a patient's conflicts, the analyst must appreciate his style of life and his singular set of acceptances and ideals. Anomalies of responsibility can be recognized in the course of analysis itself without waiting for moments when the patient's relation to society is jeopardized.

Anomalies of responsibility are analyzed in precisely the same way that any other source of conflict or paradox is analyzed. The objective limits of the world and the intrinsic limits of the person are basic factors which restrict responsibility, just as they influence the kind of reality that exists. A person's orientation with respect to reality, and to standards of excellence, may change, but the worth of reality and the reality of worth are unquestioned by psychoanalysis. Similarly, the analytic adventure in self-exploration includes questioning the very motives and acceptances, values and ideals, that the patient seems to regard as reliable guides to an uncertain world. Because what is accepted as real may be simply unchallenged illusion, his respectable codes of "oughts and shoulds," duties, and obligations may conceal self-deception, defeat, and surrender of responsibility.

Responsibility can be called upon in analysis for special purposes, much as analysis can call upon reality testing. Though no analyst will chide or exhort patients into following directives or observing prohibitions — for the practical reason that such an approach does not work — residual subjective responsibility and its related ideas can be fostered when conflict seems too acute to be tolerated. For example, many patients become terrified lest they inadvertently act upon some recurrent sadistic or sexual phantasy. In such instances the extreme phantasies may be interpreted as efforts by the patient to maintain control, and not as an indication that he is about to translate these ideas into action. Thus the analyst helps the frightened patient to summon up personal responsibility by recognizing that his apparent fears are expressions of his capacity to control. This variety of anomalous responsibility is often found in the obsessional patient, whose undoing rituals are produced both by fear of his phantasies and by fear of his own freedom. Such a patient imposes limits on his freedom by imagining the destructive acts he feels capable of committing. Then, by undoing these acts, he tests, and tests again, his subjective responsibility. In contrast, the paranoid patient may suffer from too little, not too much, freedom. Out of a conviction of weakness he may surrender his subjective responsibility and create a new world, according to his own specifications, in which he will matter. Other instances of anomalous responsibility are described below in "Strategies of the Superego" (p. 194).

Like his patients, the analyst is obliged to clarify his own autonomous, or anomalous, responsibility. This should not be confused with the institutional, categorical responsibility he has simply because he is a physician. He cannot afford to be an infallible authority, even if his patients seem sometimes to thrust their responsibility upon him. Patients often yearn for an absolute source of final appeal and are ready to surrender what remains of subjective responsibility by asking for an external judgment of praise or blame. Other patients plead for direction, advice, and information — for unequivocal intelligence about what is real, right, or good. However, they do not merely wish to have the analyst become a somewhat belated parental authority; more often they seek to reaffirm themselves by having something specific to oppose. Their sense of responsible choice is enhanced by stubborn resistance to the initiative of others. By opposing someone else's choice they compensate for their own indecision.

DECISION-MAKING

Critical decisions cannot be made for someone else because decision is one of the most highly personal and self-conscious of human acts. Most significant decisions occur at moments of crisis and in the face of conflict. Doubt is usually an indication that reality sense has become divided between different courses of potential action. Indecision is one of the most common signs of conflict. Chronic indecision, furthermore, is a disorder of responsibility. Patients who try valiantly to induce their analyst to make decisions for them are often people who would compromise his freedom as well as their own. In the relationship with the doctor, the so-called transference neurosis repeats ways in which the patient's autonomy has been compromised in the past and, perforce, foreshadows ways in which he hopes to rectify past mistakes. In exchange for the analyst's freedom, the patient offers what is left of his own. Analysts refuse gifts, not merely because it is technically inadmissible to accept them, but because gifts can bind the patient to the analyst, and the analyst to the patient, and thereby may limit the range of responsibility within which each can function. There are other, less tangible "gifts" which may be Trojan horses and, ultimately, deleterious to the analysis because they are difficult to detect. For example, a patient may beg the analyst to assume responsibility for him by ostensibly conforming to the image of the "good patient," and even by re-enacting earlier struggles over freedom with him. All of this may be consistent with the ego ideal. To idealize the analyst externalizes the ego ideal but is not necessarily synonymous with trust. In fact, idealization usually yields subjective responsibility to another in order to have greater freedom returned. In its first form, this is called *identification*; in its secondary form, it is *introjection*.

The crucial decision for an analyst to make is not how much responsibility to assume for a patient but how much to assume for himself. He discovers the reality of his own responsibility when he is free to nurture it in others. By contributing to the reality of another person he must, of course, expect to be influenced in return. Responsibility does not mean that he should control others or that he should be controlled. Occasionally he must take control when a patient falters, but only for short periods. This choice must be exercised judiciously. To assume responsibility for another is like administering a narcotic — it is life-saving in certain circumstances but life-destroying in others. Even at these critical moments the analyst should remind himself that responsibility does not bestow authority; it confers authenticity — a quality he cannot present as a gift but can only encourage in another.

THE NONJUDGMENTAL ATTITUDE

No one is free of conventional values. At best, people can be objective only in their own fashion. Why, then, has psychoanalysis scrupulously recommended a "nonjudgmental" attitude? There is a valid distinction, of course, between understanding, accepting, condoning, and approving what anyone thinks or does, but psychoanalysts strive for impartiality in order to avoid the inadvertent imposition of the criteria of objective responsibility. Unless conventional standards of responsibility are recognized, it becomes extremely difficult to recognize and rectify the anomalous subjective responsibility that the patient brings to analysis.

From the existential viewpoint, the most significant reason for withholding categorical judgment is that, were the analyst to condemn, he would also have to forgive. He cannot forgive because he has not been injured. This precept insures the patient's right to his own responsibility, which cannot substantially be changed by blame and shame. In this respect psychoanalysis is more truly existential than are many so-called existential therapies that advocate a wide range of values and ideals, from such vacuous aims as "self-realization" to whatever stops just short of religious values. Indoctrination is anti-analytic, although axiological objectives are often served by semi-analytic methods. For example, it is all too easy to imply that one viewpoint is "good" and another is "bad" simply by the way an analyst presents an interpretation. Even when the analyst is particularly careful to avoid value-charged directives and prohibitions that may accidentally contaminate his interpretations, the patient may only hear and mishear evidence of approval and disapproval. To confuse mere responsiveness with responsibility is a fallacy encouraging identification and counteridentification, not separate identities. Psychoanalysis is pragmatic, and therefore ideal, because it tests reality as it happens instead of appealing to an idealized version of what the therapist and patient think reality ought to be.

INDEX OF REALITY AND RESPONSIBILITY

Like psychoanalysis itself, responsibility has a highly practical, human meaning that applies to ordinary men, not to demigods. Its self-defining objective is that an ordinary man, who is, admittedly, quite extraordinary, can learn to respect his own aberrant, anomalous existence by understanding his private paradoxes. If he understands also that good and evil, truth and error, pleasure and pain are largely within him — not arbitrarily imposed upon him by tyrannical forces — he will understand his own participation in the unfolding of reality.

Responsible, autonomous man is not a mythical superman who is exempt from the impersonal strivings of his species and from the calamitous indifference of his era. Confidence in one's own resources and recognition that the ego ideal is a personal possession are far different from an overweening conviction of control or — what amounts to the same thing — from feeling an obligation to be in control of some limitless destiny. They are also quite different from being possessed by an image of responsibility that finds fulfillment only in a grandiose, transmundane phantasy of power, prestige, riches, or timeless survival. To believe in such unlikely dreams is not true responsibility. It is cruel self-deception, no better than whistling in a graveyard. *In short, to be responsible, man must believe in his own death.*

The discrepancy between the convictions of reality sense and the corrections of reality testing is an *index of reality*. The gap between what a man is and what he interprets himself to be is an *index of responsibility*. Self-deception is a cardinal sin of responsibility. Many of the so-called great personalities of history and fiction are, in effect, great frauds, perpetrated by men whose uneasy consciences about themselves led them to glorify, as though they were virtues, characteristics that negated their own subjective responsibility. Responsible man can appreciate his kinship with the false, evil, and sick and, by acknowledging this existential fact, still maintain his singular distinction, which he shares with no one else. Man has both an active power to cause responses and certainly a capacity to respond; each is necessary for full expression of the other. He can respond to the pains and problems of others but cannot always contribute to their relief. Responsibility, in a sense, idealizes man's limitations. This is one of the lessons taught by psychoanalysis — to those who already know it.

Responsibility and Superego

Earlier generations, preoccupied with rationalism and mechanistic interpretations of nature, once asked themselves, "Is man a machine?" Astounded by machines that mind and are mindful, today's generation asks, "Do machines have a mind?" Among the ingenious machines that carry out assignments with speed and accuracy beyond human capacity, there are some that even select the most efficient task to perform in order to reach a particular objective. Are we justified in considering these machines "responsible"?

No matter how spectacular their performance, few people would be ready to surrender the presumably human attribute of responsibility to machines. It is hard to tell which human qualities distinguish man's sense of responsibility from the almost perfect performance of these machines. However, machines lack at least three qualities properly belonging to the idea of responsibility. These are man's *culpability*, his idealized appetites, called *values*, and his *sense of freedom*.

According to the psychoanalytic interpretation of responsibility, man lives *with* his dynamic unconscious, not by it. There is a limitless disquietude about accepting coercion, even from our own unconscious. It is far more congenial to believe that, despite being rooted in obligation and conformity, we are able to recognize our own uniqueness and to make full use of freedom. Without this faith every dream of choice and responsibility would be shattered, and man might well resign himself to being a fragile, not too efficient machine, set into operation by some careless or indifferent technician.

The concept of *superego* is so much a part of our contemporary viewpoint that it scarcely needs review. But because superego rescues responsibility from the arid domain of philosophy, it also makes the feeling of responsibility worth talking about.

THE THREE-COMPONENT STRUCTURE

The structural viewpoint postulates three "mental institutions" — id, ego, and superego — which have become so firmly embedded in our thoughts that we often think of them as three structures in the mind as solid and distinct as heart, lungs, and brain in the body. Some psychiatrists believe that ego can be studied as a more or less independent unit and that superego, almost at will, can line up against id during conflict [42]. These "structures," which began only as convenient nomenclature, have now become personified, autonomous entities. It is not unusual to meet such egregious phantoms as "tyrannical superegos," "compliant egos," and "spiteful ids."

Motivated acts appear in many different forms and in varying degrees of complexity. At one end of the spectrum are the so-called instinctual responses — forms which tend to be somewhat stereotyped and relatively rigid. Next come the more differentiated and more modifiable practical acts of everyday life, with their variety of short-term aims and goals. Then, according to the different requirements of men and their society, these practical acts gradually develop into highly symbolic, abstract, and technical behavior, which might be considered identical with long-range responsible conduct.

Reality sense and reality testing require that motivated acts reach a standard of excellence as well as carry out practical aims effectively. What we do is selected not only because it can accomplish a task or solve a problem but because it is worth doing.

Reality testing, Freud [46l] maintained, is a way to compare present-day perceptions with early prototypes that offered gratification. However, reality testing is more than a primal image seeking its duplicate. Because reality sense contributes to the sense of value and the act of judgment, one important aim of ego-regulatory functions is to monitor motivated acts according to idealized values and standards of excellence. This is wholly in keeping with the theory that reality is not merely discovered but modified and created by what we do.

The unfolding of organic meaning progressively includes stereotyped, instinctual acts, emotional expressions, rational thinking, practical behavior, symbolic forms, and idealistic conduct, among many other variants. Mental events encompass manifold motivations, a highly differentiated system of regulatory operations, and a hierarchy of values. Where id leaves off and ego begins, and where superego takes over from ego, are arbitrary problems of doubtful value. This is the anthropomorphic interpretation of the structural viewpoint, in which id insists upon reckless ways of acting, an austere superego tries to hold it back, and an overworked ego attempts to mediate between the unmitigated evil of one and the uninteresting good of the other.

Instead of viewing id, ego, and superego as interlocking parts of a stationary operation, or as a single structure, it is more useful to see them as distinctions between inseparable phases of related processes. Id may be called primary processes; ego, secondary processes; and superego, tertiary processes. All three participate in motivated acts, but any one phase may be singled out for special evaluation. In general, primary processes supply the *contents*; secondary processes, the *controls*; and tertiary processes, the *correctives* of motivated behavior.

Logically enough, the psychoanalytic trinity of id, ego, and superego lends itself to quasi-scholastic speculation. This inevitably loosens its tie to intrapersonal experience, which is our principal concern. Hence, without any further elaboration, the following tabulation indicates how concepts related to the existential core of analysis can also be related to one or another structural institution.

Responsibility and Reality Sense

Id	Ego	Superego
Reality sense	Reality testing	Responsibility
Primary processes	Secondary processes	Tertiary processes
Contents	Controls	Correctives
Emotions	Thoughts	Values
Stereotyped acts	Learned behavior	Monitored conduct
Instinctual aims	Practical aims	Idealized aims
Affective equivalents	Conceptual sequences	Imperatives (directives and prohibitions)
Libidinal fields	Conceptual fields	Ego ideal
Quiescence of appetites	Mastery of problems	Fulfillment of ideals

It is possible to compare many other ideas in a similar fashion. For example, the so-called pursuit of pleasure, combined with avoidance of pain, is an id-act. When also viewed as an ego-act, id components will necessarily be included, but the emphasis will be on ways to master problems and to perform practical tasks in order to survive and to adapt. When superego factors are introduced, all of the previous factors can be elaborated from the viewpoint of different values, and appropriate acts can be defined according to more remote idealized and responsible aims.

Superego functions can be recognized in imperatives that direct and prohibit, approve and disapprove, one kind of conduct instead of another. *Superego,* then, is the common term for that phase of ego-regulatory functions which monitors the ego image, in so far as motivated acts conform with or violate the ego ideal.

Although efficiency and a sense of accomplishment can result from mutually regulated, harmonious ego functions, the judgment of excellence is belatedly conferred upon the ego image only when the effectiveness of ego functions lives up to the ego ideal. However, neither ego operations nor superego imperatives can testify about what is right or wrong, however responsible it may seem. *Superego values oppose whatever threatens to deprive a man of his responsibility and freedom.* Since society at large will not necessarily judge these values to be "good" or "bad," they may not be subject to the rules of culpability. Superego values and social values can share the same viewpoint, but this viewpoint might be considered wholly evil when judged by another responsible person within the same social system. In a word, superego designates the inner wisdom of the way we regulate our acts, according to our own standards of efficiency and excellence. It is not an independent tribunal that imposes guilty feelings when offenses are committed. Superego imperatives can evoke guilt, remorse, and dejection during conflict and can also generate sentiments such as triumph, fulfillment, and satisfaction after the successful completion of certain acts.

Internalization of parental decrees certainly influences superego values and the ego ideal, but early authoritarian correctives and controls — a kind of "determinism" — produce only a categorical extension of what a man believes he is and what he believes is worth becoming. They contribute to an image of reality without creating the superego functions which will expand reality testing into the realm of the ideal. Many of the uncompromising decrees attributed to parents, of course, are not what they have actually said or implied. But even if such dictates were literal equivalents, instead of highly selective elaborations, they would not explain how either the sense of responsibility or the process of idealization comes about. Both are necessary factors in the growth of an ego ideal. It is odd, but commonplace, to find that some patients who complain bitterly about being victimized by their parents — as well they might — also betray an idealized image of them which they impose upon the next generation.

IDEALIZATION

Just as superego functions are extensions of reality testing, and reality sense is represented in superego values, the process of *idealization* is an extension of identification. What we idealize determines what we believe controls the universe and what we strive to emulate. In a simple sense, the root meaning of responsibility — *cause* and *control* — endows parents with the capacity to control children by means of their predominant values, just as they once had the power to create them. In obeisance to total parental responsibility — an ideal of cause and control — some people deny their own subjective responsibility and blame their misfortunes on their having had uncompromising, punitive parents, as though their parents had chosen to cause and control according to an evil ego ideal. The root meaning of responsibility may be expanded to include confluent value systems whose idealized images are those of mental health and utopian societies. The concept of an idealized cause of existence, with a continuing source of benevolent control, gives rise to values and phantasies which are themselves beyond pragmatic truths.

We are, then, inclined to idealize only those people who are disposed to care, and to take care of us, and whom we would like to emulate. The idealized person is usually an extension of our own ego image, without its rapacious traits. Isolated traits of many people, presumably, are fused into a single ideal. The absence of rapacity implies that ideal images lack nothing that is desirable, and this quality, in itself, allows us to use these images to satisfy our own anaclitic and narcissistic requirements. The manner, style, character, and flair of the idealized person represent not only a system of values fulfilled but a fulfillment of what we would have to be in order to be cared for. It is not surprising that the ego ideal — the idealized image we have of ourselves — carries its measure of sexual attachments, but it is incorrect to reduce this idealization to sexual propensities alone.

One indication of an expanding libidinal field is a growing capacity to care about many different things. Correlated with this growth is an ideal called maturity. This means that when a child becomes a responsible adult he is not still dependent upon only a few people for his basic survival but capable of differentiated, modulated relationships with many people [97]. Whatever other factors are present, it may be said that aggressive patterns of mastery, lifelong erotic interest in absolutes, abiding wishes to be cared for, and, perhaps, even a persistent passion to explain give rise to our remote aspirations, ideals, and values. In the course of survival alone, the cumulative product of many disappointments and satisfactions contributes to our comprehensive image of what is worth struggling for. Existential values are not conventional social values but functions of a personal potential for self-corrective conduct.

Kant's famous "Categorical Imperative" is a classic attempt to reconcile man's personal wishes and existential value — his subjective responsibility — with society's categorical ideals and objective responsibility. In effect, Kant proposed that the criterion for personal conduct should be whatever conduct we would choose as the general rule for all people [147]. If Kant had lived later, and had been familiar with superego, his categorical imperative might have insisted that superego values and categorical values ought to be identical.

Because consent is notoriously fickle, a rule that reckons responsibility and ego ideals according to our willingness to adopt them as general rules is scarcely a reliable rule for society. In fact, the categorical imperative is the antithesis of what so many psychiatric patients demonstate, particularly those who have problems of conscience, blame, responsibility, doubt, and self-denigration. Such people are usually far more lenient toward others than they are toward themselves. They readily grant freedom, latitude, and indulgence to the rest of humanity but inflict upon themselves a degree of suffering from which they have exempted others who may be even more culpable. The categorical imperative has little to offer these unhappy people, whose high expectations of themselves are desperate attempts to salvage subjective responsibility. This kind of self-tyranny may cast a glow of altruism and forbearance, but it lacks the warmth of humanity.

In some societies the gods ordain imperatives and create the capacity to obey them. But in most societies people spend much of their lives trying to decide between impulse and imperative. In practical affairs men get along the best they can and, within limits, concede their weaknesses and utilize their strengths. However, in the sphere of morals and instincts their ideal is full compliance, as if the urges of primary processes and the imperatives of tertiary processes will not tolerate half-measures, compromises, or promises. Persistent problems of ethics are often the result of attempts to compromise the seemingly absolute antagonism between morals and instincts, and between values and appetites [44]. This is less an antagonism of substance than it is an insistence that judgments be absolute, that only values of good and bad are relevant, and that the only wish worth having is a frustrated wish. Thus when a patient suffers from too extreme a polarity between his insistent instinctual urges and his superego imperatives, it is often difficult for a psychiatrist to distinguish between them! Among patients with obsessional neurosis, for example, a rage to destroy and to defy may be concealed by an equally intense passion to be upright and to obey rules.

GOALS AND CONDUCT

What can guide man at moments of decision and despair? There is no reason to believe that everyone ought to behave in the same way or cherish the same ideals. Even were it feasible to create some all-inclusive, grand categorical canon — a law of laws — it would not insure man's freedom and responsibility. Psychoanalysis cannot demonstrate what is good or bad, cannot tell man what he ought to do. Responsibility is not an explicit code of conduct but a way to contend with the ambiguities that reality and ideals impose upon man. Subjective responsibility is not identical with values, but it makes use of them. There is, of course, no shortage of easy discourses about the "goals of man." These discourses usually advocate a jumbled inventory of directives and neglect to show the reader how his objectives can be reached. The usual "goals of man," such as security, power, pleasure, prestige, order, and acceptance, are umbrella notions that cover the combined effects of many subsidiary acts. These goals are not the *direct* result of any particular act or set of acts but the comfortable consequence of avoiding an antithetical disaster like death, disease, alienation, loneliness, and so forth. They are *judgments* about a series of acts, not genuine goals at all. For example, people often talk about seeking security, the way a poet might speak about creating beauty. However, a poet does not create beauty by the act of writing. Beauty is a superego judgment *about* what he has written. He may gladly accept this judgment, on behalf of his ego ideal, but nothing he can *do* has beauty as its principal result. Similarly, a man may work hard, watch his health, and prudently invest his money, but none of these acts will result in security as a direct goal. This is the crucial difference between *behavior* and *conduct*. Behavior can be described according to an overall pattern of motivated acts; conduct is behavior which is interpreted, or judged, according to a prevailing value system. Superego aims and responsibility help us to integrate a purposeful program of existential merit, but psychoanalysis cannot help us to decide what this program should be.

The Existential Core of Psychoanalysis

When people in conflict are torn between duties and impulses, self-punitive emotions, such as dejection, guilt, depression, or uncontrollable anxiety, are not produced by a tyrannical superego or an implacable id but by impairment of ego functions. What remains is an *apparent opposition* between id and superego, joined together by residues of ego functions and reality testing. Reality sense may be concentrated at one pole or the other. In order to preserve a modicum of responsibility, one or the other of these poles must act as a corrective, to compensate for the ameliorating and modulating operations usually carried out by secondary processes. In severe ego impairments, when conflict is extreme, the corrective factor may be experienced as a hostile *outside force*, from which there is no escape [126]. The unfortunate patient may be engulfed by both his wishes and fears, by his unmodified impulses, or by his unrestrained objective culpability. In his effort to maintain responsibility he may feel passively victimized by uncompromising social forces. For example, paranoid delusions are often made up of extremely conventional ideas. The outside, persecuting force is usually an established, highly conservative authority, such as some church or government agency. Sometimes the punitive forces manipulate natural influences, such as medicine, radiation, or even gossip, in order to exercise their choice and control.

STRATEGIES OF THE SUPEREGO

In the presence of conflict and crisis, people without serious ego impairment will often call upon certain *strategies of the superego* to help preserve harmony between reality and responsibility. Although these strategies may enlist outside forces, they are not punitive or implacable forces and, as a rule, reality testing remains intact.

Suttie [133] proposed — erroneously, I think — that the therapeutic effect of psychoanalysis depends upon the total acceptance, or "love," which permeates the consultation room. He maintained that this quality is ignored in theories about psychoanalysis. While it cannot be disputed that acceptance is a necessary part of the analytic encounter, there is no evidence that mere acceptance can restore self-esteem, relieve shame, allay guilt, lift depression, or, in short, reconcile what a man is with what he believes he is or ought to be. For such purposes, patients make use of superego strategies, some unwittingly, others at self-conscious, ritualistic lengths. A few of these strategies are *confession, masochistic surrender, scapegoating, atonement, undoing, sacrifice, reaction formation,* and *excuses, apologies,* and *justification.*

Confession has a beneficial, albeit transient, effect upon the troubled patient. By his effort to discharge an offense through the magical act of reporting it, he begs for reaffirmation of his worth as a person. However, the psychodynamic significance of confession, like that of catharsis and suggestion, is obscure. Some people confess in order to be punished, and thus to be freed of their guilt. Others seem desperately to need reaffirmation, but confession does not achieve it. A more complex version of confession is found in patients who repeatedly violate the social and analytic codes, then look upon any pertinent interpretation as a scolding. Consequently, guilt, confession, being reproached, and unsolicited promises to do better become part of the violation itself. The acts of confession and the anticipated daily chidings seem to reduce the level of conflict as well.

Some patients empty themselves of offenses the first time they consult a psychiatrist, whether or not the offenses are pertinent to the immediate problem. Their aim is not to gain forgiveness through self-denigration but to present all problems to the analyst and then turn away. This maneuver, called *masochistic surrender,* resembles the *compulsive confessions* of more disturbed patients who plead guilty to crimes they have not committed. As a strategy, confession may be used to repudiate, as well as to restore, responsibility. Not only is it possible to detach oneself from genuine problems by confession, but it is also possible to lie about facts in the act of confession. For example, a remorseful father confessed that he had beaten his daughter, but he concealed his incestuous phantasies about her.

A valid act of confession may resemble an act of intuition by bringing out some hidden truth. This is quite different, however, from merely pouring out a litany of misdeeds. There is more in psychoanalysis than is revealed by dubious confessions. The belief that confession is a demeaning act, or that it puts the participants under mutual obligation, is anti-analytic. Being able to confront oneself openly, with neither praise nor blame, is nothing more than honesty. Anything less is self-deception.

Because it is natural to hate whatever represents or reminds us of our unworthy impulses, we may attribute an offense to someone else. Then confession for *them* makes them the victim and violator, and we become righteous and retributive. This strategy is called *scapegoating*. It may also be found in a reversed form called martyrdom.

Atonement restores responsibility in the performance of an act which is a precise antidote for a previous act of violation. As a rule, atonement is prescribed by an established authority. It tends to be less original and more conservative than the offense committed, but there are special, more personal acts of atonement, called *undoing*, which are intended to reverse symbolic rather than literal offenses. Acts of undoing often give rise to some of the most bizarre symptoms encountered in psychiatry.

Alexander [1*b*] has referred to some superego stratagems as "bribing the superego" — a peculiarly ironic phrase which underscores the hypocrisy of many conventional moral standards. So-called *reaction formation* is a character trait that has many qualities of a permanent stratagem, in that it converts avoidances into positive appetites and reverses potential violations into actualized virtues. Nevertheless, distortions of reaction formation can occur when failure to act is mistaken for prudence, when self-denial is confused with moral distinction, and when large-scale avoidances are expected to satisfy "higher" appetites. In a way, prejudices are reaction formations against the putative acceptances of other people; but prejudices are also tactics because they allow some people to feel better by convincing themselves that someone else is worse.

People with an "unconscious sense of guilt" use many different strategies to insure their responsibility. They court defeat at every turn, give themselves an excess of suffering, and never find the "better life," which their misfortunes make them feel they deserve. For some of these people, to plead guilty is a privilege, and a permissible way to announce their moral superiority. *Sacrifice* is a more vigorous, related tactic which protects some people from the guilt of future offenses by prepaying a penalty. Frequently the guilt is inappropriately predicated upon future triumphs instead of upon misdeeds. Thus, sacrifice and ambition are close companions.

Far less exacting, less exciting, but more plebeian ways to reconcile acts with ideas are *excuses, apologies,* and *justification.* All of us look for categorical justification of our acts, just as we look for corroboration of our thoughts. This is simply an example of reality testing in action. Excuses are intended merely to mitigate an act, but justification transforms a blameworthy act into one that fulfills a praiseworthy objective. Apology does not promote responsibility; by conceding error it forestalls punishment, restores a relationship, and neutralizes the anger and disappointment of the other person.

GUILT AND RESPONSIBILITY

There are as many vicissitudes within the responsible life as there are in the instinctual life, and it is even more difficult to achieve responsibility than it is to recognize abiding reality. The estimate of responsibility is found not in the fact of guilt but in the meaning of guilt. There is no particular merit in suffering, only in seeking the significance of suffering. Guilt, or any other sentiment related to superego values, makes sense only when it is a way to insure harmony between motivated acts and responsible acts, and to effect a closer approximation of the ego image and the ego ideal.

For psychoanalysis, responsibility is neither a burden nor a joy, but an existential fact. Since not every human act can be expected to conform to an ego ideal, responsibility is by no means a permanent value judgment. The aims of responsibility, like the aims of reality sense, are to establish harmony between choice and necessity, freedom and obligation, the aesthetic and the practical, within the ego ideal. What "mob psychology" is to id, superorthodoxy is to superego. The ego ideal of psychoanalysis is based upon a belief that human conduct, by means of self-affirmation, can exist for its own enjoyment, edification, and enlightenment without being inflexibly chained to a specific value, ideal, or practical goal. There is nothing obligatory about either responsibility or superego, except for the loyalty and tribute demanded by our acceptances and dispositions. These are the source of every other allegiance.

The Responsible Act

Responsibility cannot mean one thing on the analytic couch and something entirely different in the world at large. If superego aims are correctives for ego functions, then these aims contribute to the corrective influence that the reality principle wields over the pleasure principle. Ultimately, the decisive issues of responsibility can be reduced to those explicit *acts* for which people are held responsible and hold themselves responsible.

The salient characteristic of a healthy nervous system is the way it learns how to fractionate gross automatic movements into differential behavior [21]. Impairment of this potential for learning, or damage to it, is a practical definition of neurological disease. Although motives for any specific neurological response are not usually considered part of its actual mechanism, motives for purposeful acts cannot be isolated, deep within the recesses of the nervous system, from the sources of any other motives. Biological action systems contribute to instinctual acts — typical of primary processes; to practical acts — typical of secondary processes; and to responsible acts — typical of tertiary processes. Except for purely visceral responses, every act is an intent to modify something in the world and, therefore, is a motivated act. Responsible acts, in particular, reveal a unique style of action that combines the perceptive and practical functions of ego with the ideal aims conferred by superego.

A responsible act fulfills a special purpose, but it is not necessarily a special act. Responsible acts are not just sober or uplifting, like reading the classics, giving to charity, or attending church. Acts that defy convention and acts that comply with custom are not, by that fact alone, either irresponsible or responsible. If a man who avoids a fight violates his ego ideal in so doing, he is irresponsible; but if, by avoiding a fight, he fulfills his ego ideal, he is responsible.

There are two ways to appreciate the reality of responsible

purpose: as an *internal observer* who watches himself and as an *external observer* who watches someone else. To the internal observer responsibility is (1) a conviction that he is wholly conscious of what he wants, (2) a confidence in his capacity to carry out his intentions, and (3) a certainty that his acts will fulfill practical and ideal criteria. In short, because he feels able to choose between alternatives, and to recognize the consequences in advance, he is sure that his choice will be a good one. If he is asked, moreover, he will not hesitate to say that he is performing a "voluntary" act.

An external observer cannot be sure about what an internal observer reports because he cannot experience the sense of reality for cause, consciousness, control, and value. To an external observer acts are purposeful only when he can establish an intelligent connection between their ostensible aims and their actual effect upon the world of people and things. His opinion about responsible acts is limited to a comparison between the social effects of purposeful acts and acceptable norms.

Neither observer can explain his observations without recognizing that every level of his physical, physiological, and psychological organization shares in the reverberating system of responses that is called intelligent behavior. The internal observer is certain that he acts purposefully, but, like the external observer, he *assigns* a purpose, or a meaning, to what he does. If no intelligent purpose can be assigned, his acts seem to be determined only by chance, or external influence alone, instead of by choice.

The internal observer, by scrutinizing his inner experience, and by being able to choose and to carry out his intended movements, is encouraged to believe that his acts are "voluntary," and that there is even a kind of super-function, called "will," or "volition." To the external observer, however, the notion of a "voluntary" act is an egregious fiction. Unlike some fictions which are useful, the concept of "will" has obstructed the analysis of responsibility. Assuredly, responsible acts are a reality, but voluntary acts are not.

The fiction of voluntary acts and volition may be attributed, in part, to an illusion, an analogy, a wish, and an insistent claim. The illusion is that whatever follows conscious anticipation is, therefore, under causal control; the analogy is that intention is to consequence as stimulus is to response; the wish is for an utterly rational personal destiny; the insistent claim is that there is a compliant universe which yields to our intentions, without disappointment or surprise.

If our intentions were, in fact, regularly followed by smooth, effective, undeviant, and conventional consequences, man would be no more responsible than a moth is, flying around a flame. Unconscious motives and inconspicuous psychodynamic processes introduce novelty, aberrance, and deviations from the rules. These unconscious factors are not alien forces that corrupt responsibility; they are factors that strengthen the search for responsibility by means of purposeful acts. An aberrant *fact* prompts the search for *reality*; in the same way, an aberrant *act* challenges the accepted system for determining *responsibility*.

Without unconscious factors there would be no sense of reality and no sense of responsibility. This means that a responsible act is not completely defined by saying that it is an act in which there are explicit aims, absolute standards, full control, and conscious intent. *We have no evidence that such acts exist.* In actual situations, where responsibility is a living issue, a responsible act is like any other act except for its accent upon superego aims. The act itself gathers force by telescoping primary, secondary, and tertiary processes into its final consummation. Not only when the act goes wrong, or turns out to be fallacious, but at every phase, it is influenced by unconscious factors.

Until recent years [48, 72], psychoanalytic theory implied that mental processes are wholly unconscious and that consciousness is a phenomenon, not a discriminative process. As a result, psychoanalysis found itself caught in a paradox between a dynamic unconscious, with processes beyond the rules and reasons of ordinary events, and the existential fact of consciousness, with its indispensable, selective participation in the analytic encounter. This paradox was partly due to perpetuation of a topographical view of mental events, which seemed to minimize the dynamic significance of "being conscious of." Another factor in the paradox was failure to recognize that the term *dynamic unconscious* is incomplete; it refers to a "dynamically unconscious system," not to a special mental domain.

Traditional psychoanalysis epitomized its aims in "Where there was id, there ego shall be" [46m]. Contemporary psychoanalysis finds it more accurate to translate this as "Where there was stereotyped behavior, there responsibility shall be." In the practice of analysis, we do not simply replace one fictitious entity with another. Instead of trying to put ego where there was id, we clarify a continuous series of motivated and purposeful acts. These acts range from the most unorganized emotional images and inclinations, through the varying complexities of relevant attitudes and practical performances, to highly abstract, idealized, and symbolic expressions of language and conduct. In the course of clarification, as repetitious, driven acts of compulsion become converted into more discriminative acts of choice, some more or less stereotyped acts will move further along on the continuum of differentiation. Accordingly, necessity, in the form of unmitigated, unconscious motives, will gradually be diluted by freedom and the corrective potential of "insight."

Psychoanalytic patients provide many examples of "ego defects" that cannot be influenced by any known means, including insight, and psychoanalytic theory does not provide adequate explanation for these supposed infirmities. In effect, the ego ideal of analytic theory is a kind of upward perfection from one level of psychosexual organization to another [52, 97]. Despite many paradoxes encountered along the way, as each level is surmounted, its traces are carried along, in sublimated form, to the next level. Fractional changes cannot be accounted for, and there is no recognition of the genuine adaptive potential of so-called ego defectives, a term that, in itself, is pejorative. That it is wholly possible to be responsible and still deviate from the norm of social and emotional equilibrium can scarcely be formulated in metapsychological terms. There is little doubt, nevertheless, that the wholly "adjusted" personality, filled with "mental health," is a vacuous verbalization having no human counterpart. Early in their careers psychiatrists learn how slight is the correlation between psychodynamic clarity and therapeutic prognosis. This is another way to recognize that awareness of motives does not mean that something can be done about them.

Regardless of its own infirmities, psychoanalysis does offer an opportunity to recognize unconscious motives, typical problems, and characteristic ways of responding to them. It provides greater latitude for the exception, or for aberrant conduct, than do those systems of existential therapy which tacitly ignore unconscious motivation and substitute a categorical value system, accessible, presumably, through the proper use of voluntary action and "will" [95, 152]. By emphasizing a spurious function like "will," it, too, becomes a prominent part of that value system. Implicitly, "will" becomes the best of all possible functions. This makes no more sense than to claim that *choice* is the best of all possible motives.

WILL AND CHOICE

The skilled, motivated acts of everyday life are usually performed so spontaneously that problems of choice, competence, consummation, and control rarely arise. Their precision is called "skill"; their inconspicuous dependability is called "habit." As James [64a] noted, habit spares us from endlessly renewing the search for a solution to the same problem every time it arises. Although habit reduces selective acts to automatic behavior, habitual acts are no less motivated than are self-conscious, willed movements. By repeated automatic performance habitual acts do not remain in the foreground of thought and perception but recede into the unobserved, unconscious components of more complex acts. Habitual acts are the mortar of complex motivated acts, and motivated acts themselves are the brick wall built within the scaffolding of responsible action.

An *act* is merely a cluster of movements until a meaning is assigned to it. Since a "voluntary" act means nothing to an external observer, its meaning depends entirely upon what an internal observer reports about his own action. From this viewpoint, therefore, a voluntary act means, "I had a purpose in mind when I did it"; a habitual act means, "That was not my main purpose in doing it"; and an incorrect act means, "That was not at all my purpose." The distinction between these acts depends upon intention, not volition. For example, were a man to dial a telephone number at random, without any apparent pattern, an observer could conclude that his purpose was amusement, and not that he was expecting to talk to anyone in particular. If, however, his dialing followed a pattern, the observer could then assume that it had a purpose (P_1). When performed in this way, "dialing" would be the means appropriate for P_1, which could be "talking to X." However, unless the total motivated act of "dialing in order to speak to X" had been fully consummated by only saying "Hello" to X, P_1 would now become an appropriate means for P_2, which could be "getting information about Y." As successive purposes snowball into a complex motivated act in order to fulfill a more or less remote purpose (P_n), each preceding act becomes an inconspicuous act, both habitual and skillful, and a subsidiary part of the total act, whatever its ultimate purpose.

The penultimate acts that are performed in order to effect a total act are usually termed *ego functions*. To have a certain skill, or competence, is not the same as performing a skillful act, but one is necessary for the other. An ego function is like "having a skill" or an available capacity to carry out an intended act competently. An obvious ambiguity in current psychoanalytic ego psychology is that sometimes an ego function is like "having a skill," but sometimes it refers to a skillful act. Because of this ambiguity, some ego functions, like "identification" and "repression," seem to have achieved a kind of Olympian autonomy, while others are held in readiness for appropriate tasks. An ego function is not an established structure but a hypothetical set of acts, joined together according to the serial and hierarchical purposes assigned to them.

If we can admit that when we call some acts voluntary we mean nothing more than "having a purpose in mind," and that "purpose" refers to an intent, and not to a special capacity, what meanings can be given to other, related qualities of internal experience, such as *willed movements, choice,* and *will?*

The division of the central nervous system into "voluntary" and "autonomic" is an antiquated fallacy. It came about by arbitrarily superimposing speculative theories of psychology upon anatomical areas. The so-called voluntary nervous system is not predicated on systematic observation but on dubious inferences. Nevertheless, the case for substantiating choice and willed movements seems more plausible than that for will. Choice and willed movements imply only that there is a functional capability — skill and discrimination — to act upon different alternatives. The concept of will implies the reality of a special function to carry out the act of willing.

Choice and willed movements are entirely psychological concepts. Although pyramidal and extrapyramidal cell clusters enter into an act of will, as Walshe [138] pointed out, willed movements do not seem to be the specific function of any part of the cerebral cortex. Denny-Brown [33] defined a voluntary act as a product of learning how to use subcortical reflex apparatuses. However, this is a skill found in any learned behavior and discriminatory act. Neurological information, in other words, tells us only what James observed years ago — that will is whatever we do, just before we do it.

Reality sense alone takes choice and willed movements out of the domain of surmise and conjecture. Although their antecedent processes are obscure, choice and willed movements are the perceptive and effective components of those motivated acts that require both clear intention and consummate skill. The human capacity to expand the range of purposeful acts is also beyond surmise; every technical advance testifies to this. But, in addition to choice and willed movements, other kinds of ego functions are required. We can choose within limits, and perform skillfully up to a point, but further progress cannot be attributed to a mythical ego function called will. Contrary to popular opinion, willing is not a separate function but a negative phenomenon. Like the phenomenon of fatigue, willing tends to occur when, in pursuit of an assigned purpose, our choice, control, and skill approach a limit.

Sermons and lectures exhorting people to use "will power" may help them to avoid irresponsible acts — but not for long. In fact, whenever will is invoked in order to buttress a faltering act, it is an indirect announcement that capitulation or collapse is about to take place. If a man wants to eat and is convinced that eating is good for him, he does not call upon his will. However, if he is averse to eating and yet knows he ought to keep up his nutrition, his faltering wish to eat may be temporarily bolstered by willing himself to eat.

The sense of willing appears only when there is conflict between two antithetical acts. Because the stronger act needs no booster, willing seems always to be on the weaker side. Actually, willing serves the purpose of "counter-willing" the consummation of an antithetical act, or the failure of a purposeful act. It does not resolve conflict, nor does it delay failure for long. Counter-willing is, therefore, a sign of *waning* responsibility. By the time the patient becomes aware that he is about to lose control of what he wants to do, he has already recognized that skill and choice are also dwindling. His responsible aims are even more remote and have been replaced by only a modest wish to avoid an imminent disaster. His ego ideal can now be visualized only from the *outside perspective* of diminished strength. Since counter-willing requires no particular skill or competence, it is a phenomenon closer to compulsive behavior than to responsible conduct.

CHOICE AND COMPULSION

Compulsion and futile counter-willing are the opposite of choice and confident skill. Nevertheless, people frequently confuse choice and compulsion when, in order to maintain a rigorous responsibility, they emphasize trivial and vital acts equally. Compulsive acts are anti-responsibility. They do not *cause* something else to happen; they are done *because* something else has happened or might happen. Subjectively, to behave compulsively is to feel influenced. Because of their unspontaneous, stereotyped patterns, compulsive acts can often be predicted by an external observer. In fact, even from the inside, the victim himself may feel like an external observer who is unable to influence the inevitable pattern of events but can only stand by and foretell what will happen. By so doing, he underscores his existential helplessness to be anything but a highly conventional categorical unit, controlled by a universe that permits no choice.

In contrast to compulsion, *choice* is essential to responsible acts because it combines cause and value with discriminatory fulfillment. Acts of choice are, for the most part, unique, differentiated, skillful acts which cannot be regularly predicted by an external observer — they seem to occur at random. In a sense, choice in human acts is like chance in natural events; they baffle prediction and defy categorical rules. Choice and chance are contrary to a compulsive universe where everything is ordered and people cannot be aberrant exceptions. There is no place for choice, chance, and counter-control in such a world and, hence, no place for responsibility.

COUNTER-WILLING AND DESPAIR

It is never enough only to profess responsibility. Even in the course of faltering and in the face of despair, responsibility demands responsible acts. Anguish and anxiety can spur a person on to one last lunge toward affirmation and responsibility. Like counter-willing, despair can produce a momentary illusion of redemptive triumph but, in itself, has no authentic healing significance. Nevertheless, periods of crisis and conflict can summon forth latent ego functions which circumstances have permitted to slumber. These fresh functions may generate new strength. By contrast to this self-enriching hypothesis, those who call upon a spurious external source of strength when none exists, inside or outside, betray responsibility.

If very little of the foregoing discussion resembles psychoanalysis as it is usually presented, be reminded that psychoanalysis tries to recognize the authenticity, or responsibility, of man as he is, not as philosophers and theologians wish he were. Ideals are the narcissism of superego, and responsible acts require fulfillment, not endless renunciation. In fact, because it is a common factor of many different motivated acts, the sense of responsibility modulates the abrupt transition between reality sense and the sense of time. If reality sense is at its height when motivation is strong and fulfillment is at a minimum, responsible acts carry the burden of reality, even when there is nowhere to go. Like a pair of tight shoes, "principles" are worn by some people for appearance rather than for practical use. When a man turns away from conflict and seeks to follow values which are only compulsive opposites of his primal fears, he will find, not responsibility, but what counter-willing has tried to avoid — annihilation.

Conflict and Responsibility

Just as there are unnoticed muscle movements that silently contribute to a single motor act, there are also levels and sequences of subsidiary motivated acts that share in the fulfillment of any final act. Fluctuations of meanings and emotions accompanying these acts join with endless networks of wishes and fears, and with peripheral and subliminal perceptions, to be recorded within the same instant of time and to exert a creative influence. These events can barely be adumbrated with the natural language at our disposal. How, then, can we understand those pyramided acts which fuse into responsible acts and, at times of stress, into emotional conflict?

In an earlier section (Chapter 5, p. 131) the inner experience of conflict was attributed to two strong appetites that have incompatible consummations, neither of which can be satisfied without exacting pain, fear, guilt, or some other emotional penalty. This is, of course, an oversimplified explanation of conflict. Although psychoanalysis has taken the problems of conflict upon itself, it cannot be dogmatic about the inner structure of conflict [101]. The physiological and psychological factors that determine the intensity of emotion, or even the specific quality of an emotion, are largely unknown; we can only guess why conflicts spring up or subside.

By "two strong appetites that have incompatible consummations" we mean that the intended purposes of two mutually inconsistent acts fall within the same context. This, too, from the existential viewpoint, is an abstraction. It is like singling out a large tree in a forest to represent the flora of the whole community. Although the tree may be a prominent part of the forest, its selection can be almost arbitrarily influenced by personal preference, or by knowledge about only trees, instead of about plants and shrubs as well. Psychoanalysis recognizes that to single out one set of acts, because it is particularly relevant for a specific purpose, and then to single out another set of acts, whose collective purpose is incompatible with the purpose of the first set of acts, is a precarious intellectual enterprise. Even under rigorous logical conditions, the final choice often seems to be determined by factors beyond the data themselves. Our knowledge of conflict is so limited that it is better to work backwards from the *fact of being* in conflict than to conjecture about metapsychological motives. Whenever this method is conscientiously practiced, using every cue and clue that clinical experience makes available, we find that the components of conflict are a tangle of wishes and fears.

Many wishes and fears swirl about in everyone's mind, each with an urgency of its own. Some combinations facilitate each other, while others are mutually incompatible. How separate acts, or sets of acts, representing different wishes and fears assist or interfere with one another, so that their combined result is mutual self-regulation or vectorial deviation, is a problem for the first and second systems of cybernetics [91], not for psychoanalysis. However, establishing a terminological distinction can make it somewhat easier to formulate conflict from the psychoanalytic viewpoint.

CONCORDANCE AND DISCORDANCE

When the success of one act — actually, a set of related acts — insures the consummation of still another intended act or forestalls a fear, the combination of such acts is called *concordant*. When the success of one act frustrates an equally imperative intended act or undermines a defense against a fear, or even when two potential acts vie for consummation, this combination of acts is called *discordant*. Psychoanalysis is not always able to disarticulate the wishes and fears that result sometimes in concordant and at other times in discordant purposes, but this is its aim. The method of *free association* is a strategic attempt to attenuate conscious selection and discrimination, so that different potential acts which impel toward the same desired objective and away from a dreaded fate may be more readily detected. Among the cues and clues to conflict none are more reliable than knowledge of how a patient's ego ideal has suffered and how he expects to correct this discordance between his image of himself and his idealized image of what he ought to be.

Everyone puts his distinctive stamp upon what he does.

Responsibility and Reality Sense

When a person has a sense of reality for his own worth, there is concordance between what he does and what he wants to do. The *sense of responsibility* is, therefore, produced by concordance between motivated acts and responsible acts. In contrast, when he is unable to act, or to choose to act, without violating his ego ideal, this discordance between motivated acts and responsible acts produces the *sense of conflict*. The conclusive factor in understanding conduct as a whole is not the decision between choice and necessity, free will and determinism, or even between compliant and culpable behavior; it is the factor of concordant or discordant acts.

An act may feel wholly natural and spontaneous, but if it violates the ego ideal it will feel worthless or degrading. Another act may be highly rewarded by society, but unless it conforms with the ego ideal it will seem like a hypocritical act of empty obedience. Because our feeling that we have choice is a mark of responsible conduct, the latitude of our choices is a sign of concordance. Acts of concordance may be gathered from sources that are longitudinal or vertical — longitudinal through a consistent series of mutually motivated acts in chronological time; vertical through stratified acts in existential time. Cause without choice is freedom without control, but control with neither freedom nor choice is compulsion, not concordance.

Ego defenses — acts that are performed to insure the success of other acts — not only foster concordance but resolve discordance. Patients do not engage in defensive struggles simply to avoid a disaster; they are trying to correct an impaired ego image and, in the presence of conflict, to muster concordant action. In attempting to understand, an analyst will put the following questions to himself: What does this patient need or do in order to feel in charge of himself? If he could choose, how would he change his image of himself? How would it differ from his present self-image? What has interfered with his capacity to choose, or to act, within his image of responsibility? What kinds of compulsion have taken over his concordance?

Every concordance of acts, within the ego ideal, binds motives and inclinations together. When potential acts are discordant, choice is impeded, compulsions and other stereotyped behavior take over, and still other symptoms of neurosis appear. Symptoms are ways to maintain concordance and responsibility and to reduce discordance, even though, because choice is impaired, it is necessary to use less differentiated means. Accordingly, some avoidances will fortify wishes that, in an earlier, healthier state, would have been restrained, and some wishes will become manifest as avoidances and fears. Phobias, for example, may arise in one situation because of "philias" in another. Furthermore, arrested and anachronistic conflicts may be reignited during conflict. As consciousness is diverted from the pragmatic present to some other phase of existence, wholly adventitious issues may force themselves into the foreground to alter images of discordance into other kinds of responsible images and different kinds of symptoms. These are the so-called reversals, displacements, projections, and other secondary changes.

A "precipitating event" that seemingly elicits conflict can cause discordance by adversely influencing more or less constant, characteristic ways of responding to reality. These typical responses to reality maintain a concordant and relatively harmonious attitude toward the capacity to choose and contend with problems as they arise. If the typical responses are ineffective, they are called predisposing factors. Since what is real is not necessarily true, a highly condensed, filtered view of reality, as seen through the lens of discordance, may be the only means a patient has to reconcile opposites, reclaim responsibility, and restore concordance.

Strategies of the superego operate from a broader base of freedom and choice than do symptoms and stereotypes. These strategies delineate areas in which responsible conduct is possible, without necessarily seeking to avoid transgression by imposing an over-control. As a result, fulfillment of responsibility carries the same feeling of triumph, vindication, and renewed control that follows remission of conflict. Epileptic patients often feel unusually optimistic, composed, even invigorated, after a seizure. Many women who have been unsure of their femininity feel at their best during pregnancy. It is possible that part of this sense of freedom is a reassurance born of reaffirmed control and concordance.

This may, however, be a deceptive control. Some suicidal patients are driven to play Russian roulette with their lives time and time again, only because they have been persuaded, by repeated survival and by the elation that accompanies renewed control, not to believe in the reality of death.

LEGAL RESPONSIBILITY

When a patient is at an impasse of discordant acts, when whatever he does imposes suffering, he is not simply *in* conflict — he *is* conflict. Similarly, responsible man does not simply *have* freedom — he *is* freedom. The inner authenticity, inherent in any ego ideal that is worth seeking, is altogether different from the scrupulous conscience. Because the purpose of responsible conduct is to expand the field of concordant acts by means of authentic choices, the narrow, compulsive conscience is quite the opposite of freedom. A man who discriminates against other superego values in himself, and surrenders to one because of a guilty conscience, is often no more responsible than the man who has ignored entirely the sanctions of his superego. Responsible man, because of his freedom, has a sense of reality for both practical and ideal aims; because he can choose, he can compromise between them [93]. His ego ideal works for him, not against him. He is certainly not just the legendary "salt of the earth," who must operate within the least common denominator of social sanction. He is even further removed from the prototype hero-criminal, who, from the viewpoint of ordinary citizens, at least, often seems to be rewarded for defying laws, values, and conventions. The ordinary criminal is more like a paranoid psychotic who is pursued by phantoms of highly conventional forces. Most offenders, it would seem, instead of being heroes or trying to be free, responsible spirits with values of their own, are simply trying to be respectable by illegal means, according to their own extremely conventional standards.

Inevitably, discussions about responsibility [99] revert to what is only a special problem — legal responsibility [2]. Psychoanalysis cannot decide for the courts, judging that this or that prisoner knew right from wrong when he broke the law. Nor can it judge whether or not a particular infraction is a "product of mental disease." The hybrid concept of "partial responsibility," like partial pregnancy, is not helpful from anyone's point of view.

Legal responsibility is an order of experience entirely different from existential responsibility. It emphasizes the act, not the one who acts, because the law assumes that responsible men have acceptable motives which are always under conscious and competent control. Legal responsibility is purely practical; it asks only that men refrain from violating the law — the least common denominator of social sanction.

In some situations, of course, reality testing is so impaired by illness that skillful acts cannot be performed within an appropriate order of conduct [92]. The external observer, who represents reality testing, concludes that if a skillful and appropriate act is possible it is also law-abiding. However, a patient with a so-called mental illness may be alert and able to behave skillfully in many situations. If the patient breaks the law, the external observer then decides that the violation is the result of responsible choice. This predicament can be reduced to a somewhat paradoxical dictum: A man is deemed responsible for a faulty motive when his act is carried out skillfully but is exempted when his capacity to perform skillfully is impaired, however faulty his motive.

What psychoanalysis cannot easily do for itself it can scarcely do for the courts. Its problem is to distinguish between the motive and the means of carrying it out. But this has only a tangential relevance to the ego ideal of subjective responsibility. Knowledge of unconscious factors is useful clinically but does not contribute substantially to the adjudicative process. Questions about legal responsibility refer mainly to objective responsibility — how society should judge acts that violate its codes, and what shall be done with the violator. These questions concern culpability and reality testing; they impinge only slightly upon reality sense.

PUNISHMENT

Nevertheless, there is an existential attitude toward lawbreakers, although it is based upon different questions. These questions, perhaps unfamiliar, are no less practical, in spite of the fact that they refer to superego strategies on a society-wide scale. They do not ask, for example, "What lawbreakers shall be punished?" but "Why is punishment necessary?" and "Who benefits from punishment?"

Punishment goes beyond the quarantine, or isolation, that society imposes upon those who are unable or incompetent to act within an expected range of behavior. It is a way to retaliate — a style of testing reality — against those who violate society's codes. The purpose of punishment, according to commonly held theories, is (1) to seek revenge, (2) to prevent further violations by instilling fear, (3) to protect both victims and violators by exacting some kind of penalty, and (4) to arouse a positive wish to obey the law. These aims overlap, and they go beyond mere retribution or social utility. Whether punishment entails vindictive retaliation or visionary rehabilitation, its collective purpose is clear: *Society retaliates against its offenders in order to forgive them.*

If this proposal is true, then punishment is as necessary for the victim of the violation as it is for the violator. It is a superego strategy — a measure that reaffirms responsibility in the victim, comparable to the effect of confession, sacrifice, or undoing — which restores responsibility to the violator. The Golden Rule and the Talion Principle are based upon similar precepts, which also are superego strategies. Their common theme is "like deserves like"; their common strategy is "retaliation in kind." There is a difference, of course. The Golden Rule is prompted by fear of retaliation, before the fact. The Talion Principle endorses retaliation, after the fact. Both are designed to preserve the responsible image of both the victim and the violator.

It is sometimes held that, because punishment ought to be reserved for the guilty, punishment is necessary in order to make offenders feel guilty. This is a semantic absurdity; it confuses an extrinsic judgment that punishment is deserved with an intrinsic conviction that punishment is deserved. Furthermore, punishment will not produce remorse in a person who already feels none. In fact, punishing a violator will often relieve his guilt feelings. In this situation, also, the purpose of punishment is largely to relieve the feelings of the victim or potential victims. It is usually difficult to tolerate offenders who feel no guilt and who evidently transgress accepted codes with impunity. The aim of retaliation, however, is not to generate guilt but to *create conflict* in the offender and to *resolve* it in the retaliator. In this way the aberrant act can be brought under the influence of conventional rules, or codes of conformity. The violator will then, presumably, follow some sanctioned superego strategy, and the victim will be able to forgive him. When we forgive an offender who has victimized us, we resolve our own conflict — that general conflict of wishes and fears represented by the precepts of the Golden Rule and the Talion Principle.

Therefore, no one can forgive for the victim; the decision to punish, to isolate, or to absolve is his prerogative. From the existential point of view, a courtroom judge is a prototype-victim who exacts the conditions for pardon of the offender. However, in doing so, he restores his own concordance. There is a common rootstock for restoration of concordance, retaliation in kind, resolution of conflict, and renewal of responsible conduct, but this does not mean that any one of these is equivalent to any other. The scales of psychological justice are poised between many kinds of alternatives, and it is not always necessary to punish in order to forgive. This is only one strategy, perhaps not even a desirable strategy, which human beings use to maintain a balance between what they do and what is demanded of them. Justice may ask, "Who deserves punishment?" Responsibility will pause before asking, "Who shall administer justice?"

THE EXISTENTIAL EVENT

Anything that abruptly reveals a specific orientation toward existence or confronts us with the necessity for decision is an *existential event*. It is not just another incident in the symbolized world of objects, people, and things (see Fig. 2, p. 42), nor is it some vivid cluster of affective equivalents. Compared with the fragmentary perspectives and deceptive generalizations that usually represent both conflict and responsibility, the typical existential event is an elusive quarry. Yet this is the object of the psychoanalyst's quest.

Responsibility and Reality Sense

When deciding what to do, or when judging the significance of what others do, man necessarily becomes involved with existence. Whether or not these involvements are typical existential events, they are surely the result of working within the limits of human illusion and fallibility and of taking responsibility for what is thought or done about some sector of reality. The giddy despair that sometimes overtakes chronic multiple sclerosis patients may lead them abruptly to deny their incapacity, to fabricate plans beyond practicality, and to declare themselves on the threshold of a new life. This is one kind of existential event. When a philanthropist one day realizes that he has generously supported many worthy and distant causes primarily to keep them at a distance, this, too, is an existential event. Existential events are unsparing truths, or affirmations of reality which reveal themselves by suddenly overthrowing a *stereotype*. Thus, *the existential event is an integer of reality sense, occurring in the here-and-now but encompassing an entire state of being.*

The long catenary that began with the existential attitude, the human conditional, and the meaning of reality sense has now ended with the core meaning of responsibility and conflict. Not only is psychoanalysis suspended between these poles, but the existential core of analysis holds their intervening links together. What, then, can be said about the open span between reality sense, grounded in organic processes, and responsibility, predicated upon choice, control, and idealized conduct?

The abstract purpose of reality sense and responsibility is to justify the ontological acceptance. In the immediacy of the present, however, their palpable purpose is to close the gap between them and to encircle existential events completely. Yet, like snatching at a bubble, packaging a principle, or, for that matter, understanding human nature, it is an objective that is doomed to fail — and *ought* to fail! No one can expect to capture existence within an airtight enclosure of existential events. Given a few scattered glimpses, we can, at best, only hope for a more or less authentic approximation between reality sense and responsibility.

The professional preoccupation of the psychoanalyst, the next chapter will show, is to confront the special existential events that are called *clinical* and *paraclinical syndromes*. But he cannot do it unless he first recognizes the kinds of existential events in which he himself is revealed and then acknowledges that his own involvements require him to walk a tightrope between what has organic meaning and what is meaningless extinction.

8. Existential Events and Clinical Syndromes

THE EXISTENTIAL CORE is the central fact of psychoanalysis; everything else is superstructure, designed to contain and explain the various events that emerge from that core. Inevitably, we are immersed in our own existence. Theories and concepts are concocted in order to lift ourselves out of the unformulated flux of experience. To maintain any other view is like confusing a topographical map with a continent. The basic concern of psychoanalysis is to assign meaning to being, but there is a vast domain of experience that separates the existential core from psychoanalytic theory. Therefore, I have introduced other ideas in order to mediate between these two extremes of meaning and being. These are the concepts of *organic meaning,* the diverse meanings of the *sense of reality* and *responsibility, intuition, affirmation* and *con-*

firmation, and so forth. I have also extended the meaning of still other concepts so that they can be articulated with more familiar psychoanalytic ideas.

Many problems remain. What, for example, is the relation between these theoretical principles and the mental disorders that the psychiatrist encounters? How can we forge a link between *existential events* — those private proceedings which affirm reality — and the various clinical syndromes with which psychoanalysis contends? How are the clinical syndromes related to the para-clinical syndromes that existentialists describe? By what means can the psychoanalyst, who must heed his own inner world before he can comprehend the acts and attitudes of others, manage to achieve dispassionate objectivity in his judgments of clinical events?

In this final chapter, these and other pertinent problems cannot be exhaustively investigated. Instead, the chapter will present a *prospectus* for future clinical application of the concepts already developed. The guiding principles, many of which may be inferred from preceding chapters, include these four: (1) Opposite ideas define each other, and exceptions evoke rules. (2) The existential event is the irreducible affirmation and basic unit of both reality sense and organic meaning. (3) Conflict consists of antithetical affects, paradoxical ideas, and incompatible acts. (4) Clinical and paraclinical syndromes are polarized versions of different existential events, particularly when each event is viewed from the perspective of one or another personal dimension.

These somewhat stark propositions will be illustrated, first, by the existential event of *being sick* — as opposed to *being responsible.* Being sick is an event which is familiar to physicians and psychiatrists because it presents itself at different times and in different forms as disease, crisis, and conflict. The second illustration is *primary anxiety,* an existential event which is familiar to mankind as a whole. Among several possible antithetical alternatives, the concepts of *eros* and *agape* will illustrate how one existential event leads to affirmation of its opposite. As a third illustration, the antithetical sentiments of *hope* and *despair,* which characteristically follow the course of any motivated act, will be described. Finally, because the psychodynamic processes of *denial* and *repression* participate in concordant as well as discordant acts, it will be shown how they reinforce hope and forestall despair in some instances but lead to annihilation and absurdity in others.

Psychoanalysis understands that external observations alone will not disclose the existential events that are at the core of subjective experience. The familiar psychiatric division of mental events into thought, emotion, and action is, admittedly, an arbitrary distinction based upon verbal reports, inferences, and external observations. At best, it is confined to secondary and peripheral manifestations of inner events. Although these outward acts and inner events take place before we have any scientific thoughts about them, existential events — primary affirmations of reality — precede them both. The various organic meanings which arise from existential events, and which are assigned to still other events, enable us to formulate psychodynamic principles to account for the distinctive forms in which clinical and paraclinical syndromes appear.

The paradoxes of opposing forces that bring events together and harmonious forces that tear them apart have been recognized by mankind throughout its history. Whether these antithetical forces and forms are called syndromes, principles, traditions, or truths, or whether they present themselves in polarities between life and death, love and hate, spirit and substance, good and evil, hope and despair, or sick and responsible, will depend upon the particular way in which we perceive the existential events and mental states that produce them. Whatever protean form conflict assumes, it, too, is characterized by a feeling of being hopelessly suspended between incompatible alternatives, paradoxical ideas, and antithetical affects. We do not know how conflict is relieved and hopeful enthusiasm for living is restored, but there is neither relief of painful emotion nor resolution of conflict without prolonged, antecedent oscillation between one form of polarized experience and another. Successfully or not, people try to solve problems of all kinds, as well as conflicts, by trial-and-error performance of whatever alternative acts may be suggested by different polarities [106b]. Organic meaning itself cannot be made explicit by definitions. It is the product of antitheses that mutually define each other. This is an important distinction between organic and objective forms of meaning. Because truth is such an evanescent entity, no formula, however acceptable and useful, does more than tolerate our ignorance; and ignorance itself means that we have an incomplete knowledge of antitheses.

Just as an object can be more accurately located in three dimensions than in one, existential events can be defined more comprehensively by locating them in different personal dimensions. These personal dimensions, as already described, include the intrapersonal, interpersonal, and impersonal, and, to some extent, the temporal dimension.

Unlike the organs and objects that scientific disciplines study and define, and unlike the physical disabilities and incapacities that are detected by more or less direct inspection of impersonal data, mental states must be comprehended, for the most part, through information acquired primarily by means of verbal reports. Because verbal reports are expressed in natural language instead of scientific notation, they are notoriously imprecise and deceptive. In the present state of technology, the meaning and content of mental states are largely inferential. Even with the most pristine intuitions to illuminate the way, so-called mental states cannot be systematically comprehended, communicated, or catalogued. We must recognize that the *meaning* of each mental state will often vary according to the perspective and personal dimension of the observer. Since we are dealing with particular versions of organic meaning, each mental state may be thought of as a *polarization* of some existential event.

Being Sick and Being Responsible

The process of polarization in mental states can be illustrated by the existential event which most patients present: *being sick*. In the impersonal dimension, being sick means to have a disease. In the interpersonal dimension, being sick signifies a *crisis*. In the intrapersonal dimension, being sick is a result of *conflict*. To have a disease is a unidimensional way of being sick. It means that mental states have been impersonalized according to the organic disability and incapacity with which they are associated. For example, a mental state associated with cerebral arteriosclerosis may be characterized by impaired retention of recently acquired information and, paradoxically, by elaboration of the details of remote events. From a disease-oriented viewpoint this aspect of the mental state will be described as "memory loss" and "perseveration." However, having an impersonal disease of any kind may also impair the way a patient customarily contends with reality and, in consequence, can interfere with his effective operation as a person in society. Even if his physical condition quickly returns to normal, being sick may provoke an interpersonal crisis and a persistent, unresolved intrapersonal conflict.

DISEASE, CRISIS, AND CONFLICT PERSPECTIVES

Disease, crisis, and conflict are not merely transmuted forms of each other; they are three distinct ways of being sick [140d]. It is fallacious to believe that ultimately one can be reduced to another. Their respective aims differ; their associated disabilities differ; and their characteristic mental states, within the existential event of being sick, also differ. From a disease perspective, a sick person's wish is to survive for survival's sake, and to be relieved of pain. From a crisis perspective, a sick person's aim is to meet the challenge of a decisive moment — a confrontation from which he will emerge with a different image of the world and of his place in it. The crises brought about by illness will vary from patient to patient, even though each patient ostensibly has the same disease. Hence, what often seems to one person to be a significant crisis, leading to a major victory or defeat, may be only a casual incident to another person, whose ego ideal and standards of performance are not so drastically impaired by illness. The crisis of impending permanent disability from anatomically similar diseases may produce a far different mental state in a father with a large family and small income than in an affluent bachelor.

Quite apart from the special crises and decisive moments of individual patients, there are transition periods in everyone's development which regularly present more or less similar problems. Appropriately enough, these are called "identity crises" [40a] because the individual is expected to change his identity in the course of solving the unique problems of that period. Inasmuch as identity crises are not, in themselves, signs of being sick, they are usually interpreted from the interpersonal viewpoint. Except when there is "identity diffusion," intrapersonal and impersonal dimensions are given far less emphasis.

From a conflict perspective, a patient's wish is that his sense of autonomous responsibility be restored, so that he can once more achieve a measure of cause and control over what he does and what his ego ideal requires. Although psychoanalysis is mainly concerned with the conflict perspective, the existential core of psychoanalysis is by no means restricted to the existential event of being sick. The existential core pertains to many kinds of conflicts and clinical syndromes and to many varieties of conflict-free affirmations of reality, including responsible conduct. Among these different existential events are the problematic states of consciousness and the aberrant acts that existentialists describe by such terms as *absurdity, annihilation, metaphysical anxiety, anguish, despair, loneliness*, and so forth. Since what they refer to are evidently different polarized views of more familiar mental states, and are not necessarily the mental states found in *psychopathological syndromes*, these events can be called *paraclinical syndromes*.

MEANINGS OF SICKNESS

Because the existential event *being sick* has equivalents in each dimension, it has several antithetical meanings. The antithesis of sickness is not physical health alone, nor does sickness negate only physical health. The antithetical meaning which helps to define sickness most comprehensively is responsibility. Sick people are usually exempted from responsibility by the law, but, aside from this legal sense, the meaning of being sick is also judged, to a great extent, by the degree to which patients have lost their perceptive clarity, thought capacity, and ability to perform purposeful tasks. The meaning of being disabled includes an awesome recognition that organs and body parts are no longer inconspicuous, compliant instruments that carry out their owner's intentions. Instead, the affected parts become alien and alienated objects, with a distinct existence — indeed, an autonomy — of their own. The sick person cannot fulfill the mandates to which his native acceptances and ego ideal have committed him. As sickness alters his image of excellence and efficiency, his self-expectations are gradually reduced to the narrowed performance of visceral functions and acquisition of the necessities of animal solace. Because he is unable to bring about significant changes in his familiar world, his sense of being able to cause and control is transformed into an antithetical sense of being acted upon by impersonal forces, interpersonal displacements, and intrapersonal anguish.

In much the same sense that anyone in conflict is prone to feel as if he were only that conflict, sickness tends to take over the patient's entire existence. In the course of many progressive, unremitting, and demoralizing sicknesses, the dignity and privacy of *being responsible* is transmogrified into bare existence and impersonal survival. The diversified mental states characteristic of the intrapersonal and interpersonal dimensions are reduced to whatever their equivalents are in the impersonal dimension. The sick person then becomes an object, to be manipulated by forces beyond comprehension and control. When this happens, motivated acts do not press for fulfillment, the inner spur to achievement becomes blunt, and the external world offers neither a residue of incentive nor a source of consolation.

Camus's account [23b] of the task of Sisyphus is not substantially different from the everyday life of many patients who must constantly reaffirm their strength against impediments within themselves. The day-by-day reckoning of sickness is determined by the way it prevents healthy concordant conduct. The least part of the healing function of medicine is to restore only physical competence, without necessarily reinstating purposeful behavior; the largest — and most laudable — part is to help replenish and encourage the sense of being responsible. This aim is often overlooked because doctors, too, suffer from their own polarizations. As a result, one version of organic meaning, one kind of objective meaning, and one polarity of sickness are emphasized while the others are ignored or are assumed to be self-corrective. Physicians cannot become so absorbed with visceral disorders that they ignore what people do with their healthy organs and functions, nor can psychoanalysts concentrate so exclusively upon skewed intrapersonal perspectives that they overlook the manifold inter-personal and impersonal forces that bear down upon any member of our society.

Antithetical Affect

Most of the objective principles that determine mental states are still to be discovered; there is no standard nosology of clinical syndromes, nor is there a universal nomenclature for psychiatric disorders. Furthermore, there is no satisfactory analytic method that can designate and describe even the unambiguously distinct conflicts and crises of either inner experience or external observa-tion. Part of this almost incredible situation may be attributed to the tendency to confuse organic meaning with objective meaning and, therefore, to force meanings of mental events into objective, categorical molds. Another part results from a failure to appre-ciate the process of polarization and its contribution to organic meaning. The inner antithesis between one meaning and another helps to interpret different motivated acts and to qualify different mental states. Without the dialectic of opposite meanings, we could neither recognize the distinction between what is real and what is true nor perceive the discrepancy between a rule and its exception.

The meaning of conflict, it is true, often begins with a conflict of meaning, and paradoxes are reliable ways to detect nearby con-flicts. But long before incompatible wishes and fears, or even paradoxical ideas, are revealed, a patient in conflict can be tenta-tively recognized by his laboring affect and inappropriate emo-tion. As a rule, the external observer allows fairly generous limits of emotional quality and intensity in any particular situation, just as one individual characteristically differs from another. Although it is difficult to state accurately what makes one emotion "appro-priate" and another "inappropriate," psychiatric observers accept the validity of such distinctions, noticing exceptions to the estab-lished, albeit arbitrary, range of acceptable responses. However, psychiatrists must assume that every emotional response is appro-priate in some context or other.

Because emotions primarily designate highly transitory, subjective experience, they have organic meaning, not objective meaning. The wide diversity of emotions in almost any particular situation is another indication that conventional language is a manifestly inadequate vehicle for organic meaning, just as a vapor cannot be carried in an uncovered pail. To speak of different "kinds" of emotion is a concession to objective meaning because the difference between one emotion and another is determined by internal polarizations instead of by innate categorical distinctions. Therefore, only at more or less extreme moments, when a definitive action is either called for or suppressed, does just one kind of emotion prevail. It is wholly possible to feel worried, angry, jealous, sympathetic, and depressed at approximately the same time. Even to use these terms is somewhat "inappropriate," for they refer to unmodulated emotional extremes. After all, "emotion" is only the general direction taken by several different inclinations to action. We habitually judge emotions to be transient only because we assume that their evocative situations are fixed and firmly defined. But according to the principle of affective equivalence, people may feel the same way toward different objects and situations, and according to the principle of the relativity of the real, they may at different times seem to have opposite feelings toward the same object and situation. Ideas are defined in order to be separated, like tangible objects; emotions are like gases — they suffuse the moments in which they confluently occur. There is no reason to conclude that one, and only one, affect permeates the present. It is consistent with what we understand about reality sense and its distribution in libidinal fields to postulate that, in its most primitive sense, organic meaning is the resultant of scattered trends and assorted affects.

How incompatible truths conceal conflict and how, unavoidably and with almost fateful necessity, antagonistic inclinations to act bring about pain, suffering, and anxiety in the act of fulfillment have already been described as distinctive clues to conflict (Chapter 7, p. 207). Similarly, antithetical affect — affect which is precisely inappropriate for the expected response in a familiar situation — is an unmistakable indication of latent conflict. Not only will antithetical affect disclose conflict, but it will also be the appropriate affect for the antithetical version of a manifest event. Thus antithetical affect, like exceptions that evoke rules, offers hints about the underlying organic meaning of otherwise objective events. Because it has this important psychodynamic significance, the spontaneous expression and deliberate evocation of antithetical affect are highly useful in both diagnosis and treatment of emotional disorders.

Although psychoanalysts are as alert to antithetical affect as they are to paradox, there is a difference in the way affects can be investigated and understood. Patients may readily recognize paradoxical ideas and, when confronted with their inconsistencies, will usually have some reasonable, if unconvincing, explanation. While the explanations are frequently rationalizations, direct confrontation with incompatible ideas is a familiar psychotherapeutic device which at least calls forth an effort to understand. In contrast, because a convincing emotion usually seems quite appropriate from the inside, few people recognize or can account for a sentiment that is opposite from what is usually expected unless, of course, they are confronted with an extreme situation in which the antithetical affect is alarming. For example, sudden panic in a familiar setting that previously presented no problem may be an alarming and mystifying aberrant fact that causes a patient to avoid similar situations thereafter, and even to seek psychiatric treatment. On the other hand, the same patient may repeatedly risk his life in manifestly dangerous adventure, perhaps relishing the thrill that narrow escapes and courageous acts generate. Both situations are characterized by antithetical affects.

Except in extreme situations, people are more inclined to legitimize their affects than to rationalize their ideas. An antithetical affect is a spontaneous clue to reality sense and therefore is more readily accepted than is evidence of its incongruity. What appears on the surface, however, is not necessarily superficial; overt acts and attitudes may only be manifestations of whatever side of conflict is most concordant with the ego ideal. Even when a patient volunteers an appraisal of how he feels, it is usually so saturated with a wish to make his feelings appropriate that the report is hardly trustworthy. For example, a person who insists that he feels "hostility" toward someone does not describe his anger; he indirectly tells us that he feels called upon to observe amenities in a situation where anger seems appropriate.

The particular form in which antithetical affect appears may be typical of certain syndromes. In some cases of conversion hysteria a patient's seeming indifference to disabling symptoms — blindness, paralysis, unlikely amnesia for highly disturbing events, and uncontrollable agitation about relatively neutral incidents — suggests to the psychiatrist that these antithetical affects are produced by excessive repression, and by displacement of affect appropriate to some unresolved problem. Analogously, when severely depressed or suicidal patients abruptly adopt a highly optimistic attitude inconsistent with the actual problem, the psychiatrist regards this as an ominous development. Inappropriate conviction that all is well, that problems no longer exist, is an affect and attitude more appropriate for an unformulated delusion than for a reliable appraisal. Spurred by a delusion of invulnerability, these patients will often consummate their attitude by a successful suicide.

PREVALENCE OF ANTITHETICAL AFFECT

Antithetical affects are more commonly met with in ordinary life than is usually recognized. Not only do obsessional characters show no concern about tragic events, and readily become enraged about trivia; many people are saddened by glad tidings, excited by the sufferings of others, regretful when misfortune is averted, and exhilarated by gallows humor. Freud was so impressed by the ubiquity of antithetical affects, reversals of meanings, transposition of objects — in general, by the polarities in mental life — that he originally called many clinical disorders "instinctual vicissitudes" [46g]. The permanent character trait called reaction formation is recognized by acts, affects, and attitudes which are socially acceptable antitheses of an original emotion. Ordinarily, most perceptive people are familiar with the special form of antithetical affect called ambivalence. They are also more or less accustomed to find fright associated with fascination, temptation preceding disgust, love disguised as hate, and tenderness concealing a wish to destroy.

The Existential Core of Psychoanalysis

Psychotherapists may elicit antithetical affect in order to relieve symptoms, suppress another kind of affect, and bring out a more appropriate, but unacknowledged, attitude toward a specific event. To ask a patient about his feelings may, in itself, modify those feelings. To insist that he feel any particular affect may either completely suppress that affect or bring about its antithesis, particularly when conflicting affects contend for recognition, and one or another is struggling against repression. It is a common observation that if a person is told in advance that he is about to hear a *very* funny story, if he laughs at all, his laugh will almost certainly be forced. Analogously, an effective way to control a patient's weeping is to urge him to cry still more, and when you tell someone that your next statement will make him angry, he usually responds cordially, without anger.

ANTITHETICAL ATTITUDE OF THE PSYCHIATRIST

Therapeutic interventions in many clinical syndromes may be effective because the psychiatrist adopts an attitude toward the patient and his problems which is completely unexpected, even antithetical to the conventional attitude that the patient assumes. Not only does the psychiatrist follow a seemingly paradoxical course of action, but his affect is altogether different from what the distressed patient has been accustomed to. Nevertheless, paradoxical or not, the appropriate therapeutic attitude may be closer to existential reality than is the more conventional, categorical position. For example, the psychiatrist does not become angry when insulted or attacked; he does not criticize patients for their shortcomings or rebuke them for misdeeds. He does not praise and he does not prod. His "antithetical affect" is part of his therapeutic attitude of impartial involvement. It enables him to confront the latent side of conflict that is not directly expressed by the patient and thus to reduce its intensity. While no psychiatrist knowingly accedes to a masochistic patient's plea for punishment, a doctor's natural compassion may lead him to sympathize with a patient who has suffered a serious loss or damaging defeat. Most deeply depressed patients are not helped by these expressions of well-intentioned but perfunctory sympathy. If, however, the psychiatrist withholds sympathy and, in some instances, asserts openly that the reason the patients feel so culpable is because they deserve punishment, and that they feel evil because they know how bad they really are, this paradoxical intervention is frequently beneficial. The doctor emphasizes, in as kindly and nonpunitive a fashion as possible, his conviction that, because only feelings of unmitigated worthlessness satisfy them, such feelings must be justified. Finally, when the psychiatrist refuses to relieve guilt, or to make futile attempts to encourage, the patient is forced to recognize for himself that he is not entirely to blame for his loss or defeat and that there is another side to his problem.

There are many analogous ways in which the psychiatrist exploits his antithetical attitude — in appropriate situations! Certain patients with psychic impotence are expressly forbidden to have sexual intercourse. Dissimulating patients who tell obvious lies are not challenged about the truth of their statements. Instead, their veracity is accepted so literally and punctiliously that the literal truth becomes de-emphasized in favor of the metaphorical truth. As a result, a less distorted account will sooner or later emerge. Negativistic patients are often frightened people who oppose the doctor, even though they know that cooperation would be in their best interests. Instead of insisting upon their cooperation, which actually demands that they yield uncritically and helplessly, the psychiatrist encourages them to resist still more, because he recognizes that their negativism contains all that remains of mastery and control. For instance, if these patients are obstinately silent, they may be advised not to speak until they are quite sure they want to.

Antithetical attitudes may also be expressed in interpretations that call attention to an antithetical affect which the patient does not recognize. An obsessional patient may become alarmed lest he act upon a destructive phantasy. It is altogether proper to point out that this phantasy is itself a protection against feelings he fears even more — tenderness and love. A similar paradoxical attitude or affect is adopted when the psychiatrist carefully becomes amiably aggressive, in order to contend with a particularly suspicious patient. Because paranoid patients anticipate chicanery, they are often reassured by an openly aggressive, but not belligerent, attitude because its opposite — tactful but wary diplomacy — may be correctly interpreted as the deception that the patients fear.

Primary Anxiety

Being sick is a fairly conventional existential event. Most people know that they feel distinctively different during an illness, although they may not be able to describe how they feel and may be unaware that disease, crisis, and conflict are three polarized versions of being sick. Existential events are mental states embodying an affirmation of reality that cannot be further reduced. In fact, existential events give rise to various organizations of ideas and observations which, collectively, become processes of one kind or another. It is characteristic of existential events to appear and reappear in different versions, and to be described in idioms appropriate to particular perspectives. Erikson [40c], for example, sees human ego identity developing through a series of crises, each of which entails changes in perspective. In turn, these perspectives determine the kinds of epigenetic processes that occur. Such processes have both longitudinal components in time and horizontal components in immediate experience, despite differences in the way events are interpreted. Thus, an existential event which a psychiatrist may call "depression" is "loneliness" to an existentialist. The overused term *security* refers to an existential event that is recognized and represented in widely divergent syndromes. The feeling of "desperation," to take still another example, presumably refers to an irreducible fact of experience, but it appears in so many different contexts that a "desperate man" may be one who is suicidal, at one extreme, or, at another extreme, a boy who has no date for the prom. Any particular version of an existential event is sharpened by being examined against a contrasting background, and the meaning of any syndrome is enhanced by being compared with its antitheses, of which it may have many.

Erikson [40] used the method of antitheses to elicit the meaning of successive psychosocial crises. His rubrics, such as autonomy vs. shame and doubt, identity and repudiation vs. identity diffusion, are not intended to define these crises precisely but to evoke, I believe, the meaning of typical existential events within each phase of transition. Mueller [100] has discussed the more metaphysical significance of opposites, and Anton [5] has analyzed their logical relationships.

The most pervasive polarity of all is that between *existence* and *extinction*. Others have termed this the polarity between Eros and Thanatos, life and death, meaning and absurdity, activity and annihilation, and so forth. Our immediate interest is in the irreducible *existential event* which underlies the polarity. This event, for example, causes us to acknowledge that death is inevitable and still to strive for unlimited survival. It prompts an existential question: How shall we find meaning for what we are when the sources of meaning — if they exist at all — are beyond our reach? Our yearning for care and concern is counterbalanced by an equally strong conviction that there is no source of meaning, care, reason, or concern beyond the frail limits of our own existence. When we seek ways to resolve this quandary, the quest for identity may become a search for an ideology, and this means, as a rule, that an adventure ends in a disaster. The way out of paradox then turns back upon itself; rubrics take the place of realities, and institutional opinions become substitutes for instrumental inquiries. If the meaning of existential events is defined only according to a fixed set of alternatives, we can understand conflict only by interpreting the shadows it casts.

The problem of *anxiety* concerns both existentialists and psychoanalysts, as well as every other man who thinks about his nature. Each in his own way, according to the polarized viewpoints toward which he is inclined, seeks an alternative to anxiety just as he seeks resolution of conflict. The mental state which he calls anxiety cries out for meaning and for relief because it seems to symbolize an event that partakes of both existence and extinction. So ubiquitous is this event that in his phantasies of a life filled with harmony, serenity, and responsibility man can even imagine an idealized, antithetical affect strong enough to sustain and protect him against the depredations of primary anxiety.

Primary anxiety is more than a state of being sick; it is anxiety about existence itself. It is more than fear or phobia, because fears have things to fear, and phobias have situations to avoid. The sense of devastation that is primary anxiety has been called by other names, such as *anomie, estrangement, dread, despair, depersonalization, alienation, abandonment,* and so on — each tending to assign primary anxiety to one or another special clinical or paraclinical syndrome.

In his meticulous survey of psychoanalytic theories of anxiety Schur [125a, b] concluded that primary anxiety and infantile anxiety are equivalent. But in the course of his argument, and in the breadth of his examples, he inadvertently demonstrated that the prototype of primary anxiety cannot be restricted to the image of a hungry or frightened infant. Furthermore, because our knowledge of what an infant experiences is largely based upon conjecture and inference, this putative anxiety seems hardly a reliable guide to the general structure of primary anxiety.

Anxiety appears in many forms, ranging from vast autonomic outbursts to genteel rustlings that accompany mild embarrassment. People differ widely in the way they experience acute anxiety, so it is not only unlikely that an acceptable general definition can be found but also improbable that the full significance of primary anxiety can be limited to any one instance [148]. The distinction between an *I* and the *other one* is a natural contingency, and even a necessary condition, for self-recognition. But this kind of obligatory separation, or "isolation," is far from the spiritual loneliness of primary anxiety, which crowds solitude into despair. Primary anxiety seems to be a prototype in itself — a prototype for whatever causes the experience of self to become meaningless existence.

Primary anxiety is an existential event without external meaning. The constancy and continuity of subjective experience disintegrate into a series of isolated images lacking direction or purpose. It is a state of limitless uncertainty in which the absence of familiar cues — even of threats — is perhaps its most intimidating aspect. There is an unbreachable schism between the isolation of the intrapersonal dimension and the impersonality of everything else. All that remains is a suspended moment of anguish or, when less intense, a single threat — imminent, meaningless dissolution. Sometimes this threat turns into a silent tedium that passes beyond fear, depression, guilt, shame, abandonment, or any other ostensive emotion. The sense of being nowhere and seeking nothing may be felt only as a heavy awareness of lost identity. Freedom has been forfeited; responsibility is only a word. To lose one's meaning, therefore, is to lose everything.

Existence without meaning is far different from statements which have no sensible negation and, consequently, are semantically meaningless (Chapter 3, pp. 53–58). Moreover, inasmuch as theories about the different forms of secondary anxiety fail to clarify the underlying existential event itself, the *experience* of primary anxiety can evidently be grasped by reality sense alone. Even the concepts of *being, becoming,* and especially *nonbeing* cannot be used to *explain* primary anxiety. The reality sense of primary anxiety precedes whatever conviction the concepts of being, becoming, and nonbeing contain and is, perhaps, the source of the distinction between them.

At this juncture we have two alternatives. We can confess our bafflement and resign ourselves to the adumbrative affirmation that primary anxiety is what happens when the darkness of the world causes even shadows to disappear. Or we can make use of the concept of polarized meaning and antithetical affect to find another way to understand primary anxiety and the existential event that gives rise to it.

AGAPE AND EROS

Because primary anxiety afflicts mankind as a whole in so many ways, its antithetical alternatives can be expected to assume different guises. The cultural circumstances in which different forms of primary anxiety occur may also elicit a wide variety of concepts to designate its polarized opposite. Here we shall briefly examine only one, the concept of *agape* [102], simply because it is so closely related to *eros* — whose relevance to psychoanalysis needs no justification — and not because belief in the reality of agape is urgently recommended.

The original meaning of eros is closer to that of agape than it is to sensual love [32], or even to its more abstract variant, "psychic energy" [30]. In its full, historical sense eros is that form of love which idealizes *both* the object loved and the process of loving. Since this is concordant with the ego ideal, erotic love is both responsive and responsible, in the loftiest sense. In its most elementary sense, agape refers to God's love, which He bestows, with unwavering devotion and without bidding, upon His own creation — man. Leaving aside its special theological significance, this general meaning of agape seems to make it an admirable antithetical alternative to the sense of hopeless abandonment and dread generated by primary anxiety. Eros is a process of seeking perfect love through the love of perfection, but agape is love that reaches down to the bereft and undeserving, as well as to the most meritorious of people. In a sense, to believe in agape is to believe that, in spite of interminable discord and despair, no one is ever beyond redemption, and no dilemma is beyond hope. Conflict has a solution; paradoxes make sense; suffering has significance — particularly at those moments of bewilderment, loneliness, and irrationality when a drastic antidote is needed. In short, we may conjecture that the complementary concepts of eros and agape are idealized versions of reality sense and responsibility, even though eros is a mythological polarization and agape is a theological polarization. Whether the idea of agape is a genuine promise or only a pious hope that infuses a fiction is irrelevant. The *concept* of agape is an antidote for the aimless flux and alienation of primary anxiety, just as the *concept* of eros is an antithesis of unreality and dissolution. Their principal significance is not that they represent some form of supreme love but that they attest to the metaphysical meaning of belief itself. They urge us to believe in a world that cares, in a limitless human potential, and in the ultimate unity of passions, perceptions, and principles, in place of unreality, anonymity, and meaningless existence.

Agape and eros do not have to show themselves for their adherents to believe in their existence. Both primary anxiety and conflict are characterized by hopelessness, and the existential event of conflict derives its augmented reality sense from the discordance between what one does and what the ego ideal requires. The reality sense of conflict, responsibility, and primary anxiety may itself contribute to the everlasting appeal borne by eros, agape, and other universal antidotes. At the very least, the fear of imminent annihilation, which seems to accompany many human enterprises, can also prompt hopeful anticipation of a pervasive love that outlasts fears, withstands despair, forgives wrongdoing, and counters every other alienating force. Even the somber writings of existentialists about loneliness, estrangement, and dread seem to imply that metaphysical support has been with them all along.

Hope and Despair

The most comprehensive antithesis of a meaningless existence is to believe that whatever happens has significance. The fundamental opposition between primary anxiety and agape is reflected less dramatically, but no less emphatically, in the antithesis between *hope* and *despair*. Oscillation between hope and despair seems to follow the fluctuations of existence and extinction within any dimension [50]. This is most clearly witnessed in the ultimate instance when disease, crisis, and conflict converge and polarities fuse in the existential event of *death and dying*. Man cannot conceive of his own death, although he accepts it as a reality. He fears death because the act of dying reminds him of the sense of imminent extinction experienced in primary anxiety. This, too, is understood only by means of antithetical alternatives. If the dying need the living, so, also, do the living need the dying. Only through the presence of the dying can the living reaffirm what being alive means. By an open confrontation with imminent obliteration, both the living and the dying may find themselves caught up in a resurgence of hope and despair [141c].

Patients who are faced with inevitable death will often demonstrate a paraclinical syndrome as they near the threshold. This has been called the *bereavement of the dying* [141b]. Although the syndrome arises from the hopelessness and loss of meaning that inevitable extinction exacts, it is the specific result of being abandoned by the living before actual physical death occurs. Those who survive withdraw themselves, and the patient is consigned to a kind of premortem burial. There is no evidence that religious belief, by itself, prevents or neutralizes the fear of death, the fear of dying, and the bereavement of the dying. Nevertheless, the crisis of dying calls for something like a concept of agape to contend with conflicts about dying. If a person facing nothing but death can retain a sense of awe for the inner affinity of existence, and for his own significance, the inevitability of extinction can become a necessary harmonic among the antitheses of life, not just a tragic and meaningless interruption. Much of this task of affirmation and confirmation belongs to the psychiatrist, the physician, and those who stand to lose most by the person's death. In mundane, human terms, *agape is acceptance of another person on existential terms*. If this state can be achieved, primary anxiety can yield to reality and responsibility, since nothing is without significance and no act is without motivation.

This does not mean, of course, that the best treatment for primary anxiety is to stand at the bedside of a dying patient. At such a moment, however, the witness will discover two significant existential events: a prelude to his own death and a fleeting, secret celebration, mingled with compassion, that he has been spared, at least for a time. These events are like a superego strategy in which guilt, triumph, depression, and elation — antitheses that define one another — pass beyond paradox and suddenly become concordant. In the existential core, which psychoanalysis attempts to fathom, purposeful acts are joined at either end by absurdity; objects, people, and things become instances of annihilation; encounter stretches into solitude; and intuition comes face to face with negation.

There are many gradations of motivation and purpose between hope and despair. Hope is not blind optimism, nor is despair untempered self-excoriation. Because confidence is to performance what intuition is to perception, they are necessary components of whatever sentiment extrapolates organic meaning into the unfolding acts and innovations of the future. The purpose of such concepts as eros and agape is not only to neutralize primary anxiety but to surround purposeful acts with a penumbra of hope. Hope, in other words, is the sense of reality for future events, whereas despair denies that there is, or can be, a future different from the past. In some states of despair there is loss of reality sense for the task at hand, as well as for the likelihood of future choice between genuine alternatives.

Imminent death is only one instance of despair. Despair can

occur in any personal dimension and in many clinical and para-clinical syndromes. Some of these syndromes are dominated by depression, others by paranoia. Another paraclinical syndrome, located somewhere between depression and paranoia, is called self-pity. All of these disorders include isolation, impoverishment, and interminable self-rebuke. Melancholic patients are more likely than others to feel unexplained, seemingly unjustified guilt and, as a result, to seek punishment as a way to relieve their distress. Their despair is so intense that they do not merely ask for punishment but offer to be the victim of another crime, similar to the unknown crime they have perpetrated. By this kind of sacrifice they express some measure of hope that their despair can be neutralized.

Paranoid patients attribute their best, and worst, motives to others and turn their appetites into aversions. Consequently, although the world becomes a conspiracy against them, they no longer must fear alienation. The interpersonal polarization is preserved, even though it becomes a relationship between the hunted and the hunter. The victim of self-pity protests about the neutrality of the world. He blames others for not trusting him more than he trusts himself, and indirectly he blames himself for wanting others to take care of him. Since victims should be treated tenderly, he finds both solace and vindication in suffering. As a victim, he escapes guilt and reaffirms hope.

If these few examples seem to be extreme illustrations of despair, we can only wonder how, in the presence of failure, frustration, illness, misfortune, deception, and sheer illusion, such a fragile sentiment as hope is able to survive at all. However, hope often survives on meager rations. In fact, to question the grounds upon which hope can be reaffirmed is itself almost an admission of despair [460].

Denial and Repression

The curious discrepancy between the pain of life and the persistence of hope suggests that the origins of hope depend upon inner processes, not upon outward satisfactions. Hope and despair are antithetical affects that accompany both concordant and discordant behavior. In order to carry out various kinds of motivated acts, secondary processes and ego functions control the strategic deployment of appetitive and aversive motives and meanings. Two of the more familiar ego functions — those penultimate acts performed for the sake of an ulterior act — primarily have an aversive effect but secondarily have an ancillary effect upon appetitive acts. These processes, known as *denial* and *repression*, selectively influence the conscious content of experience by negating, redirecting, modifying, muting, and augmenting wishes and fears. Hence denial and repression complement acts of affirmation, concordance, and responsibility.

A detailed study of negation, denial, and repression is out of place here and so must be postponed. Nevertheless, we should acknowledge their contribution to the concordance of diversified action and, presumably, to the preservation of hope in the presence of repeated and inevitable disaster. This does not mean that denial and repression guarantee hope, or that hope is a product of processes that conspire to ignore the ominous potential of existence. Psychoanalysis has constantly sought ways to overcome repression and to undercut denial [20]. But even mental health, that putative ideal, cannot require the elimination of repression and denial on every front. They are necessary factors in the smooth enunciation and performance of those acts which conscious intelligence — a party to the same conspiracy of hope, and a partial product of denial and repression — deems worth performing.

Although denial and repression are often discussed together, they differ in several important respects. These differences may be crucial inasmuch as denial and repression help to shape the polarization of different meanings and to define the quality of existential events.

Common usage notwithstanding, denial is a particular *quality* of an interpersonal relationship and *not* a special ego function. Its effect is to annihilate a portion of *object meaning* within a field of experience that is shared with someone else. Thus we can bend reality to conform with an inner wish, or phantasy. Reaffirmation of the residual object meaning, embellished with phantasy, also defines the conditions upon which certain kinds of interpersonal relations can be maintained.

Existential Events and Clinical Syndromes

Repression is distinct from denial in that it is an inner *process* which negates a portion of *organic meaning* associated with a potential act. The fact of repression is fairly well established, but the component acts that bring about repression are still controversial. We can be sure, however, that neither repression nor denial permanently annihilates experience — the way wind extinguishes a candle, for instance. In spite of denial, objective meaning is preserved, to be used another time, on another occasion, in relation to another person — when there is a more favorable attitude toward unwelcome reality. In spite of the partial deactivation attributed to repression, it should be clear that repression refers to organic meaning on several different levels of psychological activity. It does not apply merely to recorded memories and amnesias, to emotions and extinctions, or to potential acts and inhibitions. Because organic meaning comprises acceptances, inclinations, symbolic forms, and the full scope of conditioned and conditional experience, there can be only a vast panel of partial deactivations, with secondary distribution in other centers of expression. Although their unavailability at certain centers and in certain contexts may determine the *fact* of repression, there are undoubtedly many different processes engaged in subsidiary *acts* of repression. In any case, the augmented product is affirmation.

Denial is not a simple act of ignoring an obvious fact, nor is repression equivalent to fractional forgetting. The primary purpose of denial and repression is to facilitate concordant acts by minimizing discordant motives and meanings. In the presence of conflict, however, denial and repression will often distort organic meaning. Conflict itself can produce enhanced reality sense. As a result of distorted meaning and enhanced reality sense, the ego functions which attempt to resolve conflict may ultimately give rise to antithetical affect, regressive acts, and wholly inappropriate, albeit harmonious, behavior. Quite typically, patients may discover that their best efforts are expended in pursuit of trivial goals, that every serious enterprise ends in empty disappointment, that the values which guide their lives are simply pockets of hypocrisy, or, most tragically, that the conduct which justifies their aspirations also destroys the meaning of responsibility.

The Existential Core of Psychoanalysis

One of the themes of this book has been that knowledge is without beginning or end and that there are no isolated facts, only facts beheld in isolation. Denial and repression, operating without our expressed consent, alter the meanings of both inner and outer reality. Denied facts are at least shared with other people, but repressed organic meaning is wholly unshared. Hence, whatever we know about existential events is at best an approximation — and perhaps an antithetical approximation at that. This is the nuclear meaning of the *human conditional*.

Annihilation and Absurdity

In the end, we return to man himself, who discovers his own reality and his motivation rooted in the soil of primary processes. Out of this soil grows the sense of reality for the world and the means by which heterogeneous acts can be united in a sense of purpose. In the quest for meaning and fulfillment we find that reality sense and primary anxiety, conflict and responsibility, are inseparable. Every conflict occurs in an atmosphere of hopelessness; every responsible act takes place in the shadow of despair. Hope is no less a quality of existential events than is despair. Unfortunate ancillary meanings force us to separate existential hope from the hope of pious impossibility and from the hope of an unlikely reward. Existential hope is, simply, the animal optimism for survival that leads a suffocating man to smash a window with unquestioning confidence that — somewhere — there is air to revive him. In spite of discord, anxiety, depression, or futility, it is this transmuted image of concordant processes, steeped in reality sense and spread throughout existence, that generates an intuitive affirmation of life.

In paradoxical contrast, this image of life demands that man also affirm the inevitability of depletion and death. The dry fare of fixed categorical attitudes and impersonalized attitudes, like the short rations on which hope subsists, is useful for the purposes of reality testing, rational thinking, and pragmatic operations. However, when organic meanings are completely replaced by object meanings, so that the reality of existential events is overlooked in the search for knowledge, then reason, logic, categorical thinking, and effective performance destroy their own sources. This is true annihilation.

The meaningless absurdity and annihilation of reality that are found in primary anxiety cannot be produced by denial and repression alone. Some forms of annihilation and absurdity are as comprehensive as the affects of hope and despair. Annihilation occurs whenever man insists upon defining himself only according to what he is not. Then, at the moment when he discovers how he has impersonalized himself in the cause of conformity, or sacrificed himself for the sake of categories, annihilation becomes absurdity. It is true that a dying man, for example, disbelieves the fact of his own death and hopes that he is an exception. But what happens when any man becomes aware of the gap between his unique reality and all the attributes with which he has adorned himself? Impersonal death is an inescapable existential event, but intrapersonal death is a form of absurdity.

Annihilation is meaning without man; absurdity is man without meaning. When existential man splits away from categorical man, the result is either a bare, inscrutable being or a stark meaning unrooted in reality. Reduced to conditions of animal survival, it is the dread of extinction and anguish of loneliness that initiate every motivated act. In its idealized form, beyond that of survival, dread of extinction becomes loneliness, and this, in turn — glamorized beyond recognition — becomes preoccupation with human "involvement." In its still more personal and poignant form, dread of extinction is fear that, despite being a thing unique, we shall become nothing in particular. Annihilation and absurdity are, therefore, the defining alternatives and antitheses of reality and responsibility.

The pervasive polarizations of existence are apparently so inexhaustible that anyone who claims to explain everything understands nothing. Object meaning is a product of man's intellect and perception, but his organic meanings emerge from his cells and tissues and have no fixed or final significance. A psychoanalyst who approaches the study of human beings with only the equipment provided by the technical tools and plausible blueprints of his particular polarization is absurd. Without reality sense for each human being, including himself, and without a sense of being responsible for his own being and nonbeing, his task has already been annihilated. *The existential core of psychoanalysis is whatever nucleus of meaning and being there is that can confront both life and death.* Unless he accepts this as his indispensable reality, the psychoanalyst is like a man wandering at night in a strange city. His incredible isolation is both tragic and ludicrous, because he is never sure whether his assignment in this darkness is to deliver a message or to receive one.

Bibliography

1. Alexander, F.   (a) A metapsychological description of the process of cure. In *The Scope of Psychoanalysis, 1921-61: Selected
   Papers of Franz Alexander*. Basic Books, New York, 1961, pp.
   205-224.
   (b) *Psychoanalysis of the Total Personality*. Tr. by B. Glueck
   and B. Lewin. Nervous and Mental Disease Publishing Co.,
   New York and Washington, 1930, pp. 139-157.
   (c) Impressions from the 4th International Congress of Psychotherapy. *Psychiatry* 22:89-95, 1959.
2. Alexander, F., and Staub, H.   *The Criminal, the Judge and the
   Public*. The Free Press, Glencoe, Ill., 1956, pp. 125-131.
3. Allport, G.   *Personality and Social Encounter*. Beacon Press,
   Boston, 1960, pp. 59, 71 *et seq.*, 137 *et seq.*
4. Angel, R.   Jackson, Freud and Sherrington on the relation of

brain and mind. *Amer. J. Psychiat.* 118:193-197, 1961.

5. Anton, J. *Aristotle's Theory of Contrariety.* Routledge and Kegan Paul, London, 1957.

6. Bahm, A. *Types of Intuition.* University of New Mexico Press, Albuquerque, 1960, pp. 16-58.

7. Barclay, J. *Franz Brentano and Sigmund Freud: An Unexplored Influence Relationship.* American Psychological Association, Washington, Sept. 6, 1960.

8. Barrett, W. *Irrational Man: A Study in Existential Philosophy.* (Anchor ed.) Doubleday & Co., Garden City, N. Y., 1958.

9. Bellak, L. (Ed.) Conceptual and methodological problems in psychoanalysis. *Ann. NY Acad. Sci.* 76:973-1134, 1959.

10. Benjamin, J. (*a*) Some considerations in biological research in schizophrenia. *Psychosom. Med.* 20:427-445, 1958.
    (*b*) Prediction and psychopathological theory. In *Dynamic Psychopathology in Childhood*, L. Jessner and E. Pavenstedt (Eds.). Grune & Stratton, New York, 1959.

11. Berggren, D. The use and abuse of metaphor. *Rev. Metaphysics* 16:237-258, 1962; 16:450-472, 1963.

12. Bergson, H. *An Introduction to Metaphysics.* Tr. by T. Hulme. G. P. Putnam's Sons, New York and London, 1912.

13. Berne, E. (*a*) The nature of intuition. *Psychiat. Quart.* 23:203-226, 1949.
    (*b*) Intuition IV. Primal images and primal judgment. *Psychiat. Quart.* 29:634-658, 1955.
    (*c*) Intuition V. The ego image. *Psychiat. Quart.* 31:611-627, 1957.

14. Bibring, E. (*a*) The development and problems of the theory of instincts. *Int. J. Psychoanal.* 22:1-30, 1941.
    (*b*) The conception of the repetition compulsion. *Psychoanal. Quart.* 12:486-519, 1943.

15. Binger, C. Freud and medicine. *New Eng. J. Med.* 256:297-303, 1957.

16. Binswanger, L. Symptom and time. *Existent. Inquiries* 1:14-18, 1960.

17. Board, R. Intuition in the methodology of psychoanalysis. *Psychiatry* 21:233-239, 1958.

18. Boss, M. *Psychoanalysis and Daseinsanalysis.* Tr. by L. Lefebre. Basic Books, New York and London, 1963.

19. Bradley, F. *Appearance and Reality: A Metaphysical Essay.* George Allen and Unwin, London, 1897.

Bibliography

20. Breuer, J., and Freud, S. *Studies on Hysteria.* Tr. by J. Strachey. Basic Books, New York, 1957.
21. Brickner, R. A neural fractionating and combining system. *Arch. Neur. Psychiat.* 72:1-10, 1954.
22. Burton, A. Schizophrenia and existence. *Psychiatry* 23:385-394, 1960.
23. Camus, A. (*a*) *The Rebel: An Essay on Man in Revolt.* Tr. by A. Bower. (Vintage ed.). Alfred A. Knopf, New York, 1956.
    (*b*) *The Myth of Sisyphus and Other Essays.* Tr. by J. O'Brien. Alfred A. Knopf, New York, 1955.
24. Cassirer, E. (*a*) *Substance and Function.* Tr. by W. and M. Swabey. Dover Publications, New York, pp. 112-233.
    (*b*) *An Essay on Man: An Introduction to a Philosophy of Human Culture* (Anchor ed.). Doubleday & Co., Garden City, N. Y., 1953.
25. Caudill, W. Anthropology and psychoanalysis: Some theoretical issues. In *Anthropology and Human Behavior*, T. Gladwin and W. Sturtevant (Eds.). Anthropology Society of Washington, 1962.
26. Caudill, W., and Scarr, H. Japanese value orientations and culture change. *Ethnology* 1:53-91, 1962.
27. Chisholm, R. (Ed.) *Realism and the Background of Phenomenology.* The Free Press, Glencoe, Ill., 1960.
28. Cohen, F. What is a question? *Monist* 14:350-364, 1930.
29. Cohen, M. *A Preface to Logic.* Meridian Books, New York, 1956, pp. 80-93.
30. Colby, K. *Energy and Structure in Psychoanalysis.* Ronald Press Co., New York, 1955.
31. Collingwood, R. *An Autobiography.* Oxford University Press, London, 1939, pp. 29-43.
32. D'Arcy, M. *The Mind and Heart of Love.* Meridian Books, New York, 1956.
33. Denny-Brown, D. The nature of apraxia. *J. Nerv. Ment. Dis.* 126:9-32, 1958.
34. Deutsch, F. Creative passion of the artist and its synesthetic aspects. *Int. J. Psychoanal.* 40:1-14, 1959.
35. Dewey, J. (*a*) *Reconstruction in Philosophy.* Henry Holt and Co., New York, 1920, pp. 103-131.
    (*b*) The development of meanings. In *Intelligence in the Modern World*, J. Ratner (Ed.). Modern Library, Random House, New York, 1939, pp. 857-867.

(c) *Essays in Experimental Logic.* Dover Publications, New York, 1953, pp. 1-74.

36. Dodds, E. *The Greeks and the Irrational.* Beacon Press, Boston, 1957.

37. Ellenberger, H. A clinical introduction to psychiatric phenomenology and existential analysis. In *Existence*, R. May, E. Angel, and H. Ellenberger (Eds.). Basic Books, New York, 1958.

38. Embler, W. (a) Metaphor and social belief. *ETC.* 8:83-93, 1951.

    (b) Metaphor in everyday speech. *ETC.* 16:323-342, 1959.

39. Engel, G. Selection of clinical material in psychosomatic medicine. *Psychosom. Med.* 16:368-373, 1954.

40. Erikson, E. (a) The problem of ego identity. *J. Amer. Psychoanal. Ass.* 4:56-121, 1956.

    (b) The nature of clinical evidence. *Daedalus* 87:65-87, 1958.

    (c) Identity and the life cycle. *Psychological Issues, I.* Monograph I, International Universities Press, New York, 1959.

41. Fales, W. *Wisdom and Responsibility: An Essay on the Motivation of Thought and Action.* Princeton University Press, Princeton, N. J., 1946.

42. Fenichel, O. *The Psychoanalytic Theory of Neurosis.* W. W. Norton and Co., New York, 1945, pp. 19, 129, 168, 543.

43. Fingarette, H. Psychoanalytic perspectives on moral guilt and responsibility: A re-evaluation. *Phil. Phenom. Res.* 16:18-36, 1955.

44. Flugel, J. *Man, Morals and Society.* International Universities Press, New York, 1945, pp. 16-28.

45. Frankl, V. *The Doctor and the Soul: An Introduction to Logotherapy.* Tr. by R. and C. Winston. Alfred A. Knopf, New York, 1957.

46. Freud, S. (a) On the psychical mechanism of hysterical phenomena: A lecture (1893). In *The Standard Edition of the Complete Psychological Works of Sigmund Freud*, tr. and ed. by J. Strachey with others. The Hogarth Press and the Institute of Psycho-Analysis, London, 1962, p. 38.

    (b) The neuro-psychoses of defence (1894). In *ibid.* Vol. III, 1962, pp. 47, 49.

    (c) Obsessions and phobias: Their psychical mechanism and their aetiology (1895). In *ibid.* Vol. III, 1962, p. 81.

    (d) *Interpretation of Dreams.* Basic Books, New York, 1959, pp. 509-621.

Bibliography

(e) Character and anal erotism (1908). "Standard Edition." Vol. IX, 1959, pp. 167-176.

(f) Antithetical meaning of primal words (1910). In *ibid*. Vol. XI, 1957, pp. 153-162.

(g) Papers on metapsychology: On narcissism, pp. 67-104; Instincts and their vicissitudes, pp. 109-140; Repression, pp. 141-158; The unconscious, pp. 159-204; Metapsychological supplement to the theory of dreams, pp. 217-236; Mourning and melancholia, pp. 237-258. In *ibid*. Vol. XIV, 1957.

(h) Criminals from a sense of guilt, in some character types met with in psychoanalytic work (1916). In *ibid*. Vol. III, 1962, p. 332.

(i) The ego and the id (1923). In *ibid*. Vol. XIX, 1961, pp. 12-59.

(j) Negation (1925). In *ibid*. Vol. XIX, 1961, pp. 235-242.

(k) The resistances to psychoanalysis (1925). In *ibid*. Vol. XIX, 1961, pp. 213-222.

(l) Project for a scientific psychology. In *The Origins of Psychoanalysis: Letters to Wilhelm Fliess, Drafts and Notes: 1887-1902*, M. Bonaparte, A. Freud, and E. Kris (Eds.). Imago Publishing Co., London, 1954, pp. 347-445.

(m) Anatomy of the mental personality. In *New Introductory Lectures on Psycho-Analysis*. Tr. by W. Sprott. W. W. Norton and Co., New York, 1933, pp. 82-112.

(n) Explanations, applications and orientations. In *ibid*., pp. 186-215.

(o) A philosophy of life. In *ibid*., pp. 216-249.

(p) The 'uncanny' (1919). "Standard Edition." Vol. XIX, 1961, pp. 217-252.

47. Fromm-Reichmann, F. Clinical significance of intuitive processes of the psychoanalyst. *J. Amer. Psychoanal. Ass.* 3:82-88, 1955.

48. Gill, M. Topography and systems in psychoanalytic theory. *Psychological Issues, III*. Monograph 10, International Universities Press, New York, 1963.

49. Gitelson, M. The curative factors in psychoanalysis. *Int. J. Psychoanal.* 43:194-205, 1962.

50. Goldstein, K. *Human Nature in the Light of Psycho-Pathology*. William James Lectures, 1938. Harvard University Press, Cambridge, Mass., 1940.

51. Gooddy, W. Time and the nervous system: The brain as a clock. *Lancet* 2:1155, 1959.

52. Greenacre, P. Early physical determinants in the development

of the sense of identity. *J. Amer. Psychoanal. Ass.* 6:612-627, 1958.

53. Hackett, T., and Weisman, A. Psychiatric management of operative syndromes: I. The therapeutic consultation and the effect of noninterpretive intervention. *Psychosom. Med.* 22: 267-282, 1960. II. Psychodynamic factors in formulation and management. *Psychosom. Med.* 22:356-372, 1960.

54. Hartmann, H. (*a*) On rational and irrational action. In *Psychoanalysis and the Social Sciences*, Vol. I. International Universities Press, New York, 1947, pp. 359-392.
(*b*) Notes on the reality principle. *Psychoanalytic Study of the Child*, Vol. XI. R. Eissler, A. Freud, H. Hartmann, and M. Kris (Eds.). International Universities Press, New York, 1956.

55. Hartmann, H., and Kris, E. Genetic approach in psychoanalysis. *Psychoanalytic Study of the Child*, Vol. I. International Universities Press, New York, 1945.

56. Hartmann, H., Kris, E., and Loewenstein R. The function of theory in psychoanalysis. In *Drives, Affects, Behavior*, R. Loewenstein (Ed.). International Universities Press, New York, 1953, pp. 13-35.

57. Heidegger, M. *Being and Time*. Tr. by J. Macquarrie and E. Robinson. Student Christian Movement Press, London, 1962.

58. Heinemann, F. *Existentialism and the Modern Predicament* (Torchbook ed.). Harper & Brothers, New York, 1958.

59. Herberg, W. (Ed.) *Four Existentialist Theologians* (Anchor ed.). Doubleday & Co., Garden City, N. Y., 1958.

60. Hook, S. (Ed.) (*a*) *Determinism and Freedom in the Age of Modern Science*. New York University Press, New York, 1958.
(*b*) *Psychoanalysis, Scientific Method and Philosophy: A Symposium*. Grove Press, New York, 1959.

61. Hora, T. (*a*) Existential psychotherapy. In *Current Psychiatric Therapies*. J. Masserman (Ed.). Grune & Stratton, New York, 1962, pp. 30-40.
(*b*) Ontic perspectives in psychoanalysis. *Amer. J. Psychoanal.* 19:134-142, 1959.

62. Hospers, J. Meaning and free will. *Phil. Phenom. Res.* 10:307-330, 1950.

63. Jacobson, E. Depersonalization. *J. Amer. Psychoanal. Ass.* 7:581-609, 1959.

64. James, W. (*a*) *The Principles of Psychology*. Vol. I, Habit, p. 104; Consciousness of self, p. 291. Vol. II, Perception of

Bibliography

reality, p. 283; Will, p. 486. Dover Publications, New York, 1950.

(b) *Essays in Pragmatism.* The sentiment of rationality, pp. 3-36; The dilemma of determinism, pp. 37-64; The will to believe, pp. 88-109. Hafner Publishing Co., New York, 1948.

65. Jaspers, K. *Truth and Symbol.* Tr. by J. Wilde, W. Kluback, and W. Kimmel. Twayne Publishers, New York, 1959.

66. Johnson, A. (a) *The Interpretation of Science: Selected Essays of Alfred North Whitehead.* A. Johnson (Ed.). Bobbs-Merrill Co., Indianapolis, 1961, p. 149.

(b) *Whitehead's Theory of Reality.* Beacon Press, Boston, 1952.

67. Jones, E. (a) *Life and Work of Sigmund Freud.* Vol. II, Libido theory, p. 282. Vol. III, Metapsychology, p. 265. Basic Books, New York, 1955, 1957.

(b) Free will and determinism. In *Essays in Applied Psychoanalysis.* Hogarth Press, London, 1951, Vol. II, pp. 178-189.

68. Kardiner, A., Karush, A., and Ovesey, L. A methodological study of Freudian theory. I. Basic concepts. *J. Nerv. Ment. Dis.* 129:11-19, 1959. II. Libido theory. *J. Nerv. Ment. Dis.* 129:133-143, 1959. III. Narcissism, bisexuality and the dual instinct theory. *J. Nerv. Ment. Dis.* 129:207-231, 1959. IV. The structural hypothesis, the problem of anxiety and post-Freudian ego psychology. *J. Nerv. Ment. Dis.* 129:341-356, 1959.

69. Kaufmann, W. *The Owl and the Nightingale: From Shakespeare to Existentialism.* Faber and Faber, London, 1959.

70. Kaufman, W. (Ed.) *Existentialism from Dostoevsky to Sartre.* Meridian Books, New York, 1957.

71. Kierkegaard, S. Concluding unscientific postscript to the "Philosophical Fragments." In *A Kierkegaard Anthology*, R. Bretall (Ed.). Princeton University Press, Princeton, N. J., 1946.

72. Klein, G. Consciousness in psychoanalytic theory: Some implications for current research in perception. *J. Amer. Psychoanal. Ass.* 7:5-34, 1959.

73. Kluback, W., and Weinbaum, M. (Eds.) *Dilthey's Philosophy of Existence.* Bookman Associates, New York, 1957.

74. Knight, R. Determinism, "freedom," and psychotherapy. In *Psychoanalytic Psychiatry and Psychology*, Vol. I. Austen Riggs Center. International Universities Press, New York, 1954, pp. 365-381.

75. Knight, R., and Friedman, C. (Eds.) *Psychoanalytic Psychiatry and Psychology*, Vol. I. Austen Riggs Center. International Universities Press, New York, 1954.

76. Kohut, H. Introspection, empathy and psychoanalysis. *J. Amer. Psychoanal. Ass.* 7:459-483, 1959.

77. Krapf, E. Psychoanalysis and the self-understanding of man. *Acta Psychother.* 6:1-15, 1958.

78. Kris, E. On inspiration. In *Psychoanalytic Explorations in Art.* International Universities Press, New York, 1952, p. 291.

79. Lafitte, P. *The Person in Psychology: Reality or Abstraction.* Routledge and Kegan Paul, London, 1957.

80. Langer, S. *Philosophy in a New Key: A Study in the Symbolism of Reason, Rite and Art.* Penguin Books, New York, 1948.

81. Levine, I. *The Unconscious: An Introduction to Freudian Psychology.* The Macmillan Co., New York, 1923, pp. 176-178.

82. Levy, D. (a) Capacity and motivation. *Amer. J. Orthopsychiat.* 27:1-8, 1957.
    (b) The "act" as an operational concept in psychodynamics. *Psychosom. Med.* 24:49-57, 1962.

83. Lichtenstein, H. Identity and sexuality: A study of their interrelationship in man. *J. Amer. Psychoanal. Ass.* 9:179-260, 1961.

84. Lindzey, G., and Hall, C. Psychoanalytic theory and its applications in the social sciences. In *Handbook of Social Psychology.* G. Lindzey (Ed.). Addison-Wesley Publishing Co., Reading, Mass., 1954, Vol. I, pp. 143-180.

85. Lipton, S. A note on the compatibility of psychic determinism and free will. *Int. J. Psychoanal.* 36:355-358, 1955.

86. Little, M. On delusional transference. *Int. J. Psychoanal.* 39:134-138, 1958.

87. Lyons, J. An annotated bibliography on phenomenology and existentialism. *Psychol. Rep.* 5:613-631, 1959.

88. Macdonald, J. The concept of responsibility. *J. Ment. Sci.* 101:704-717, 1955.

89. Marcel, G. *Metaphysical Journal.* Tr. by B. Wall. Rockliff, Salisbury Sq., London, 1952.

90. Maritain, J. (a) *Creative Intuition in Art and Poetry.* Meridian Books, New York, 1955.
    (b) *Existence and the Existent.* Tr. by L. Galantiere and G. Phelan. (Image ed.). Doubleday & Co., Garden City, N. Y., 1956.
    (c) Freudianism and psychoanalysis. *Cross Currents* 6:307-324, 1956.

91. Maroyama, M. The second cybernetics: Deviation-amplifying mutual causal processes. *Amer. Sci.* 51:164-179, 1963.

Bibliography

92. Maudsley, H. *Responsibility in Mental Disease.* D. Appleton and Co., New York, 1883.

93. May, R. Will, decision and responsibility: Summary remarks. *Rev. Existent. Psychol. Psychiat.* 1:249-259, 1961.

94. May, R., Angel, E., and Ellenberger, H. (Eds.) *Existence: A New Dimension in Psychiatry and Psychology.* Basic Books, New York, 1958.

95. Mazer, M. The therapeutic function of the belief in will. *Psychiatry* 23:45-52, 1960.

96. Menninger, K. *Theory of Psychoanalytic Technique. Menninger Clinic Monogr.* 12. Basic Books, New York, 1958, pp. 15-42.

97. Michaels, J. Character structure and character disorders. In *American Handbook of Psychiatry.* Basic Books, New York, 1959, pp. 353-377.

98. Morris, C. *Signs, Language and Behavior.* George Braziller, New York, 1955, pp. 123-152.

99. Morris, H. (Ed.) *Freedom and Responsibility: Readings in Philosophy and Law.* Stanford University Press, Stanford, Cal., 1961, pp. 392-435, 463, 500-527.

100. Mueller, G. *The Interplay of Opposites: A Dialectical Ontology.* Bookman Associates, New York, 1956.

101. Nemiah, J. *Development of the Concept of Intrapsychic Conflict in Freud's Writings.* Panel on Intrapsychic Conflict. American Psychoanalytic Association, New York, December, 1962.

102. Nygren, A. *Agape and Eros.* Tr. by P. Watson. Westminster Press, Philadelphia, 1953.

103. Ogden, C., and Richards, I. *The Meaning of Meaning.* Harcourt, Brace and Co., New York, 3d ed., 1946.

104. Papez, J. A proposed mechanism of emotion. *Arch. Neurol. Psychiat.* 38:725-743, 1937.

105. Parsons, T. The role of ideas in social action. In *Essays in Sociological Theory.* T. Parsons (Ed.). The Free Press, Glencoe, Ill., rev. ed., 1954, pp. 19-33.

106. Pepper, S. (a) *World Hypotheses: A Study in Evidence.* University of California Press, Berkeley and Los Angeles, 1948. (b) *The Sources of Value.* University of California Press, Berkeley and Los Angeles, 1958.

107. Peters, R. *The Concept of Motivation.* Routledge and Kegan Paul, London, 1958.

108. Plotinus. *The Enneads.* Tr. by S. MacKenna (2d ed.), rev. by B. Page. Pantheon Books, New York.

109. Popper, K. *The Logic of Scientific Discovery.* Basic Books, New York, 1959, pp. 78-92.

110. Pribram, K. On the neurology of thinking. *Behav. Sci.* 4:265-287, 1959.

111. Pumpian-Mindlin, E. (*a*) Position of psychoanalysis in relation to the biological and social sciences. In *Psychoanalysis as Science*, E. Pumpian-Mindlin (Ed.). Stanford University Press, Stanford, Cal., 1952, pp. 125-157.
    (*b*) Propositions concerning energetic-economic aspects of libido theory: Conceptual models of psychic energy and structure in psychoanalysis. *Ann. NY Acad. Sci.* 76:1038-1065, 1959.

112. Rank, O., and Sachs, H. *The Significance of Psychoanalysis for the Mental Sciences.* Tr. by C. Payne. *Nerv. Ment. Dis. Monogr.* 23. Nervous and Mental Disease Publishing Co., New York, 1916.

113. Rapaport, D. (*a*) *Emotions and Memory. Menninger Clinic Monogr.* 2. International Universities Press, New York, 2d. ed., 1950, pp. 129-137.
    (*b*) On the psychoanalytic theory of thinking. In *Psychoanalytic Psychiatry and Psychology*, Vol. I. Austen Riggs Center. International Universities Press, New York, 1954, pp. 259-273.
    (*c*) The structure of psychoanalytic theory: A systematizing attempt. *Psychological Issues*, II. Monograph 2, International Universities Press, New York, 1960.

114. Rapaport, D., and Gill, M. The points of view and assumptions of metapsychology. *Int. J. Psychoanal.* 40:1-10, 1959.

115. Reichenbach, H. (*a*) *Elements of Symbolic Logic.* The Macmillan Co., New York, 1947, pp. 4, 7, 25, 241, 346.
    (*b*) *The Rise of Scientific Philosophy.* University of California Press, Berkeley and Los Angeles, 1951.

116. Rogers, C. (*a*) *Counseling and Psychotherapy.* Houghton Mifflin Co., Boston, 1942.
    (*b*) A process conception of psychotherapy. *Amer. Psychologist* 13:142-149, 1958.

117. Rosen, V. Abstract thinking and object relations. *J. Amer. Psychoanal. Ass.* 6:653-671, 1958.

118. Runes, D. (Ed.) *Dictionary of Philosophy.* Philosophical Library, New York, 1942, pp. 149-150.

119. Ryle, G. *The Concept of Mind.* Hutchinson's University Library. Hutchinson House, London, 1949, pp. 83-115, 195.

120. Sachs, H. *The Creative Unconscious: Studies in the Psycho-*

analysis of Art. Sci-Art Publishers, Cambridge, Mass., 2d ed., 1951, pp. 147-242.

121. Sartre, J. (*a*) *Existentialism.* Tr. by B. Frechtman. Philosophical Library, New York, 1947.
    (*b*) *Existential Psychoanalysis.* Tr. by H. Barnes. Philosophical Library, New York, 1953, pp. 41-89.
    (*c*) *Being and Nothingness: An Essay on Phenomenological Ontology.* Tr. by H. Barnes. Philosophical Library, New York, 1956, pp. 233-252.

122. Schilder, P. *Mind: Perception and Thought in Their Constructive Aspects.* Columbia University Press, New York, 1942, pp. 213, 233, 243, 346.

123. Schmidl, F. Sigmund Freud and Ludwig Binswanger. *Psychoanal. Quart.* 28:40-58, 1959.

124. Schrodinger, E. *Science Theory and Man.* Dover Publications, New York, 1957, pp. 39-51.

125. Schur, M. (*a*) The ego in anxiety. In *Drives, Affects, Behavior,* R. Loewenstein (Ed.). International Universities Press, New York, 1953, pp. 67-103.
    (*b*) The ego and the id in anxiety. In *Psychoanalytic Study of the Child,* Vol. XIII. R. Eissler, A. Freud, H. Hartmann, and M. Kris (eds.). International Universities Press, New York, 1958, pp. 190-220.

126. Schwartz, D. A review of the "paranoid" concept. *Arch. Gen. Psychiat.* 8:349-361, 1963.

127. Sears, L. *Responsibility: Its Development Through Punishment and Reward.* Columbia University Press, New York, 1932.

128. Sherrington, C. *Man on His Nature* (Anchor ed.). Doubleday & Co., Garden City, N. Y., 2d ed., 1953.

129. Shorey, P. *What Plato Said.* University of Chicago Press, Chicago, 1933.

130. Smith, J. The metaphor of the manic-depressive. *Psychiatry* 23:375-383, 1960.

131. Strawson, P. *Introduction to Logical Theory.* John Wiley and Sons, New York, 1952, pp. 185-212.

132. Strupp, H. (*a*) Some comments on the future of research in psychotherapy. *Behav. Sci.* 5:60-71, 1960.
    (*b*) Nature of the psychotherapist's contribution to the treatment process. *Arch. Gen. Psychiat.* 3:219-231, 1960.

133. Suttie, I. *The Origins of Love and Hate.* Penguin Books, Harmondsworth, Middlesex, England, 1960.

134. Szasz, T. (*a*) A contribution to the psychology of bodily feelings. *Psychoanal. Quart.* 26:25-49, 1957.
   (*b*) A critical analysis of some aspects of the Libido theory: The concepts of libidinal zones, aims, and modes of gratification. *Ann. NY Acad. Sci.* 76:975-1009.

135. Tillich, P. *The Religious Situation.* Tr. by H. Niebuhr. Meridian Books, New York, 1956.

136. Vaihinger, H. *The Philosophy of 'As If': A System of the Theoretical, Practical and Religious Fictions of Mankind.* Tr. by C. Ogden. Routledge and Kegan Paul, London, 2d ed., 1935, pp. 97-100.

137. Waelder, R. (*a*) The problem of freedom in psychoanalysis and the problem of reality testing. *Int. J. Psychoanal.* 17:89-108, 1936.
   (*b*) The principle of multiple function. *Psychoanal. Quart.* 5:45-62, 1936.
   (*c*) Book review of *Psychoanalysis, Scientific Method and Philosophy* (Ref. 60*b*). *J. Amer. Psychoanal. Ass.* 10:617-637, 1962.

138. Walshe, F. *Critical Studies in Neurology.* Williams and Wilkins Co., Baltimore, 1948, pp. 191-237.

139. Watts, A. *The Way of Zen.* Thames and Hudson, London, 1957.

140. Weisman, A. (*a*) Reality sense and reality testing. *Behav. Sci.* 3:228-261, 1958.
   (*b*) Psychodynamic formulation of conflict. *Arch. Gen. Psychiat.* 1:288-309, 1959.
   (*c*) The Psychotherapeutic "Encounter" and Clinical Research. Proc. 3d World Cong. Psychiat. McGill University Press, Montreal, 1961.
   (*d*) Crisis, Conflict and Disease. 3d Connecticut Conf. Pastoral Counseling, Windsor, Conn., 1963.

141. Weisman, A., and Hackett, T. (*a*) Psychosis after eye surgery. Establishment of a specific doctor-patient relation in the prevention and treatment of "black patch" delirium. *New Eng. J. Med.* 258:1284-1289, 1958.
   (*b*) Predilection to death: Death and dying as a psychiatric problem. *Psychosom. Med.* 23:232-256, 1961.
   (*c*) The dying patient. In *Special Treatment Situations.* Forest Hospital Publications, Vol. I, Des Plaines, Ill., 1962, pp. 16-21.

142. Wheelis, A. (*a*) *The Quest for Identity.* W. W. Norton and Co., New York, 1958.
   (*b*) Will and psychoanalysis. *J. Amer. Psychoanal. Ass.* 4:285-303, 1956.

Bibliography

143. Whitehead, A. *Adventures of Ideas* (Mentor ed. 1955). New American Library, New York. Originally published by The Macmillan Co., New York, 1933.

144. Whitehorn, J. The scope of motivation in psychopathology and psychotherapy. *Amer. J. Psychoanal.* 14:30-39, 1954.

145. Whyte, L. *The Unconscious Before Freud.* Basic Books, New York, 1960.

146. Wilde, J., and Kimmel, W. (Trs. and Eds.) *The Search for Being: Essays from Kierkegaard to Sartre on the Problem of Existence.* Twayne Publishers, New York, 1962.

147. Windelband, W. *A History of Philosophy, with Especial Reference to the Formation and Development of Its Problems and Conceptions.* Tr. by J. Tufts. The Macmillan Co., New York, 2d ed., 1926, pp. 551-559.

148. Winnicott, D. The capacity to be alone. *Int. J. Psychoanal.* 39:416-420, 1958.

149. Wisdom, J. Determinism and psychoanalysis. *Int. J. Psychoanal.* 24:140-147, 1943.

150. Wittgenstein, L. *Tractatus Logico-Philosophicus.* Routledge and Kegan Paul, London, 8th impr., 1960, pp. 31-43, 111.

151. Woodger, J. *Biology and Language. An Introduction to the Methodology of Biological Sciences Including Medicine.* Cambridge University Press, Cambridge, England, 1952, pp. 344-356.

152. Wyschograd, M. Sartre, freedom and the unconscious. *Rev. Existent. Psychol. Psychiat.* 1:179-186, 1961.

153. Yakovlev, P. (a) *Anatomy of the Human Brain and the Problem of Mental Retardation.* Proc. 1st Int. Conf. Mental Retardation. P. Bowman and H. Mautner (Eds.). Grune & Stratton, New York, 1959.
    (b) *Brain, Body and Behavior. Stereodynamic Organization of the Brain and of the Motility-Experience in Man Envisaged as a Biological Action System.* James Arthur Lectures. American Museum of Natural History, New York, 1961.

154. Young, J. *Doubt and Certainty in Science: A Biologist's Reflections on the Brain.* Clarendon Press, Oxford, England, 1951.

Index

Index

Aesthetics of mental life, 115-116
Affect
  antithetical, 218, 219, 222, 224-230
  clusters of, 87, 88, 214
Affective equivalence, 81-82, 84, 93, 103, 115, 117, 124, 155, 214, 225
Affirmation, 147, 148
  by analyst, 109
  and community of belief, 113
  deductive corollaries of, 161-162
  definition of, 101-104
  in depth, 149
  disjunctive, 130
  and inferences, 103
  intuitive, 69-70, 138, 155
  and metaphors, 117
  from open-end questions, 143
  by patient, 112
  of propositions, 116
  and understanding, 141
Agape, concept of, 218, 233-235, 236
Alexander, F., 108, 196
Ambiguity of propositions, 55
Ambivalence, 227
Analysis and validation, 148-152
Analyst, function of. See Psychoanalysis
Analytic method to reconcile opposites, 137
Anguish, 222
Annihilation, 206, 219, 222, 231, 234, 240-242
Anomalies of responsibility, 181-183, 194-197
Answers and questions, 141-152
  See also Questions and answers
Anticipation and intuition, 161, 162
Antithetical affects, 218, 219, 224-230
  prevalence of, 227-228
  in sickness, 222
Antithetical attitude of psychiatrist, 228-230
Anton, J., 231

Anxiety
  development of, 108
  infantile, 232
  metaphysical, 222
  primary, 218, 230-235, 240
  secondary, 233
Apologies as superego strategy, 197
Aquinas, St. Thomas, 8
Atonement, 196
Attenuation, 95
Attitudes toward experience, 18
  changes in, 4
Authenticity, 168
Autonomous man, 172-174

Becoming, concept of, 60-62, 63-65, 69, 233
Behavior, 53, 193
Being
  and becoming, 63, 69
  concept of, 60-62, 63-65, 233
  and meaning, 14
Beliefs
  and convictions, 17
  open examination of, 18
Bereavement of the dying, 235
Bergson, H., 9, 66
Biological forces, impersonal, 26
Body, distinct from mind, 168-170
Bradley, F., 84
Breuer, J., 124

Camus, A., 153, 223
Categorical Imperative, 191, 192
Categorical time, 90
Categorical views of man, 7, 166, 169
  challenge of, 11
  existential views compared with, 27-32, 166, 169
  language of, 31-32
Caudill, W., 25
Causality and prediction, 161, 163
Cause and choice, 29
Cause-effect, 78
Certainty
  axioms of, 18
  and doubt, 133-134

258

Index

Index

and extinction, 231
I at center of, 25
and meaning, 57
Existential, modulated, 127
Existential events, 214-216
 and clinical syndromes, 217-242
 polarization of, 219, 220
Existential language, 31-32
Existential levels of experience, 7
Existential meaning, 58
Existential time, 63, 90
Existential views, categorical views
 compared with, 27-32, 166, 169
Existentialism
 and psychoanalysis, 3-15
 and theology, 9-10
Experience
 attitudes toward, 18
 four levels of investigation, 7-8
Explanation
 and affective equivalence, 81-82
 credibility of, 78, 79
 idea, intention, and inclination
 in, 77-80
 and judgments, 43-45
 and libido concept, 87-89
 and meaning, 46-48
 in psychoanalysis, 82-85
 reality sense of, 60, 76-82
 of reality sense, 82-89
 and theories of Plato and Freud,
 85-87
Extinction and existence, 231
 See also Annihilation
Extrinsic meaning, 41-48
 explanations and judgments, 43-
 45
 explanations and meaning, 46-48
 of reality sense, 60, 74-89

Fallacies, of disciplines, 52
 of philosopher, 40
 of physiologist, 40
 of psychoanalyst, 40
 of psychologist, 40
Fate, notion of, 26
Forces and systems, 50
Forgiveness, 171-172, 214
 existential, 173

Formulations
 existential, 10
 psychoanalytic, 10, 12, 49
Fragmentation, 95
Frankl, V., 12
Free association, 93, 111, 208
Free will, 174
Freedom
 and choice, 170, 174-175
 existential, 29-30
 fear of, 175
 sense of, 186, 189
Freud, S., 3, 4, 6, 9, 13, 49, 50, 52,
 55, 67, 71, 84, 95, 109, 115,
 124, 133-134, 135-136, 155,
 178, 179, 187, 227
 and Plato, 85-87
Fulfillment of wishes, 139-140
Function, structure, and operation,
 45
Functional transformations, 95
Future, statements about, 160-163
 See also Prediction

Generalizations
 and affirmation, 103
 types of, 49
Genetic viewpoint, 47, 51
Gill, M., 49, 50
Goals and conduct, 193-194
Golden Rule, 213
Goldstein, K., 120
Gratifications, achievement of,
 108
Guilt
 legal and personal, 172
 and punishment, 213
 and responsibility, 197
 unconscious sense of, 196

Habit, 202
Heidegger, M., 61
Heinemann, F., 8
Homeostasis, 96
Hope, 240
 and despair, 218, 235-237
Hopelessness, 234, 240
Human condition, 21-22

Index

Index

Index

Object relations, 25
Objective facts and subjective experience, 8, 14
Objective meaning, 36-38, 42, 220, 224, 239
and relevance, 143
Objective reality, 24
Objective responsibility, 166-167, 168-170
Objects
affective equivalence of, 117
operations affecting, 45
of thought, 23-24
Obsessional patients, 182, 192, 229
Ogden, C., 37, 84
Ontological acceptance, 22-23, 26, 52, 65, 102, 132, 152
Operation
and activity, 51
and structure and function, 45
Operational viewpoint, 47
Opposites, significance of, 137, 231
Orderly perspectives, 39-41
Organic activity, 24
Organic meaning, 15, 34, 35, 36-38, 188, 219, 239, 240, 241
intrinsic and extrinsic meaning, 41-48
and metapsychology, 48, 49-53
and objective meaning, 36-38, 42
and orderly perspectives, 39-41
and polarization, 224
and relevance, 143
of responsibility, 166-174
scope of, 51-53
tests of meaning, 53-58
and value judgments, 44
versions of, 50-51

Paraclinical syndromes, 222
Paradox, 125-130, 224
basis of, 125
conflict beyond, 131-133
evocative property of, 126
and genuine hypotheses, 148
in insight, 138
in psychoanalysis, 128-130
reality sense of, 127-128
of time, 90-93

Paradoxical judgments, 20-21
Paranoid patients, 182, 194, 211, 229, 237
Paraphrasing, 56-57
Parental responsibility, 190
Perception
and consciousness, 67
three worlds of, 25-27
Phenomenal levels of experience, 7
Phenomenology, 17
Philosopher, fallacy of, 40
Philosophy, related to other fields, 5-6
Phobias, 210
Physiologist, fallacy of, 40
Plato, 85-87, 96
Pleasure principle, 88
and reality sense, 89
Plotinus, 8
Polarization
of existential events, 219, 220
and organic meaning, 224
Positivism, 17
Postulated entities, 24
Postulates of psychoanalysis, 140
Precipitating events, 123, 124, 210
Prediction
and causality, 161, 163
and intuition, 159-163
Prejudices, 196
Primal words, 119
Process
concept of, 78
primary, 95-96
and structure, 63-65, 187-190
versions of, 45
Projection, 210
Proof, purpose of, 67
Propositions
to interpret meanings, 111, 112, 116
significant, 145-146
Pseudohypotheses, 148-152, 155
Pseudoquestions, 144-145, 148
Psychic apparatus, 50, 187-190
Psychic determinism, 161, 165
Psychic energy, 50-51, 84, 87
release of, 108

Index

Psychic structure, fixed, concept of, 64

Psychoanalysis, 3-15
  acceptance in, 194
  affective equivalence in, 82
  analyst as element in encounter, 106
  antithetical attitude of psychiatrist, 228-230
  changes in attitude, 178-181
  changing image of analyst, 107-109
  communication in, 110-116
  couch data, 124-125, 142-143
  criticism of, 10
  and determinism, 175, 178
  development of, 108-109
  differing viewpoints in, 12-13
  encounter in, 104-116
  existentialist contribution to, 10-11, 13, 14-15
  explanations in, 82-85
  fallacy of analyst, 40
  formulations of, 10, 12
  gap between theory and practice, 10, 12, 49, 114
  insight and conflict in, 138-140
  intuition in, 68, 70
  key events in, 123-124
  mental apparatus in, 10
  and metaphor, 119-125
  and neurology, 179
  pact between analyst and patient, 63, 65
  paradox in, 128-130
  personal contributions of analyst, 7
  philosophical issues in, 6
  postulates of, 140
  questions and answers in, 141-152
  reality of analytic experience, 13-14
  and reality of content, 62-63
  reality sense of, 106
  therapeutic alliance in, 180-181
  and time, 91, 93-94
  training analysis, 109-110

Psychoanalytic encounter, 104-116

Psychoanalytic meaning of responsibility, 170, 172, 173, 174-186

Psychodynamic levels of experience, 7

Psychogenesis, theories of, 98-99

Psychologist, fallacy of, 40

Psychology, philosophical issues in, 5-6

Psychophysical levels of experience, 7

Psychotherapy, existential, 13

Punishment, 172, 212-214

Purposeful activity of consciousness, 68

Questions and answers, 141-152
  and hypotheses, 146-148
  open-end questions, 142, 143-144
  pseudoquestions, 144-145, 148
  relevance of, 142, 143
  significant propositions, 145-146

Rank, O., 106

Rapaport, D., 49, 50, 67, 160

Rationalism, reaction against, 9

Rationality, 122

Rationalization, 84, 226

Reaction formation, 196, 227

Real, relativity of the, 127, 225

Reality
  and acceptances, 18
  of analytic experience, 13-14
  boundaries of, 15
  conflict with instincts, 108
  of the I, 22-23
  index of, 185-186
  making sense of, 14
  man's sense of, 4
  objective, 24
  personalized, 25
  principle of, 89
  and responsibility, 5, 11, 14, 15
  of suffering, 11, 14

Reality sense, 27, 30, 54, 57, 240
  as activity, 60, 65-74, 124
  and aesthetics of mental life, 115
  and analysis, 148

265

Index

Index

Index